The Border Crossed Us

Rhetoric, Culture, and Social Critique

The Border Crossed Us

Rhetorics of Borders, Citizenship, and Latina/o Identity

Josue David Cisneros

THE UNIVERSITY OF ALABAMA PRESS
Tuscaloosa

The University of Alabama Press
Tuscaloosa, Alabama 35487–0380

Manufactured in the United States of America

Typeface: Dante and Letter Gothic

Cover image: Courtesy of iStockPhoto.com
Cover design: Mary Elizabeth Watson

∞

The paper on which this book is printed meets the minimum requirements of American National Standard for Information Sciences—Permanence of Paper for Printed Library Materials, ANSI Z39.48–1984.

Library of Congress Cataloging-in-Publication Data

Cisneros, Josue David, 1981–
The border crossed us : rhetorics of borders, citizenship, and Latina/o identity / Josue David Cisneros.
pages cm. — (Rhetoric, culture, and social critique)
Includes bibliographical references and index.
ISBN 978-0-8173-1812-3 (hardback) — ISBN 978-0-8173-8723-5 (e-book)
1. Mexican Americans—Ethnic identity. 2. Mexican Americans—Civil rights—History. 3. Mexican-American Border Region—Ethnic relations—History. 4. Mexican-American Border Region—Emigration and immigration. 5. Citizenship—Social aspects—United States. I. Title.
E184.M5C57 2013
973'.046872—dc23

2013021478

Contents

Preface

> But I am writing here now: is it too late? Can this writing, can any writing, refuse the terms by which it is appropriated even as, to some extent, that very colonizing discourse enables or produces this stumbling block, this resistance?
>
> —*Judith Butler*

Usually, the preface of a monograph such as this recounts the origins of the work, from its germination to completion. With this expectation in mind, when I sat down to write this preface, I tried to pinpoint the catalyst that gave rise to this project and with which I could begin such a narrative. Thinking about the genesis of this book, I traced it through political events, collaborations with colleagues, conference presentations, workshops and colloquia, and informal conversations with friends. I even saw the threads of this book running through family history, experiences, and relationships. Journeying through the history of this project has cast into doubt my ability to authoritatively narrate its origin. In this, the ironic questioning of authorial power precisely at the moment when it needs to be invoked, I feel some of the trepidation expressed by Judith Butler in the epigraph. "But I am writing here now: is it too late?" Thus rather than narrating the birth of this book, as a preface traditionally does, I will unweave some of the tangled threads that have influenced this project and that can help provide a picture of where this book is coming from and what it hopes to contribute. On this last point the epigraph is instructive in a second sense, because it signals one of the main concerns of this book: the possibility of vernacular discourses to challenge and remake the borders of citizenship and belonging. What are the possibilities that rhetoric possesses to rewrite these boundaries and redefine political and cultural space?

In the most immediate sense, these questions were sparked by the nationwide wave of demonstrations and protests by Latina/os and immigrants throughout 2006, which took place in response to proposed federal immigration legislation. The subject of chapter 3, these demonstrations featured millions of protestors organizing to oppose restrictive immigration policy and to demand immigrant rights and a clear path toward nationalization. Watching people march through the streets, risking backlash or, in the case of undocumented immigrants, legal prosecution, I was motivated to question how Latina/o and immigrant rights movements might challenge our conventions of borders, citizenship, and immigration. These demonstrations seemed to refute the presumption that the protesting groups (Latina/os and immigrants) were apolitical or solely the victims of marginalization and exclusion. On the contrary, these groups seemed to stake out political and cultural space despite their otherwise marginal status in U.S. society, particularly in the case of unauthorized immigrants. The demonstrations also brought into question standard notions of cultural assimilation and naturalization that are usually associated with immigrants. The 2006 immigrant rights protests pushed me to think about how minoritarian groups, such as Latina/os and immigrants, might be crafting alternative forms of citizenship. Could the contestation and controversy over immigration, borders, and citizenship going on in U.S. society provide any lessons about the past and potential future of belonging or national identity? And, surely these protest movements were not taking place in a vacuum, so how could historical struggles over borders, citizenship, and identity by Latina/o and immigrant groups help to contextualize and challenge our thinking about these important and contemporary topics? These broad questions about borders and citizenship, national identity, and political agency motivate this project.

However, I could also point to a second and earlier source of inspiration for the questions I take up in this book. The experiences I had and the stories I heard growing up as the child of immigrants and as part of a diasporic Latina/o immigrant family also have been a motivation for the questions about physical and cultural borders, citizenship, and Latina/o identity animating this project. My mother immigrated to the United States along with her mother, sister, and brother in 1965, leaving their native Cuba behind (as well as their oldest brother, my uncle Tito, who was conscripted and thus could not immigrate). My maternal grandfather had already been living in the United States for four years as a political refugee and former member of the anti-Castro movement, and thus, like most Cuban immigrants of that time, my mother and her family were legally welcomed as part of the United States' efforts to undermine the new Cuban government and to combat Communism in the hemisphere. In contrast, my father, who immigrated to the United States in 1972 from El Salvador (though he was born in Honduras), encountered a very different migrant experience. His family also came in waves: first his mother, who later arranged to be joined by her youngest son and daughter (my father and aunt). My father also left behind siblings who could not or would not follow. Despite political and economic turmoil in the region, however, Central American immigrants were not officially welcomed by the U.S. government to the same degree as other groups of immigrants. Thus without immediate legal avenues for migration, and faced with both economic and family troubles, my paternal grandmother had to arrange for unauthorized entry into the United States for both my father and aunt.

Despite these different migration experiences, as a child I remember hearing stories of my parents' and family's successful economic and cultural assimilation. It was only later that I started to inquire about the struggles behind those stories—experiences of physical and cultural displacement and dislocation or emotional battles to secure legal status and forestall deportation. Telling these stories is outside the purview of this present project, but needless to say, this family history invoked ill-defined questions about borders, belonging, and national identity long before I had the academic and theoretical language to think about these topics systematically. How do borders work not only physically but also figurally in the lives of legal and illegal immigrants? What does it mean to belong and to be a citizen? Also, growing up in a diasporic Latin American immigrant family, surrounded by an even more diverse Latina/o immigrant community—with Puerto Ricans, Venezuelans, Colombians, Salvadorans, and Mexicans—I could often witness the affective pull of a "pan-Latino" or "Hispanic" identity that could provisionally unite very different groups of people and experiences. At the same time, I was aware of the very real differences and disagreements between national groups and cultures that forestalled any such Latinidad (disagreements that were as pronounced in discussions about immigration or politics as they were in tastes for music or food). In sum, my family members' struggles and stories about citizenship and immigration, cultural and national identity, helped to spur and still inspire my thinking about issues such as borders, citizenship, immigration, and Latina/o identities. In this respect, we could say that the questions animating this book have an even longer generation than I first suggested.

It is because of this complex and multilayered history that I have been unable to trace a definitive starting point or origin for this project. In a sense, these trajectories that I have identified—the academic interests, political commitments, and personal experiences—help to form the backdrop for this project. They shape my theoretical, critical, and political focus on borders and citizenship, immigrant rights and questions of Latina/o identity. Each source of inspiration, as well as many others, has played a role in germinating the arguments that I advance and the commitments that I take. With this background in mind, let me briefly explain the project at hand and address some methodological and terminological issues.

The Border Crossed Us is about the way that borders and citizenship are created and contended through rhetoric. As I explain in the introduction, the title of the book is drawn from a long-standing slogan among Chicana/o and immigrant movements—"We didn't cross the border, the border crossed us"—that encapsulates the main themes of the book. Mainly, I trace how borders and U.S. citizenship crossed Latina/o communities and analyze the rhetorical strategies through which particular Latina/o groups contended with and challenged the borders of belonging. My assumption is that borders and citizenship are not just the causes of rhetoric but that rhetoric constitutes and contests borders and citizenship. At the same time, I approach borders and citizenship as sources of rhetorical and hegemonic struggle, both by those who are defined inside the bounds of citizenship and by those who are defined as alien. The chapters that follow explore this rhetorical and hegemonic struggle by analyzing situated rhetorics of borders and citizenship in the context of Latina/o groups.

One issue that I should discuss before moving on is the question of terminology. A number of ethnic identifiers have been used to refer to Latin American people or their descendants who live in the United States. These terms include Latino, Hispanic, Chicano, Latin, Spanish, and many others. Such identifiers are often deployed monolithically to refer to all people of Latin American descent and thus can be rife with inaccuracies and fraught with dangers of homogenization or essentialism. At the same time, racial and ethnic identifications such as these can serve as a source of solidarity, political activism, and group assertion in a democratic polity. For example, "Chicana/o" (or the original "Chicano") is a politicized referent for U.S. citizens of Mexican descent. Chicano (an adaptation of "Mexicano") was originally a derogative ethno-racial slur used against Mexican Americans in the early twentieth century. This negative term was redeployed as a form of political and racial identity and solidarity in the Southwest during the civil rights movements of the 1960s and 1970s (that is, the Chicano movement). As we shall see in chapter 2, Chicano identities served as a source of cultural pride and political solidarity for self-identified Chicanas and Chicanos as well as other Mexican Americans throughout the time period. The historical complexity embedded in this one word demonstrates that the terms used to discuss Latina/o populations are implicated in "the weight of history [and] governmentality" as well as in the "acts of self- and group assertion" and self-identification of particular Latina/o groups. As "Chicano" demonstrates, terms for (self-)identification touch on factors including history, governmental control, and political and cultural agency.[1]

Given these considerations, clarity about my terminological choices is important. In this book I will use the term "Latina/o" to refer to people of Latin American descent living in the United States, including Mexicans, Mexican Americans, Puerto Ricans, Dominicans, Guatemalans, and others. I prefer "Latina/o" over "Hispanic" because of its origins and because it does not define people exclusively in relation to Spanish colonization and thus is more inclusive. For example, the official use of the term "Hispanic" began with the U.S. Census Bureau as an ethnonym to refer to people with Spanish surnames, language, or Spanish ancestry. In contrast, the term "Latino" rose to prominence as a sort of alternative to the more exclusive, colonialist, and state-sanctioned "Hispanic." Apart from this history, I have also chosen to use "Latina/o" because it promotes more gender inclusivity than the implicit masculine gendering of the Spanish language and of "Latino." As a general rule I use gendered identifiers (such as "Latino") only to refer to particularly gendered individuals or groups and gender-inclusive terms ("Latina/o") in all other instances.[2]

In addition, particular chapters use terms of identification that are specific to the groups I am studying. These include "Californio" to reference Mexican Californians in the nineteenth century, "Chicana/o" or its gendered variations to reference self-identified Mexican Americans activists in the Southwest during the 1960s and 1970s, and "Hispano" to reference rural northern New Mexicans. These terms are self-identifications particular to each community under analysis and are explained in context. To some degree this book will move back and forth between general and specific identificatory terms and cultural groups. In doing so my goal is not to homogenize Latina/o nationalities, cultures, or identities but to search for meaningful commonalities and differences between these groups. In the end, I will advocate for understanding the terms used to refer to Latina/os (as well as Latinidad itself) as contingent, strategic, and performative identifications that entail pitfalls as well as possibilities for identity and agency.

A related point is the use of italics to demarcate foreign words and quotations. This is another issue, like that of terminology, which creates heated debates. The convention is to italicize unfamiliar, non-English-language terms to set them apart for the reader and thus to aid in comprehension. However, I have chosen not to italicize unfamiliar Spanish-language terms in this book. I believe that to do so poses a risk of entrenching hierarchies and negative differences between English and "foreign" languages and peoples. In my view, using italics to signal Spanish words as "foreign" would seem to imply that the reader is a monolingual, English-speaking, Euro-American who will find such non-English words foreign and unfamiliar. This is an assumption that might entrench a particular and exclusionary image of the ideal audience. In particular, since my concern in this book is to question such assumptions and the borders that are imposed on citizenship and identity, to differentiate and heirarchicalize the languages in the text would subtly reinforce those very same cultural and linguistic borders. Instead, I have chosen to maintain both Spanish and English languages in roman type to promote equality between the two languages and encourage bilingualism.[3]

Ongoing political controversies about border "security," the sanctity of U.S. citizenship, and the status of Mexican and Latina/o immigrants in the United States all demonstrate that demarcating or enforcing borders (territorial, legal, and figural) helps to define the space of belonging. This process of exclusively defining borders and citizenship has concrete effects on the lives of those living on their boundaries. Thus one goal of this book is to understand better the ways in which borders and citizenship are constituted and contested through rhetorical and performative practices. Because of continuing efforts to rigidify and naturalize the often-exclusionary borders of national and cultural community, I approach this process of critical rhetorical analysis as a partially political task. In other words, a second goal of this book is to uncover the possibilities for marginalized groups to struggle with and against restrictive and dominant logics of citizenship and to redefine political, cultural, and national community. Alternative visions of belonging are articulated within marginalized rhetorics, which may or may not hold promise for expanding or even reimagining our national community. Though the book focuses on the rhetorics of Mexican Americans, Chicana/os, and Latina/o immigrants, I also attempt to answer broader questions about the contours of U.S. citizenship.

One of the central arguments this book advances is that Latina/o and immigrant groups have used the (exclusionary) language of borders and citizenship to simultaneously claim belonging and challenge conventions of national identity. Again, this relates to the quotation in the epigraph, where Butler suggests that the "very colonizing discourse" of dominant society may be reappropriated to enable or produce a form of resistance. In this vein, I argue that the rewriting of citizenship by Latina/o and immigrant groups (for our purposes we could expand "writing" to all forms of rhetoric, including written, spoken, visual, and embodied) can enact belonging while also contesting borders, citizenship, and national identity. Of course, we will also see that, though the reappropriation of dominant rhetorics can enact a form of "stumbling block" or "resistance," these minoritarian discourses can also risk entrenching the very same boundaries and divisions of dominant logics. *The Border Crossed Us* unpacks this argument by examining precisely how borders and citizenship have been rhetorically articulated and naturalized as well as by analyzing particular moments in which Latina/o and immigrant groups contest and challenge those selfsame borders of belonging. My hope is that the specific case studies and theoretical perspectives considered in the following chapters can cast these themes into new light and provide new avenues for understanding the ongoing rhetorical struggles over borders, citizenship, and Latina/o identity.

Acknowledgments

It would be impossible for me to acknowledge in this limited space all those to whom I am indebted for helping to bring this project to fruition. This book is truly the labor of a multitude of colleagues, friends, professionals, and loved ones who guided, supported, encouraged, and inspired me over the last several years. However, here I want to publicly acknowledge some of the individuals and groups that have been instrumental in helping me to complete this project.

I owe a tremendous debt of gratitude to a number of wonderful colleagues, teachers, and friends for their help throughout the development of this book. I am immeasurably indebted to Dr. Vanessa B. Beasley, who has invaluably contributed to my writing, thinking, teaching, and professional development. Most of all, I am grateful to her for being the model of an engaged scholar, mentor, and friend. I also thank a number of other teachers who helped me to ask hard questions and to expand my thinking. Thanks to Dr. Celeste M. Condit, Dr. Kevin M. DeLuca, Dr. Bonnie J. Dow, Dr. Thomas M. Lessl, Dr. John M. Murphy, Dr. Edward M. Panetta, and Dr. Pamela Voekel. I would also like to thank my colleagues while at Northeastern University for their continued support during the completion of this book. I am especially grateful to Dr. Greg Goodale and Dr. Thomas K. Nakayama for their generosity and kindness. Both of them were wonderful colleagues, volunteering to read, discuss, and comment on many of the chapters in this book, and they continue to be great friends. Finally, I should thank other friends and colleagues who have helped me develop this project through less formal but no less significant ways. In particular, to Dr. Matthew P. Brigham, Dr. D. Robert DeChaine, Dr. Anne T. Demo, Dr. Eric S. Jenkins, Dr. Kristen L. McCauliff, and Dr. Darrel Allan Wanzer—thank you.

I have been honored to present some of the ideas in this book at conferences, talks, and writing workshops throughout the last few years. These discussions have been a true joy and have greatly enhanced the arguments in this book. In particular, I thank the members of the Athens of America Rhetoric Reading Group (AARRG!) in Boston for reading and commenting on early versions of chapter 3. Thanks are due to the participants in the 2010 Summer Workshop on Critical Latina/o Communication Studies at the University of North Texas (organized by Dr. Darrel Allan Wanzer), who discussed some of the ideas in chapter 2 with me. I have also presented selections from this book in front of audiences at the University of Minnesota and Wake Forest University in the last several years; I am honored to have had those opportunities and very grateful to these audiences for their engagement with my work. In addition, conference reviewers and audiences at the National Communication Association, the Rhetoric Society of America, the National Association of Chicana and Chicano Studies, and the Tepoztlán Institute for Transnational History of the Americas have all listened to and commented on my work.

Parts of the book have been previously published. Chapter 3 is an expanded version of an article that appeared as "(Re)Bordering the Civic Imaginary: Rhetoric, Hybridity, and Citizenship in *La Gran Marcha*" in the *Quarterly Journal of Speech* 97, no. 1 (2011): 26–49. Some portions of the introduction and chapter 2 appeared in slightly different form in the article "Reclaiming the Rhetoric of Reies López Tijerina: Border Identity and Agency in 'The Land Grant Question,'" published in *Communication Quarterly* 60, no. 5 (2012): 561–87. I thank Taylor and Francis for granting permission to reprint portions of these essays.

Research professionals have greatly supported this project and often do not get the credit they deserve for their tremendous work. I am grateful to librarians at Northeastern University and the University of Georgia, who helped to point me in new directions and broaden my conversation with relevant literature. I also thank the Center for Southwest Research at the University of New Mexico Libraries for permission to publish material from their Reies Tijerina Papers. The staff was absolutely wonderful during my time there: in particular, Ann Massmann and Nancy Brown-Martinez, who were immensely helpful in orienting me during what was my very first visit to the archives and who also engaged me in conversations about chapter 2 that significantly improved the final argument.

It has been a joy to work with the editorial staff at the University of Alabama Press. They have been incredibly helpful and professional, and I am very grateful for their assistance and especially for their patience with my many mistakes. In particular, I should thank the editor in chief, Daniel Waterman, who has been incredibly generous of his time and support and who has expressed an unwavering confidence in this project, and Robin DuBlanc, who enthusiastically and graciously guided me through the editing process. I also thank the reviewers of this manuscript for their very helpful suggestions, which substantially improved the final product.

On a personal note, I would like to thank my family and loved ones for supporting me during the writing of this book. As I stated in the preface, my parents, siblings, and extended family can be given much of the credit for inspiring and supporting the questions that animated this project. They too have engaged me in the ideas presented here through informal conversations and personal stories. Most important, however, my family has been a fountain of encouragement, motivation, and love. For these reasons, this book is dedicated to my parents Rene and Debora and to my grandparents Arquímedes, Hortensia, and Leticia, whose love, loss, and struggles have helped to shape who I am and what I do with my life. Finally, I want to thank my wife, Betsy, for her love and support. Perhaps more than anyone she has helped and sustained me in a staggering multitude of ways. She has been a motivational speaker, life coach, copy editor, and, most important, a wonderful and caring partner and best friend. Betsy, thank you for the patience, love, and kindness you have shown me.

The Border Crossed Us

Introduction

On Border Crossings and the Crossing Border

The border is also a migrant.

—Rebecca Solnit

We didn't cross the border, the border crossed us.

—Popular slogan in the immigrant rights movement

The "problem" of the U.S.-Mexico border and of the borders of U.S. identity seems to grow ever larger in the political debate and public discourse of the United States. This is reflected in more and more instances of anxiety over the sanctity of the border (or lack thereof), increasing efforts to shore up border security, and greater contestation over the meaning and potential pliability of the borders between "citizen" and "foreigner." As evidence of these observations, consider a few examples from the last decade.

In the summer of 2005, the "Minutemen Civil Defense Corps" and the "Minuteman Project" organized in Arizona to take border enforcement into their own hands. Angered by what they perceived as the "crisis" of illegal immigration, the Minutemen groups organized their own efforts at border enforcement: policing the border between the United States and Mexico, confronting border crossers, pressuring the U.S. Border Patrol to step up its own enforcement efforts, and creating an all-around mass media spectacle for the twenty-four-hour TV news networks. Concurrent with and also partly because of these vigilante border movements, then-president George W. Bush mounted a nationwide campaign for immigration reform, the efforts of which culminated in debate over HR 4437 (known as the Sensenbrenner bill) in late 2005 and early 2006. In response to this proposed immigration reform bill, Latina/o and immigrant groups across the country organized dozens of protests throughout the summer of 2006, claiming that the legislation would enact a number of overly restrictive immigration provisions. By the end of 2006, several million protestors had organized to demand rights and paths to naturalization for undocumented immigrants.[1]

In the wake of these mass mobilizations, a number of state and local governments—from Arizona and Utah to Georgia and Virginia—instituted some of the most restrictive immigration legislation in decades. Though differing in the details, these measures were part of a concerted effort to step up border enforcement by further criminalizing undocumented immigration as well as legalizing police surveillance and profiling of suspected "illegal aliens." Protests, boycotts, and court battles that arose in response to one of these specific laws, Arizona's SB 1070, attracted national attention. Much of that law was eventually overturned by the U.S. Supreme Court in a high-profile case. At the same time, immigrant rights groups, emboldened by the limited success of the 2006 protests, organized for the passage of the DREAM Act (Development, Relief, and Education for Alien Minors), which would provide avenues for naturalization of immigrant youth. Despite a variety of protests and media spectacles by DREAM activists, the DREAM Act was defeated in Congress in 2010.[2]

These contemporary examples demonstrate that political controversy about the "problem" of the border and the borders of U.S. citizenship has reached renewed intensity. On one hand, border anxiety has bred attempts to militarize the border, enforce immigration policy, and police the boundaries of U.S. identity. On the other, these efforts have been met with protests, contestation, and attempts to negotiate the parameters of citizenship. Contemporary controversies over borders, immigration, and U.S. identity attest to the shifting nature of borders, both physical and figurative—to their porousness and pliability, to the prevalence and persistence of border transgressions, and to the impossibility of keeping borders intact.[3]

The Border Crossed Us explores these and other efforts to restrict and expand U.S. citizenship and the borders of national belonging. The title of the book is drawn from a popular saying of contemporary immigrant activists—"We didn't cross the border, the border crossed us." This slogan exemplifies two important themes of the book. First, it encapsulates my emphasis on performative rhetorics of borders and citizenship: how public discourse creates, contests, and moves the borders of belonging, both metaphorically and materially. Second, the slogan points to my particular focus on Latina/o vernacular discourses of borders and citizenship—on rhetoric about borders and citizenship that emerges from Latina/o communities.

Through critical rhetorical analysis of public discourse, *The Border Crossed Us* explores case studies of debate over borders and citizenship in the context of U.S. Latina/os. I pay particular attention to how Latina/o groups—including Mexicans, Mexican Americans, Chicana/os, and Latina/o immigrants—cooperated with, challenged, and contested the restrictive borders of nation, citizenship, and U.S. identity. Latina/o discourses concerning borders and U.S. citizenship demonstrate that borders move, migrate, and cross individuals and groups for good or ill, that borders are more than territorial boundaries but rather constitute a rhetorical process of demarcating and defining identity and social space. The U.S.-Mexico border and the borders of U.S. citizenship have been constituted across time, in concert with shifting power relations, to define the parameters of belonging. Latina/o groups have been subject to (and the subjects of) these logics of borders and citizenship, working at various times within or against them. The four case studies I examine represent moments in which Latina/o groups crossed and were crossed by borders and include debates about Mexican American citizenship after the Mexican-American War, the advocacy of 1960s Chicano civil rights movements, and modern-day immigrant activism. When borders and U.S. citizenship crossed Latina/o communities (both materially and rhetorically), Latina/os struggled with border rhetorics and enacted U.S. citizenship to cross into or challenge the borders of belonging and U.S. national identity.

Though my primary focus is on the ways that specific Latina/o groups in the United States have contributed to and contested dominant understandings of borders and citizenship, the book also advances a broader critical approach to the study of border rhetorics. I argue for studying borders and citizenship as they are created and contended through public discourse. Thus if the book foregrounds stories of Latina/o groups and individuals struggling with belonging, the background of the book demonstrates the importance of historicizing particular configurations of borders and citizenship. Latina/o rhetorics examined in this book illuminate and challenge our thinking about citizenship, race, identity, and nationality. By tracing the rhetorical evolution of U.S. citizenship, the boundaries that demarcate it, and the new challenges and possibilities facing these conventions, my hope is to push us to denaturalize borders and to rethink citizenship. To orient the reader and preview these arguments, this introduction explains some of the key assumptions and concepts featured throughout the book, including my critical rhetorical approach to borders and citizenship and the importance of focusing on Latina/o vernacular discourses.

Citizenship, Borders, and Critical Rhetoric

As the introductory pages suggest, the U.S.-Mexico border and (the borders of) U.S. citizenship form crucial "problems" in contemporary politics and culture. Beyond this simple observation, however, the concept of the border and its relation to citizenship demands more sustained consideration. This task can seem daunting since, as D. Robert DeChaine notes, the trope of the border is "variously invoked as a geographical term for delineating territories, a political expression of national sovereignty, a juridical marker of citizenship status, and an ideological trope for defining terms of inclusion and exclusion."[4] The work on border studies and citizenship studies is voluminous, spanning areas such as history, law, political economy, and cultural politics.

In conventional terms, borders are understood in a limited way as the strict territorial boundaries defining a nation-state. Though we tend to understand borders exclusively as physical places, border studies scholars remind us that borders are also figurative spaces of identity, culture, and community.[5] The border should be thought of more broadly than as a territorial or juridical boundary—not only as physical but also as figurative or ideological. Here we are interested not only in the territorial borders of a nation-state but also in the boundaries of political and cultural community. This notion of the border as a psychical and figurative zone of division and contact is articulated most paradigmatically in Gloria Anzaldúa's germinal *Borderlands/La Frontera*. Anzaldúa makes clear that the border is both a physical place, "*una herida abierta* [an open wound] where the Third World grates against the first and bleeds," and also a figural space "wherever two or more cultures edge each other, where people of different races occupy the same territory, where under, lower, middle and upper classes touch, where the space between two individuals shrinks with intimacy."[6] Borders involve the process of dividing and constituting community and take shape through both material and ideological practices. As José David Saldívar explains, borders describe "what happens when different social worlds confront one another, or when boundaries between worlds are crossed."[7] In this sense, both the physical and the "figural border" serve multiple functions, drawing lines between "citizen" and "alien or "us" and "them" (whether in the form of territorial borders or ideological divisions), creating a space for community and for border zone contact. We should take care not to collapse the physical and figurative registers of borders as there are important differences, but connecting these two senses of the border illuminates the contestability of borders. As Kent A. Ono writes, "Borders go beyond borders, and so does their function."[8]

Perhaps even more than the concept of the border, citizenship is a fundamentally contested term. It can be understood very narrowly as a legal status that defines membership in a nation or as a broader contract of rights and responsibilities with the state. Some scholars view citizenship as a standard of political engagement (as in, the norm of the engaged citizen), while others emphasize the cultural and social dimensions of citizenship (as a form of "belonging").[9] It would be impossible here to provide a full account of the many different scholarly treatments of citizenship, and more important, such a review would only demonstrate the extreme variation in thought regarding what citizenship means and how far it extends. What we should emphasize, however, is that citizenship is one of the predominant "social imaginaries" by which we understand civic identity and organize social spaces like the nation-state. As an "imaginary," citizenship entails legal and institutional as well as figurative and cultural dimensions; citizenship indexes legal status and political rights but also refers to one's inclusion in a sociocultural and "imagined" community.[10]

These legal, political, social, and cultural dimensions of citizenship are mutually "reinforcing or undermining." That is, they can work together to strengthen one's citizenship status or can stand in contrast to one another, preventing full belonging.[11] For example, access to legal status and political rights depends upon symbolic recognition of one as a member of the "imagined" community. At the same time, however, minority groups often develop the cultural competencies of citizens or become members of the sociocultural community without receiving full recognition.[12] With the integration of the global economy and the greater flow of people across national borders, some scholars even call for the abandonment of a strictly national paradigm of citizenship, advancing transnational, flexible, or cosmopolitan models of citizenship that seem to belie its very foundation as a mode of national membership.[13] Because of the extreme variability and reach of the concept of citizenship, many criticize what they see as its conceptual incoherence. However, as Jeffrey A. Bennett succinctly explains, the "radical indeterminacy" in the meanings of citizenship "does not suggest it has no material or political capital," but only that citizenship "is a fluid concept whose meaning is" contextual and contestable.[14] This "radical indeterminacy" and extreme contestability in the concept of citizenship suggests the intimate connection between borders and citizenship. Borders are important because they help us define who is a citizen and who is not, who belongs and who is "alien," indeed, what citizenship is and what it is not.

The border is physical and ideological; it constitutes identity as well as exclusion. In the case of citizenship, borders define the parameters of the physical nation, demarcate identity and "belonging," and regulate exchange between political and cultural communities. Thus borders and citizenship go hand in hand. As Linda Bosniak notes, whether we think of citizenship in strictly legal terms or more broadly as political or cultural identity, citizenship has both *internal and external borders*. Citizenship references insiders, members within a political or cultural community, but concurrently, citizenship is defined in relation to outsiders, to those who are exterior to its borders. "The community's boundaries"—physical, legal, and cultural—help distinguish a "citizen" from an "alien," demarcating identity and belonging. Whether we think of citizenship as legal status, political rights, or even as social/cultural community, borders are "threshold citizenship matters . . . pertaining to the formation and maintenance of the community within which matters of substantive citizenship are enacted."[15]

In sum, on the outside, borders delimit citizenship, while on the inside, citizenship provides a sense of identity—an organizing logic for a political and cultural community—by indexing the difference between "us" and "them." As I said, borders work to bound territories and the parameters of belonging, thereby providing the possibility for community. But although citizenship promotes identification between people, it does so through "alienization" of the foreigner who does not belong, who is "other."[16] This is why, borrowing from Vanessa B. Beasley, we could call citizenship a "double-edged sword," for it promotes transcendent, "shared identity" between people but is constituted through the persistence of "exclusion, intolerance, and even inhumanity."[17] Thus, borders and citizenship are intricately related. Borders not only demarcate and divide but also regulate relationships of contact, exchange, and equivalence between communities. Meanwhile, citizenship rests in part on "bordering," demarcation, exclusion, and alienization. In this sense, citizenship takes shape through and helps materialize both internal and external borders, and borders help to define citizenship.

A number of the recent events I mentioned above, from restrictive immigration legislation to immigrant rights protests, should make clear that borders and citizenship are intricately connected sites of "hegemonic struggles."[18] More specifically for my purposes, I am interested in how borders and citizenship are constituted and contested through public discourse and in relation to power. Before I unpack this claim, I should note that rhetoric means more here than the adornment of speech, verbal manipulation, or simply hot air, which are its usual connotations in popular culture. Instead, I define rhetoric as persuasive communication addressed to public audiences.[19] Rhetoric extends beyond the podium or lectern to describe any number of symbolic practices that contribute to public identity and public culture.[20] Rhetoric does not refer just to public speeches but to a broad array of discourses that address publics, including public rituals, mass media, visuals, and even public monuments. Regardless of its medium, rhetoric is performative; it is aesthetically and instrumentally marked and staged for an audience.[21] Rhetoric constitutes identity, incites emotions, and motivates actions. More than hot air or manipulative language, rhetoric refers to the power of symbols when performed to move people to collective beliefs, identifications, and actions.[22]

In this book I will focus on borders and citizenship as they are constituted and contested in the public sphere through their rhetorical enactment. This approach centers our study of borders and citizenship on how, why, and to what end they take shape in interactions that define citizens and noncitizens. Rather than focus on borders or citizenship as static entities, I examine rhetoric that *enacts* and *contests* borders and citizenship: from the political and mass media debates that help define civic identity to the "everyday" rhetorics of citizens and those striving to be recognized as citizens. Rhetorics of borders and citizenship define social space and identity. Struggles over the meanings and boundaries of national belonging are articulated through discourses that concretize these "imaginaries" into reality.

Several scholars encourage us to think about citizenship and borders, in this vein, as rhetorically enacted. Robert Asen, for example, advances a view of citizenship "as a performance, not a possession." According to Asen, a rhetorical perspective on citizenship necessitates that we shift our view of citizenship "from a status attribute to a way of acting," that we attend to the "how" of citizenship enactment rather than the "what" of citizenship status.[23] From a different perspective, Lauren Gail Berlant argues that "citizenship may best be thought of as an intricate *scene* where competing forces, definitions, and geographies of freedom and liberty are *lived concretely*" through "personal and political *acts*."[24] Similarly, in his discussion of the U.S.-Mexico border, DeChaine urges scholars to attend to borders less as static entities and more as rhetorical enactments. "Whatever else they may be," writes DeChaine, "borders are products of human symbolic action, created by human agents through particular and often complex rhetorical practices."[25] Similarly, Kent A. Ono and John M. Sloop explain that "rhetoric *shifts* borders, changing what they mean publicly, influencing public policy, altering the ways borders affect people, and circumscribing political responses. . . . Rhetoric at times even determines where, and what, the border is."[26] Collectively, these scholars encourage us to think about how rhetorics of citizenship and borders crystallize into institutional realities, govern social relationships, and define the difference between "citizen" and "alien." The "shifting" of the border, to use Ono and Sloop's term, draws groups into or out of citizenship based on their race, culture, gender, sexuality, and/or language. Whether found in grand civic rituals or the quotidian actions of citizen-subjects, rhetoric constitutes borders and civic identity.

I want to build on these existing theorizations by emphasizing the connection between borders and citizenship as rhetorical performances. In other words, and as I mentioned above, borders and citizenship are "rhetorical and relational performances"[27] that exist side by side. Rhetorics of the border not only define spatial relations but also materialize the boundaries of belonging. Since borders define the parameters of citizenship, attempts to tighten borders, such as those of the Minutemen or of anti-immigrant legislators, serve to restrictively define citizenship and civic identity. Similarly, enactments of citizenship occur in relation to an "other" who is exterior to the borders of the civic imaginary. Efforts to expand citizenship to those who are "outside" of it, including recent immigrant rights movements, necessarily challenge the territorial, legal, and cultural borders of U.S. identity. Thus, enacting citizenship *borders* the civic imaginary just as border rhetorics *demarcate* and define the space of citizenship. The border is articulated through rhetorical practice, distinguishing those who do and do not "belong" and "bordering" citizenship.

It should probably go without saying that rhetorics of citizenship and borders are imbued with and in power, influencing material realities, cultural identity, and social relationships.[28] The examples I mentioned above, such as the border patrolling of the Arizona Minutemen and the efforts to pass restrictive immigration legislation, demonstrate the broader point that public discourse figurally and materially enacts the border, constitutes the citizen, and constructs the "alien."[29] This is not to say that citizenship and borders are wholly discursive, for laws, practices, and institutions granting formal inclusion (or exclusion) still exist. But the material realities of borders, citizenship, and U.S. identity take shape through their consistent reiteration and naturalization, from the vested interests of those who wish to maintain strict borders on the civic imaginary.[30] By rhetorically enacting and defining a specific, restrictive, and contestable form of U.S. citizenship, these recent anti-immigrant movements, for example, border the U.S. social imaginary and define the citizen and the alien. One could even see the checkpoints and fences at the U.S.-Mexico border as bordering practices in the sense that they publicly invoke, give (material) presence to, and persuade us to obey the otherwise unseen lines on a map between "us" and "them." Both historical and contemporary rhetorics of borders define social space and normalize social identities.[31]

At the same time, recent events such as immigrant social protest movements or the efforts of the DREAM activists mentioned above also exemplify how rhetoric works to reconstitute the borders of the civic imaginary. Even those individuals who are excluded from formal dimensions of citizenship often enact belonging and challenge the borders of the national community. This reminds us that even those who are not recognized as belonging can (re)constitute and contest conventions of belonging. Rhetorical struggles over the meanings of borders and citizenship involve competing attempts at "self-making and being-made within webs of power linked to the nation-state and civil society."[32] These discourses become moments of subjectivation, of creating citizen-subjects, and of subjectifying oneself to the state and to power. As we shall see, this can have both empowering and constraining dimensions: positioning oneself as a citizen-subject draws one into the borders of belonging and provides access to political visibility and subjectivity, but drawing upon institutional rhetorics of borders and citizenship subjects oneself to governmentality through which one risks becoming the "target" of surveillance, control, and even exclusion.[33] Though bordering most often defines the citizen in exclusionary terms in relation to an alien "other," the citizen and the alien "are not fixed identities but fluid subject positions in and out of which subjects move" with constraining and enabling effects on subjectivity, belonging, and agency.[34]

In this section I have emphasized the rhetorical and performative connections between borders and citizenship. Rhetorical bordering oftentimes defines citizenship in restrictive ways, bounding the civic imaginary. However, enacting citizenship itself expands and contracts the borders of belonging and draws oneself into (or others outside of) the space of citizenship. Borders and citizenship take shape in the doing, in the sense of being discursively produced in situated moments to serve practical, political, and ideological purposes. The legacy of progressive social movements struggling for full citizenship could be seen as examples of the ways in which social groups reborder the civic imaginary and *enact* citizenship despite their formal and informal exclusion.[35] Historical and contemporary examples such as these demonstrate that borders and citizenship are continually challenged, expanded, and redrawn not only through mainstream discourses that define the ideal citizen-subject but also in the "everyday" or "vernacular" discourses through which citizenship is enacted and contested.[36] Studying social and hegemonic struggles over borders and citizenship provides opportunities to understand how they have been defined and "naturalized," as well as alternative possibilities for cultural and political belonging.[37] With this broad theoretical framework in mind, the next section explains why I have chosen to focus on rhetorics of the border and of citizenship in the Latina/o context and on Latina/o vernacular discourses specifically.

Border Crossings: Latina/os at the Borders of U.S. Citizenship

The U.S.-Mexico border and the place of Latina/os in the United States both represent long-standing sources of contestation over U.S. national identity and citizenship. From the Mexican-American War of 1846–48 to contemporary debates about the immigration "problem" and border "security," borders and citizenship have long defined the relationship of U.S. society to its southern border/neighbor Mexico and to Latina/os more broadly. These histories highlight how U.S. citizenship has been rhetorically and materially bordered in exclusive and exclusionary ways. Likewise, in contemporary efforts to demarcate citizens from aliens and draw the parameters of belonging, we see the same physical and figurative bordering of the civic imaginary. These observations highlight how the Latina/o context is crucial to understanding the rhetorical construction and contestation of borders and citizenship.[38]

At least as far back as the mid-nineteenth century, concern about the U.S. border with Mexico, about its constraining effect on America's Manifest Destiny, and about the "others" living to its south and west propelled the United States' violation of the Mexican border and the forceful takeover of what is now the U.S. Southwest in the Mexican-American War. The war lasted two years, ending in 1848 with the signing of the Treaty of Guadalupe Hidalgo, by means of which the physical and figurative borders of the United States crossed Mexicans through the granting of land and transfer of national sovereignty. Puerto Ricans, like Mexicans, were also "crossed" by the U.S. border and the "imposition of U.S. citizenship," though under a different context, following the 1898 recolonization of the island by the United States after the Spanish-American War. Both cases, the reimposed southern boundary with Mexico and the relationship of Puerto Rico as a colonial territory, catalyzed heightened concern about the linguistic and cultural boundaries of Americanness. Fears about the potential dilution or contamination of U.S. citizenship by these (nonwhite) "foreigners" resulted in decades of de facto segregation of Mexican American and Puerto Rican citizens, who struggled for full citizenship rights.[39]

Controversies about Mexican/Latina/o immigration also have a long and complex history marked by the crossing of and by borders—racial, national, and cultural. Throughout the first half of the twentieth century, Latin Americans were enticed to immigrate to the United States and then exploited as a labor force. The result was "a punishing route of arrivals and departures," of migrant exploitation and deportation campaigns.[40] Even though these migrants were enticed and exploited, nevertheless, they promoted concern about the racial and cultural makeup of the U.S. polity as well as about the integrity of U.S. borders. Mexicans, Mexican Americans, and other Latina/os became exteriorized as a foreign problem "out there" threatening to violate us "over here" despite the fact that their presence within the national body was both necessary and encouraged. Rhetorics of border threat and security and the figure of the "illegal alien" saw their birth in these efforts to define the borders and U.S. citizenship in the face of Mexican immigration. By the last half of the twentieth century, greater numbers of Central American, South American, and Dominican immigrants were coming to the United States, refugees of war and economic impoverishment that in many cases were the result of the political and economic "crossing" of U.S. borders throughout the hemisphere in the form of military intervention and economic exploitation.[41] Though the demographic and cultural makeup of Latina/o immigration shifted, the predominant cultural assumption of contemporary society that all Latina/o- or Mexican-"looking" people are immigrants was entrenched in this historical process of constituting the border, the citizen, and the "illegal alien."[42]

The historical racialization and alienization of Latina/os, immigrants, and other subaltern groups demonstrate how rhetoric defines the "ideal" conditions of citizenship and demarcates the citizen from the noncitizen. These historical struggles also illuminate the significance of Latina/os in the constitution and contestation of U.S. borders and citizenship. As the history of immigration and citizenship policy as well as those contemporary examples I raised above attest, Latina/o groups have consistently created the impetus for *bordering* by U.S. society: literally, in the case of the physical and legal borders of the nation, and figuratively, in the continuing struggle over the demarcations of the "ideal" U.S. citizen. Anxieties about immigration and the "threat" of Latina/o communities continue to this day, as does the rhetorical and material bordering of the nation and of citizenship.[43]

Moving from these historical considerations, researchers from a variety of fields, including communication studies, Latino studies, and Chicano studies, mine contemporary discourses and dominant logics that often become the reiterative rhetorical materials out of which borders are rebuilt and Latina/o identity is defined. For example, a number of studies document long-standing fears of invasion, economic destruction, and cultural contamination that still frequently influence representations of Latina/o immigrants in mass media and politics. These images have become engrained in media coverage of immigration even when that coverage is favorable to immigrants.[44] As part of this overarching narrative, a number of racialized and gendered depictions position Latina/os as "ethnic," "spicy," "brown," or "foreign."[45] These representations are evident not only in political debate about the "Hispanic explosion" or immigrant "breeders" but also in the celebration of "Latin culture" or in the treatments of Latina icons such as Jennifer Lopez or Shakira.[46] Similarly, images of a "sleeping giant" or of a new Latina/o consumer demographic are prevalent in marketing rhetoric or political campaigns seeking to appeal to Latina/o communities. These dueling images of Latina/os as "spicy" newcomers *and* as border encroachers, as a threatening "Hispanic invasion" *and* as an "awakening" political and economic community work together, often positioning Latina/os as a group that must be policed or assimilated into mainstream U.S. society.[47]

These studies demonstrate how mass media and political discourse border civic identity, often defining Latina/os and immigrants as outside the bounds of the civic imaginary. Whether in the form of news media coverage, television, film, books, popular music, or even political/public address, Latina/o communication and cultural studies scholars outline fairly persistent schema of metaphors, portrayals, and dominant images of Latina/os and their role in U.S. society. They argue that racialized logics and stereotypes work collectively to define the parameters of U.S. identity and to police those boundaries from encroachment by Latina/o immigrant "others." Bordering is a rhetorical practice written on bodies and by bodies—"through the constitution of viable subjects and through the corollary constitution of a domain of unviable (un)subjects."[48] Often, rhetorics of the border and of citizenship position Latina/os outside the bounds of the U.S. nation and work alongside concrete efforts to police the borders and exclude those deemed not worthy of belonging. In sum, the borders of U.S. citizenship have multiply crossed, cut across, and have been crossed by Latina/o communities since the nation's inception. As the popular saying among Chicana/os and immigrant rights activists states, "We didn't cross the border, the border crossed us."

Though its exact origins are hard to determine, this saying has been popular since at least the 1960s, when it was deployed within the context of Mexican American and Chicana/o struggles for civil rights. Since then, the slogan has broadened into a point of political solidarity used in literature, music, and art as well as in a number of contemporary immigrant rights protests.[49] The slogan is an example of the rhetorical figure known as antimetabole, a phrase that employs parallel structure but inverts the key terms in a sort of mirror image (AB/BA). Antimetabole argues through contrast and rhetorical reversal.[50] "We didn't cross the border, the border crossed us" inverts the common notion of borders as static and natural entities that humans must encounter and cross. In this way, the slogan foregrounds my argument that borders and citizenship are dynamic, mobile, and sources of rhetorical enactment and contestation that have crossed over and constituted the identities and social space of Mexican Americans, Chicana/os, Puerto Ricans, and Latina/os throughout U.S. history. "We didn't cross the border, the border crossed us" points to the historical crossing of the border and citizenship across and by Latina/o communities—including Mexicans, Chicana/os, and other Latina/os—through war, colonial expansion, international treaties, and federal laws.

Yet this slogan also points to another significant theoretical and programmatic assumption of this book. It centers our perspective on the discourse and experience of those crossed by borders of citizenship, race, colonialism, and nationalism. It demonstrates that civic identity has long been negotiated and contested and that borders are sites of hegemonic struggle. "We didn't cross the border, the border crossed us" raises another set of questions. How have Latina/o groups contributed to or contended with the border's crossing? How have they crossed into or challenged the boundaries of citizenship? What Latina/o voices reverberate from these historical struggles over the borders of belonging? "The border crossed us" exemplifies my focus on Latina/o vernacular discourses of borders and citizenship. On one hand, the slogan "We didn't cross the border, the border crossed us" suggests that the border is not static, that it moves, crosses, and is imposed to limit the parameters of the civic imaginary. On the other hand, it also draws attention to Latina/o vernacular discourses that contest the border's crossing and (re)define the boundaries of belonging.

Crossing Borders: Theorizing Latina/o Vernacular Discourse

As I mentioned above, vernacular discourse describes communication that emanates from and/or is addressed to minoritized communities, counterpublics, and the disempowered. In their essay "The Critique of Vernacular Discourse," rhetorical scholars Kent A. Ono and John M. Sloop highlight "a specific need, given historical power relations, to study communities that have been systematically ignored" and the voices of the "historically oppressed."[51] The reason for studying vernacular voices is akin to that which Foucault gave for recovering "subjugated knowledges," those knowledges that have been "disqualified as inadequate" and are "located low down on the hierarchy."[52] According to Foucault, resurrecting these forgotten ways of thinking and knowing could illuminate the workings of power and knowledge in society and open up alternatives. In the same way, attention to vernacular rhetorics can have two important effects. First, vernacular rhetorics highlight the workings of power and interest in defining subjectivities and subjects such as citizens. Second, vernacular rhetorics help us understand vernacular communities and alternative forms of identity, agency, and belonging that have been deemed inadequate or inferior. In other words, to understand borders and citizenship as sites of rhetorical struggle, we must put vernacular rhetorics in conversation with hegemonic voices and histories.[53]

Importantly, attention to vernacular rhetoric means not only voicing vernacular communities (with all the attendant pitfalls and problems that this task entails) but also examining how these discourses materialize identity, agency, and cultural forms. Scholars of black vernacular culture, for example, theorize a number of "distinctively African American modalit[ies] of cultural expression within the larger American context"—from blues to black vernacular English to a number of specific literary tropes—that serve as modes of "invention, or reinvention, forged out of historical, sociopolitical, and cultural necessities."[54] In addition to serving as modes of cultural expression, vernacular rhetorics can also cross over to challenge materiality and power and to constitute the civic imaginary and affirm the space of citizenship.

Vernacular rhetorics of borders and citizenship do not just assert social space but also have the potential to radically restructure the boundaries of belonging and the parameters of civic identity. This is because, as I mentioned above, rhetorics of borders and citizenship are primary modes of materializing and contesting civic imaginaries into concrete realities. At the same time, we should not presume that vernacular rhetorics, because they can emanate from or resonate within marginalized communities, will necessarily be progressive or liberatory. In fact, vernacular discourses may often reify and repackage dominant assumptions and exclusions, demonstrating their purchase among many different communities. Put differently, vernacular voices are not necessarily "politically resistant" and "should [not] necessarily be valorized" as representing authenticity. Rather, vernacular discourses should be understood on their own terms and for the effects they have.[55]

In this context, my primary goal in the case studies to follow is to elaborate the vernacular rhetorics that have been used by particular Latina/o groups to contribute to or contest borders, to negotiate their position within the U.S. civic imaginary, and to perform citizenship, sometimes in the face of its explicit denial. Michelle A. Holling and Bernadette Marie Calafell describe Latina/o vernacular discourses as "the rhetorical-performative acts self-produced by and within Latina/o communities in visual, verbal, written and/or performative form" that involve "both liberatory and constraining" dimensions.[56] Latina/o vernacular discourses contribute to, contest, and reimagine the parameters of citizenship and belonging, entailing the simultaneous process of identity affirmation, cultural expression, and sometimes even social protest of marginalization. A focus on Latina/o vernacular discourse includes tensions of identity, solidarity, and resistance.

Latina/o vernaculars may both contribute to exclusionary logics of citizenship and also attempt to remake the U.S. civic imaginary from the ground up. In this sense, the variety of Latina/o discourses, from artistic expression to social movement agitation, represents the ways in which vernacular rhetoric breaks apart, borrows from, and rearranges a variety of cultural forms and discourses into a creative whole.[57] Latina/o vernacular discourses entail the constitution of identity, the articulation of agency, and the attempt to (re)define borders and citizenship. Thus, whether in the form of performance art or even in the performance of political identities through political debate and social protest, Latina/o vernaculars reappropriate and stage enactments of citizenship and identity in the public arena.[58]

Of course, Latina/o discourse is not of one voice, nor is it inherently a more liberatory challenge to some larger "American" voice, seeing as there is no one such dominant voice. Rather, Latina/o vernaculars are multivocal, rooted in multiple traditions, and sometimes involve reification of dominant logics as well as "self-assertion" and "challenge" to "oppressive social and political conditions." The designation of a vernacular discourse is in part itself a rhetorical maneuver since discourse may be vernacular for some communities but more "mainstream" or "civic" for others.[59] However, I designate these case studies as instances of vernacular discourse because they highlight the ways in which particular groups of Mexicans, Mexican Americans, Chicana/os, and Latina/os negotiated U.S. citizenship and national/cultural borders in light of attempts to define them outside of those bounds. Such vernacular discourses provide an orientation for understanding the ways that borders and U.S. citizenship have crossed and been crossed by marginalized or counterpublic communities throughout U.S. history.

"The Border Crossed Us"

The contemporary examples of struggles over borders and citizenship introduced at the beginning of this introduction demonstrate that the borders of the nation and the parameters of belonging are sites of rhetorical struggle through which we can glean insights about citizenship, identity, and political agency. As we have seen, one of the greatest instances of contemporary struggle over borders and citizenship can be found in ongoing debates over the U.S.-Mexico border and the status of Latina/os within the U.S. civic imaginary. In this light, *The Border Crossed Us* examines historical and contemporary moments of contestation over citizenship and borders, moments in which Latina/o and immigrant groups—primarily Mexican American citizens and Latina/o immigrants along the U.S.-Mexico border and in the Southwest—claimed, challenged, and contested citizenship from within. I argue that borders and U.S. citizenship have materially and rhetorically crossed Latina/o communities throughout history and that Latina/os in the United States have long struggled with and sought to cross into or challenge the borders of belonging (including race, culture, language, and gender).

The case studies that follow illuminate how Latina/o and immigrant groups have contended with the encroachment and crossing of the border, both figuratively and materially, across time and place. They focus on how Latina/o vernacular rhetorics have rhetorically redrawn, delimited, and disputed the borders of belonging. In tracing these four moments of rhetorical struggles over borders and citizenship, my emphasis will be on how, why, and to what end these particular groups enacted citizenship and challenged borders. In other words, I will focus on the kinds of citizenship that were enacted and the specific vernacular rhetorical strategies that were used. At the same time, these individual moments collectively tell a story about rhetorical efforts to define the border and to demarcate the space of citizenship in more or less expansive ways. They argue that performing citizenship, even in the face of its formal or de facto absence, can reborder the civic imaginary and redefine belonging.

While this introduction has focused on border rhetoric as a form of demarcation and division, the first two case studies emphasize that it can also encourage cultural contact, challenge boundaries, and forge new forms of identity and agency. Chapter 1, "Negotiating the Border," focuses on nineteenth-century debates about Mexican American citizenship, in particular the California Constitutional Convention debates of 1849 and 1879. The chapter examines how newly colonized Mexicans negotiated their U.S. citizenship with their Anglo fellow citizens, struggling to articulate a middle ground between Mexican and U.S. American racial and colonial logics. This case study evinces a vernacular border rhetoric that attempted but ultimately failed to successfully negotiate the racial and colonial borders between Mexico and the United States in the wake of the Mexican-American War. In chapter 2, "Inhabiting the Border," I study the discourse of the Alianza Federal de Mercedes, an activist group spanning the Chicano movements of the late 1960s and early 1970s that both problematized U.S. citizenship and civil rights and simultaneously performed U.S. identity. The Alianza's rhetoric, I argue, was betwixt and between the recognized traditions of citizenship of the time; the group's vernacular rhetoric embraced the both/and of the borders of belonging, negotiating multiple citizenship traditions and crafting identity and agency.

If chapters 1 and 2 focus on vernacular rhetorics that navigated the boundaries of identity and belonging, chapters 3 and 4 examine those that sought to integrate and transcend conventions of borders and citizenship, of inclusion and exclusion. In response to the stresses of transnational migration, globalization, and multiculturalism, the Latina/o and immigrant movements discussed in these chapters enacted hybrid vernacular rhetorics that fused new forms of belonging and identity. Chapter 3, "Rebordering the Nation," examines the 2006 nationwide immigration protests, especially the Los Angeles protest known as La Gran Marcha (the Great March), to highlight contemporary bordering practices and Latina/o vernaculars. Through hybrid verbal, visual, and embodied rhetorics, Latina/o and immigrant protestors merged multiple forms of racial, national, and cultural community. Chapter 4 extends this analysis forward to the 2010 protests against restrictive state and local immigration legislation, such as Arizona's SB 1070. These protests, as well as other recent Latina/o activism, evince a performatively enacted citizenship that is confluent and that transcends national borders. Despite the particular historical and cultural contexts from which they emanated, each type of vernacular discourse engaged and worked with, through, and against dominant logics of borders and citizenship to craft alternative imaginaries of community.

Tracing these forms of Latina/o vernacular discourse, some of which were more liberatory than others, all of which struggled with the racial and colonial tensions of national belonging, can help us understand ever-evolving struggles over U.S. borders, citizenship, and Latina/o identities. These chapters serve as touchstones in the book's broader argument that bordering is a rhetorical practice and that citizenship is a performative enactment. These historical and contemporary case studies provide both a broad and in-depth picture of border rhetorics and citizenship enactment in Latina/o contexts. From nineteenth-century legislative debates to contemporary protest movements, from archival sources and textual analysis to ethnography, the case studies appeal to a variety of methodological and theoretical orientations. Despite these differences, they each illuminate the myriad ways Mexican Americans, Chicana/os, Latina/os, and immigrants enact vernacular rhetorics that reify or challenge borders and citizenship.

Undeniably, the groups I analyze in each case study are very different in terms of their national origins, legal status, and racial/cultural identifications. Chapters 1 and 2, for example, are heavily Mexican American and Chicana/o focused, while chapters 3 and 4 center on groups of migrants (largely from Mexico and Central America but also from South America and elsewhere) and their allies. While the migrant movements of chapters 3 and 4 focus on people with different legal statuses and national origins, chapters 1 and 2 feature the struggles of legal U.S. citizens for full recognition and inclusion. My goal is to track discourses of borders, citizenship, and identity across these different contexts and historical periods, instead of erasing or subsuming their differences. As much as these case studies differ, they speak to the commonality of racialization and coloniality as organizing logics in the experiences and identities of Mexican Americans, Chicana/os, and Latina/os in the United States. They also demonstrate the breadth and depth of Latina/o vernacular discourses and that Latina/o vernacular rhetorics serve as acts of position and opposition, claiming belonging as part of the U.S. nation but challenging, stretching, and skewing the borders of national identity in new ways.

These chapters are not meant to be representative of some authoritative Latina/o history or an essential Latina/o identity. In fact, one of the arguments I advance throughout this book is that there is no such "authoritative," "authentic," or "unified" Latina/o identity and history but rather that Latinidad is a rhetorical, provisional, and strategic construction in the same way that borders and citizenship are rhetorically constructed. Instead of elevating these case studies to canonical status or forwarding them as representative of some authentic Latina/o voice, I present them as four moments of vernacular rhetoric that illuminate how borders and citizenship are constituted and contested through public discourse.The chapters focus on the contextual effects of border and citizenship rhetorics and on how each vernacular discourse constructs particular forms of identity, agency, and subjectivity. I have chosen these case studies because they present four rich moments to understand the construction and contestation of borders, citizenship, and identity in the United States. Other cases and examples are worthy of study, and in the conclusion I will broaden the arguments of the book to other examples. To the degree that I encourage a purposeful slippage between Chicana/o, Mexican American, and Latina/o in this book, the purpose is to make a political and theoretical argument for the necessity of understanding Latinidad as a performative, positional, and partially essentialist identification constructed in the context of and in opposition to colonial and racial legacies. In this respect, to call these very different voices Latina/o vernacular discourses is a conscious choice meant to perform my approach to Latinidad.[60]

Furthermore, I have chosen to study what might be considered progressive or liberal discourses that challenge conventional ideas of borders and citizenship, in part because of my commitment to a critical rhetorical approach. This acknowledges scholarship as a political act that can "advance different social relations and possibilities."[61] That said, it is important not to put the cart before the horse, so to speak, by presuming that all Latina/o and immigrant discourses of citizenship are inherently decolonial and progressive, or that they all help to secure belonging in more inclusive ways. The question, rather, is what kinds of citizenship are discursively enacted and how? What are the tensions of identity and agency animating these vernacular discourses? How can they aid in the decolonization of Latina/o and immigrant identity, of borders and citizenship? As an attempt to uncover and analyze heretofore understudied voices of Latina/o communities both past and present, this book contributes to the rewriting of a collective memory of Latina/o citizenship struggles in the United States. *The Border Crossed Us* argues that it is U.S. borders, rhetorical, geographic, and legal, that have moved and that are moving—that "the border is also a migrant."[62] In the broadest sense, this study helps to illuminate the enduring significance and rhetorical evolution of borders and U.S. citizenship and provides programmatic and theoretical suggestions for the continued study of these important topics.

To this end, we can begin to understand the process of rhetorical and material bordering of U.S. citizenship and identity by turning to the mid-nineteenth century, during which Mexican citizens were forcibly transformed into American citizens along with the exchange of Mexican territory after the Mexican-American War. This period features one of the earliest moments of rhetorical and political struggle over borders and U.S. citizenship in the context of Mexican Americans and thus evinces a very early instance of Latina/o vernacular discourse.

Negotiating the Border

Race, Coloniality, and Citizenship in Nineteenth-Century California

The U.S.-Mexican border *es una herida abierta* where the Third World grates against the first and bleeds. And before a scab forms it hemorrhages again, the lifeblood of two worlds merging to form a third country—a border culture.

—*Gloria Anzaldúa*

The signing of the Treaty of Guadalupe Hidalgo on February 2, 1848, marked the formal end to a two-year war between the United States and Mexico. This war is known in the United States as the Mexican-American War (which connotes a fair war among equals justly won) and by some in Mexico as la intervención norteamericana en México, the North American intervention into Mexico, (connoting imperialism and conquest). Though it lasted only a few short years, nevertheless the war, and the treaty that marked its ending, helped to cement the United States' position as an ascending global power. Through the Treaty of Guadalupe Hidalgo, the United States won a vast swath of territory (most or all of the land that now constitutes California, Texas, New Mexico, Arizona, Colorado, Utah, Nevada, and Wyoming) and gained control of the territory's Mexican and indigenous inhabitants, who became subjects of the U.S. government. Apart from (or perhaps because of) these monumental changes, the treaty is also important because it helped give birth to the contemporary U.S.-Mexico border and the border "problem." As Richard Griswold del Castillo shows, colonial relations influenced the drafting of the treaty, which the United States "virtually dictated," contributing to ongoing relationships of imperial control and dependence. This is why Gloria Anzaldúa refers to the U.S.-Mexico border as an open wound, "una herida abierta," where the violence of conquest and colonialism continually "hemorrhages" the "lifeblood" of two nations and peoples.[1]

Anzaldúa's quotation in the epigraph raises questions of the border's crossing and of the borders of citizenship that took shape after the Mexican-American War. The Treaty of Guadalupe Hidalgo represents what in the introduction we referred to as a moment of rhetorical and material bordering. Though this is obvious in the sense that the treaty redrew the territorial border between the United States and Mexico, the Treaty of Guadalupe Hidalgo also bordered the U.S. civic imaginary, reconstituting the legal and figural borders of citizenship in light of an influx of new Mexican (American) citizen-subjects. Specifically, the treaty guaranteed access to U.S. citizenship to all colonized Mexicans contingent on their renunciation of Mexican citizenship. That is, Mexicans could choose to remain Mexican citizens and forego the rights and protections of U.S. citizenship, becoming marginalized inhabitants of the nation, or they could take on the mantle of "Americanism" to receive (provisional) recognition. As we shall see below, this bordering took shape under the racialized contours of U.S. citizenship at the time, which extended only to white males. Thus the border was drawn not only across a territory but also across a colonized group of people (themselves part of a colonial society), who had to choose between assimilation into the conqueror's society or face exclusion. The border's crossing took shape through rhetorics of race and gender, coloniality, and nationality. It is this same legacy of bordering that shapes contemporary economic, political, cultural, and migratory relationships between the United States and Mexico. If we wish to understand the contemporary practices of bordering U.S. citizenship and identity, then the nineteenth century is a crucial starting point.[2]

Thus far we have approached the border as a dividing line or demarcation. However, the quotation by Anzaldúa in the epigraph also suggests that the border can be thought of in another way. Anzaldúa claims that the border(lands) not only create exclusion and division but spur connection and crossing and can give rise to a "border culture." Though we have emphasized how the borders and/of U.S. citizenship work to divide the citizen and the alien, border rhetorics can also entail the contestation and regeneration of identity. Anzaldúa, then, inaugurates a notion of the borderlands as a space of division as well as contact and crossing. Though borders create "hatred, anger, and exploitation"—in Anzaldúa's case the U.S.-Mexico borderlands, as well as borders of citizenship, race, gender, and sexuality—borderlands are also a space of contradiction in which individuals cultivate new identities and mold "ambivalence into something else." The border(lands) here represent both the (physical and figurative) place of racialization, colonialism, and exclusion faced by Mexican Americans and Latina/os in U.S. society and a space from which Mexican Americans and Latina/os craft a borderlands identity.[3]

In sum, the historical moment after the Mexican-American War is significant in our effort to explore the historical process of bordering as well as Latina/o vernacular discourses struggling with borders and citizenship. The transference of U.S. citizenship to colonized Mexicans gave rise to some of the first moments in which Mexicans rhetorically contested borders and enacted U.S. citizenship. This chapter focuses on one of those efforts: the 1849 California Constitutional Convention, which took place barely a year after the signing of the Treaty of Guadalupe Hidalgo during a time when the territory of California faced rapid changes that accelerated the process toward self-government. In the 1849 Constitutional Convention, which would determine the conditions for California's acceptance into the Union, Anglo-Americans debated with Californios (native Mexican Californians) about territorial boundaries, governmental structures, and the terms of citizenship in the new state. During the convention, Mexican Californios faced critical questions concerning the terms of their newly granted U.S. citizenship. Would they be accepted as full members of the U.S. political and cultural community, or would they be excluded from or forced to assimilate into traditions of U.S. citizenship? How far would their newly granted membership in the national community extend?[4]

The 1849 convention was significant because it represented an early moment of formal contestation between dominant and vernacular discourses of citizenship, race, and identity—between Mexican Californios and Anglo settlers. Only a year and a half after the birth of the modern U.S.-Mexico border (with the exception of the area added in the Gadsden Purchase of 1853), newly conquered Californios met with Anglo conquerors to negotiate the parameters of a new state government and to exercise their newly granted U.S. citizenship. A few decades later, by the late nineteenth century, Californios and Mexican Americans throughout the Southwest had been racialized and relegated to a second-class citizenship. Given this historical and cultural upheaval, vernacular rhetorics of citizenship and borders enacted in the California Constitutional Convention of 1849 speak to broader contestation over race, citizenship, and nation. Analyzing the transcripts of the 1849 California Constitutional Convention in their rhetorical/historical "milieu,"[5] this chapter focuses on the interplay between the dominant rhetorics of race, coloniality, and U.S. American identity, all of which played a role in Mexicans' marginalization, and the vernacular discourses that contributed to, contended with, and contested these dominant logics. Citizenship and (racial) identity were defined and delimited by delegates during the convention debates and, in turn, Californios negotiated the (literal and figurative) borders of U.S. citizenship.

Drawing on this aforementioned notion of the border(lands) as productive of cultural identity and political agency, this chapter will argue that the Californio delegates in the 1849 Constitutional Convention crafted a form of border rhetoric that worked at the intersections of race, coloniality, and citizenship. The Californios' vernacular discourse (unsuccessfully) tried to integrate Mexican and U.S. American citizenship traditions; the delegates performed their newly granted U.S. citizenship while also providing a subtle critique of some of its racialized dimensions. Through rhetorical analysis of the convention transcripts, I show that the Californios' border rhetoric (or "border thinking," to use Walter Mignolo's term) consisted of imitation laced with difference that "work[ed] . . . from the double bind between assimilation . . . and marginalization," that both resisted and reified coloniality and the racialized/gendered dimensions of citizenship. In this sense, the Californio delegates provided a vernacular discourse that sat at "the intersection of hegemonic and subaltern" traditions of citizenship and identity. Their enactments of citizenship imitated and appropriated but also challenged elements of U.S. citizenship traditions, drawing themselves into the borders of the national imaginary while undermining some of these exclusionary parameters of belonging.[6]

Despite the challenges posed by the Californios' vernacular border rhetoric, I conclude that their discourse during the 1849 Constitutional Convention was ultimately a failure because it entrenched the racial and colonial logics of borders, citizenship, and U.S. identity, which contributed to Mexicans' marginalization in the new state and country. As evidence of this, we will see how, just thirty years after the 1849 convention, the pressures of whiteness, coloniality, assimilation, and exclusion circumscribed the options for Mexican Americans in the new state. These nineteenth-century rhetorics of borders and citizenship illuminate the liberatory and constraining possibilities of Latina/o vernacular discourse and the legacy of Latina/o citizenship struggles throughout U.S. history.

Before examining the California Constitutional Convention debates, the next section develops the historical and rhetorical context of the Constitutional Convention of 1849—including the colonial legacies of Spain, Mexico, and the United States and their respective traditions of racial identity and citizenship. Also key to understanding the specific border discourse of Californios in the 1849 convention are the concepts of coloniality (and its relationship to colonialism) and border rhetoric as a decolonial project. The next section turns to this historical and theoretical/conceptual background.

Race and Coloniality in Nineteenth-Century California

The calling of the California Constitutional Convention of 1849 in the wake of U.S. conquest was but one significant moment in decades of radical change on the western frontier. Over the course of a quarter century, California saw the contact and overlap of various forms of colonial powers. It was transformed, during the first half of the nineteenth century, from the frontier of the Spanish colonial empire (New Spain) to a semiautonomous Mexican province to a U.S. military territory and finally to a

U.S. state. These changes in the colonial administration of the territory—from Spanish to Mexican to U.S. American—rapidly transformed the political, economic, and cultural context of nineteenth-century California, including the conditions and parameters of citizenship. In spite of this instability and change, however, many of the underlying relations of coloniality, including understandings of racial/ethnic identity and its connection to personhood and citizenship, remained remarkably stable over these decades and across various political administrations. An understanding of these legacies of colonialism and coloniality in nineteenth-century California helps us to situate the specific debates about race, citizenship, and identity in the 1849 Constitutional Convention.

First, however, I should clarify an important theoretical point that informs this discussion, namely, the conceptual distinction and relationship between "coloniality" and "colonialism." As Nelson Maldonado-Torres explains the difference, "Colonialism denotes a political and economic relation in which the sovereignty of a nation or a people rests on the power of another nation, which makes such nation an empire. Coloniality, instead, refers to long-standing patterns of power that emerged as a result of colonialism, but that define culture, labor, intersubjective relations, and knowledge production well beyond the strict limits of colonial administrations."[7] While colonialism describes a relationship of imperial domination and subordination between nations/peoples (for example, Spain and its colonies), coloniality is broader, more systemic, and more persistent than material or historical colonialism(s). Coloniality sits deep "in the modern/colonial capitalist/patriarchal world-system" and is expressed in the "intersectionality . . . of multiple and heterogeneous global hierarchies . . . of domination and exploitation," including those based on sex, gender, race, class, epistemology, spirituality, and so on.[8] The concept of coloniality resonates with what Stuart Hall referred to as the "displacement" and "internalization" of colonial power relations "within the decolonised society itself."[9]

This distinction is instrumental in understanding the bordering of racial identity and citizenship in nineteenth-century California. Both before and after Mexico's independence from Spain (in 1821), California society was organized largely around a racial and class caste system known as castas. The casta system provided "an elaborate hierarchy of race-based inequality built around combinations and degrees of racial mixture among Spaniards, Indians, and African slaves who had been brought to the Americas." As a system of classification, the castas were based on racialization of indigenous (indio), black (negro), and mixed-race (mestizo, mulatto, and so on) people in opposition to white, Christianized Europeans (peninsulares, or Spanish immigrants, and criollos, or native-born whites). This process of racialization was itself tied inextricably to discourses of gender and sexuality (ideas of feminized natives, masculine conquerors, virgin lands, and the like).[10] On one hand, the casta system served as a way of making sense of the complexities of colonial society, where racial mixture was not only prevalent but officially sanctioned and encouraged by the state and the church. On the other hand, the casta system functioned to arrange these differences into a hierarchy through the locus of race or "purity of blood [limpieza de sangre]."[11] That is to say, the casta system both helped to explain and to produce colonial racial and epistemic identities. The casta system was both mapped onto and helped to justify a rigid economic class system, where large-property-owning and fully enfranchised whites stood at the top and where (de facto if not de jure) economically and politically disenfranchised indigenous people and African slaves (who admittedly were much less prevalent in California) stood at the bottom. According to historian David Tavárez, the casta system "could index both putative ethnic category and perceived socioeconomic status," and thus it provided the "colonial lexicon" both for Spanish colonialism and for the ensuing political and economic relations between groups throughout Mexico after its independence.[12]

The interconnecting phenotypic, socioeconomic, and epistemic/ideological dimensions of this racial caste system, as well as its persistence after Mexican independence, highlight how coloniality (that is, epistemic/ideological hierarchies) worked alongside but also separate from colonialism (that is, political and economic relationships of colonial domination). Coloniality took shape in ideological distinctions between the Christian, civilized/white conquerors (Spanish, English, and later American) and the supposedly heathen/savage/nonwhite indigenous peoples of the "New World" and of "the West" who were conquered. These ideologies of superiority and inferiority both facilitated the physical conquest and subjugation of indigenous people—and, later, Mexicans—and helped to constitute a sense of a colonial superiority that sustained colonialism. The casta system and its production of (racial, gender, and class) identity was a primary "epistemic operation" of coloniality.[13] Social ideas about who was human and who was barbarian, who was civilized and who was not, who was white and who was not, as Aníbal Quijano explains, "served not only to impede the cultural production of the dominated, but also as a very efficient means of social and cultural control, when the immediate repression ceased to be constant and systematic."[14] The distinction between colonialism and coloniality helps explain how ideological dimensions of colonialism (coloniality) continued to impact Mexican society in the absence of Spanish colonial administration. After Mexican independence, many of the vestiges of Spanish coloniality remained, including the socioeconomic and racial segregation of the caste system. This system was used as the basis of legal status, citizenship, and social identity in Mexico even in the absence of Spanish colonial institutions.

After Mexican independence the Spanish casta system was formally slackened (for example, with the abolition of slavery and the extension of citizenship to white, indigenous, and mestizo men). Nevertheless, supposedly "liberal" ideas of Mexican citizenship still expressed the coloniality of knowledge and being stemming from racial classification and social class/caste. By the nineteenth century citizenship in Mexico increasingly revolved around two (originally Spanish) colonial concepts: vecindad (neighborhood, neighborliness) and gente de razón (people of reason). Nonwhite, non-Europeans, like indigenous people or mestizos, were recognized as citizens as long as they became vecinos—good neighbors integrated into local community life—through the ownership of property, the paying of taxes, and the performance of community engagement.[15] Similarly, the status of "person of reason"—originally a colonial designation for Spanish colonizers and any Indians who converted to Christianity—came to designate in nineteenth-century Mexico the assimilated (Europeanized, Hispanicized, whitened) indios or mestizos who accepted their new national identity and embraced it by speaking Spanish, wearing European clothes, practicing European customs, and embracing citizenship. Mexican "federal officers assumed in theory that if Indians were granted full political rights they would choose to acculturate and thus would become tax-paying Mexican citizens."[16] Those indios or mestizos who could perform neighborliness and reasonableness (who could "pass") theoretically gained an elevated position in the social caste system and could exercise limited citizenship rights.

On the other side of the racial/class divide, criollos (white, native born) found it increasingly necessary to protect their racial and social status in the absence of Spanish colonialism and as a tool of nationalism. By the time of Mexican independence, writes historian Martha Menchaca, "most people in Mexico were racially mixed," therefore, "racial boundaries [were] becoming blurred." Nevertheless, or perhaps because of this racial mixing, anxiety persisted about "purity of blood" and racial status. Historian Douglas Monroy explains, "Californios were well aware of the fact that they were part Indian, or, if they weren't, how an unfortunate marriage could taint the family's blood. . . . Those without Indian blood . . . strove to keep their families that way, and those gente de razón with Indian blood, quite apparent in many of the leading families, sought to distance themselves from it" through marriage or through their performance of reasonability and neighborliness (which could "whiten" their social status).[17]

In one sense, notions such as vecindad and gente de razón structuring Mexican citizenship left open the possibility of inclusion for racial minorities like indigenous people and mixed-race Mexicans as long as they assimilated, whitened/Westernized themselves, and (thus) became vecinos (neighbors) and reasonable. In another sense, however, these ideologies of citizenship and race were only deceptively flexible and, crucially, continued the subordination of coloniality. Through ideological concepts such as limpieza de sangre, vecindad, and gente de razón, "cultural Europeanisation was transformed into an aspiration" and "a way of participating" in and "reach[ing] the same material benefits and the same power as the Europeans."[18] European knowledge and racial performance became markers of one's caste position. As Gabriel Gutiérrez explains, "[D]uring the Mexican period[,] non-assimilating Indians and *mestizos* were marginalized from access to power while those who assimilated were more readily accepted, albeit patronized, for productive roles in society."[19] These dominant "imaginaries" of citizenship, race, and identity, then, rested on "a hierarchy of superior and inferior knowledge and, thus, of superior and inferior people." This explains why, according to a number of historians, Mexico's legal and cultural promises of citizenship based on assimilation for indios, mestizos, and other racial minorities often went unfulfilled.[20]

Thus far I have focused on the contexts of citizenship and racial identity in Mexican California, yet the relationship between colonialism and coloniality also helps us to understand the period of U.S. conquest of California, which saw both radical changes and some continuity in the conditions of citizenship, race, and identity. Throughout the early nineteenth century, U.S. Americans had immigrated into Mexican California, where some were admitted into Mexican citizenship once they became settled, acquired land, and assimilated into society. The relative number of U.S. settlers in California in the early nineteenth century was small enough to cause little alarm among the Californios, but beginning in the 1840s the number of migrants grew to such an extent that they began to threaten Mexican control of the region. Governor of California Pío Pico warned Californios of the "hordes of Yankee emigrants" whom he saw as a threat to the established way of life, and these "Yankees" became a central problem for the Californios because, generally speaking, U.S. settlers' disdain for Californios and California society grew as they increased in numbers.[21]

Even before the U.S. conquest of California, relations between Mexican Californios and U.S. settlers were complex, with a number of stereotypes creating regular culture clashes. In fact, it was the combination of logics about U.S. racial superiority and the myth of Manifest Destiny (racial nationalism) that justified the conquest of California. Just as coloniality contributed to and was produced by Spanish colonialism (and continued to influence Mexican society), coloniality was also an integral element in the imperial struggles of the United States to expand its western boundaries. Despite its reputation as an increasingly "democratic" era, the mid-nineteenth century tied U.S. citizenship to a larger colonial project that was rooted in white, Christian, Western European maleness and that excluded women, African Americans, and Native Americans from full personhood. This exclusionary side of U.S. citizenship was evident not only in the legal and institutionalized practices of racial exclusion of the mid-nineteenth century, such as slavery, but also in popular beliefs about superior U.S. (racial) identity. Rogers Smith writes, "Inegalitarian racial and gender conceptions were more directly and pervasively endorsed in [citizenship] law" during the nineteenth century "than ever before" because (white, male) citizens "agreed that white Christian male dominance must prevail."[22] To be a full person/citizen was to exercise the public privileges of white, Christian, American maleness.

U.S. immigrants to California could map existing racial beliefs about the inferiority of blacks and Indians onto the new racial groups they encountered in Mexico, including indios and mestizos. However, Californio elites presented a challenge to Anglo-Americans' binary racial logics. Anglo immigrants saw the (white, criollo) Californio elite as like them because of their European language, Christian religion, skin color/phenotype, economic wealth, and political prestige. However, many stereotypes existed about Californios as a carefree people, racially mixed, mentally inferior to Anglo-Americans, hedonistic, idle, lazy, and indolent, which justified Anglo feelings of superiority. As Douglas Monroy writes, "To the Americanos some Californios 'looked' Indian, many of them 'looked' somewhat European in their phenotype and especially their dress, but they all 'looked' to be different in their deportment." Anglo immigrants found Californios strange and foreign, but they also saw that Californios shared U.S. Americans' identification with a European heritage and a social and epistemic distance from indios. Racialization of Californios was complex and contingent: sometimes Californios were seen as not fully white because of their status as "mixed" and at other times they were portrayed as culturally inferior whites, owing to their Hispanic, Catholic lineage. As Tomás Almaguer summarizes, "The Californios were neither truly 'white' in the northern European or Anglo-Saxon sense of the term, nor were they simply 'uncivilized' Indians. Terms such as 'semicivilized' or 'semibarbarian' best capture the collective judgment European Americans made of Mexicans prior to the U.S.-Mexico war."[23]

In the Anglo immigrants' eyes, race, gender, and class/caste intersected so that a few Californios were distinguished while mestizos and especially Indians were at the bottom of the hierarchy. Thus coloniality helps us understand how these ideologies of identity, and particularly the (racialized) myth of America's Manifest Destiny, contributed to the conquest of California and the subsequent marginalization of Californios. As José David Saldívar puts it, "Americanity's coloniality of power did not stop at the Rio Grande."[24] Cultural and racial stereotypes about indios, mestizos, and Californios intersected with and fueled an already-growing feeling of Manifest Destiny among U.S. Americans. Amy S. Greenberg argues that by the mid-nineteenth century, "Manifest Destiny's discourse had become largely martial in tone, nurtured by scientific race theory and a growing acceptance that the imaginary race of American 'Anglo-Saxons' was destined to dominate lesser races." It was believed that "America's" destiny was to tame the wilderness (the West), rule over the supposedly inferior Mexicans, and subjugate the territory's women and feminized natives. Thus Manifest Destiny took shape through feminization and/or racialization of women, indigenous people, and Mexicans; coloniality justified the violent westward expansion of the United States.[25] Josiah Royce, a nineteenth-century Californian, summarized this belief: "Nowhere else were we Americans more affected than here [in California], in our lives and conduct, by the feeling that we stood in the position of conquerors in the new land." In this respect, because U.S. Americans believed they stood in a unique and superior position in relation to the nonwhite (or 'semiwhite') natives of the Southwest, "to overtake [them] was no crime, for Anglo Americans were required to follow God's injunction to make the land fruitful . . . and attain their divinely appointed calling."[26]

These racial and cultural theories of superiority (rooted in the coloniality of power) provided justification for revolts by a group of U.S. American "filibusters" in 1846 to wrestle California from Mexican control. Filibusters were private armies that sought to extend America's reach throughout the Western Hemisphere as part of the nation's Manifest Destiny. Similar groups led interventions into Texas, Florida, Mexico, Cuba, and parts of Central and South America. In California, groups of U.S. settlers banded together, led by filibusters like John C. Frémont, spurred on by an expansionist president, and inspired by the example of the newly annexed state of Texas. They conspired to create insurrection and "liberate" California for U.S. Americans, capturing Californio government officials and taking control of pueblos until the escalating conflict expanded the Mexican-American War into California and New Mexico.[27]

In addition to ending the war, the 1848 Treaty of Guadalupe Hidalgo transferred the land of California to the control of the United States and defined Californios as U.S. subjects. However, though the treaty legally provided access to citizenship, Mexicans' citizenship status was contingent not only on their renunciation of Mexican citizenship but also on the exclusionary parameters of U.S. citizenship, which was legally available only to European white males at that time. As a case in point, though the Treaty of Guadalupe Hidalgo provided for the protection of the land and political rights of Mexican citizens, within a year of the treaty's ratification the racialization and exclusion of Californios and other Mexicans, as well as the organized theft of Mexican-owned land, began in earnest throughout the Southwest. Federal, state, and territorial governments "refused to uphold" their promises of citizenship and rights and "imposed [their] own racial laws on the conquered territories."[28] Californios' usurpation was exacerbated by the discovery of gold in California in 1848. The subsequent gold rush, with its unexpected influx of Anglo settlers and its resultant rise in lawlessness, helped to further displace wealthy Californios from their land and political power and depressed the economy, confining poorer Californios and mestizos to brutal jobs in the mining industry. These changes strained already tense relations between natives and conquerors and provided fodder for the stereotypes of Mexicans as racially and culturally inferior and thus unworthy of full inclusion.

Wealthy Californio elites had more economic and social capital and thus were seen as more "white" by Anglos; they enjoyed more political and social mobility, and there were intermarriages between Californios and Anglo settlers as a means to solidify both groups' socioeconomic position. Yet even this class distinction rapidly changed as the Californio elites lost their land and political power and as the coloniality of power defined the relationships between Anglo conquerors and Californio natives. As Linda Heidenreich notes, after the Mexican-American War "a new racial order was articulated . . . one that was rooted in Euro-American racism and 'Hispanophobia'" and that positioned Mexicans "as 'greasers.'"[29] In order to achieve a modicum of social acceptance, "the conquered Mexican population" would have to seek "accommodation" and "entry into Anglo society" through whiteness.[30] In this way, some Mexicans were able to become privileged members of Anglo society, while the majority of Mexicans were racialized and relegated to the lower classes. Just as performances of assimilation and Europeanization were the key for indios to achieve rights and social mobility in Mexican society, now, under U.S. colonial control, a few privileged criollo Mexicans assimilated through adapting to U.S. ideologies and customs while a larger number of indios, mestizos, and others were further racialized and marginalized.

Tracing the Spanish, Mexican, and U.S. American colonial and racial logics of citizenship across three decades of California history, we can see the clear relationship between the coloniality of power (as an epistemic and ideological mode of social organization) and the political and economic conditions of colonialism. In the decades leading up to the 1849 Constitutional Convention, Californios were Spanish, then Mexican, and finally U.S. citizen-subjects. Changes in colonial administration brought significant upheaval to Californios and wrought changes in the parameters of citizenship and personhood, yet there was also some continuity in the racial, gender, and class dimensions of citizenship and in the epistemic and ontological coloniality that helped to shape nineteenth-century California. Echoing Darrel Enck-Wanzer, we can say that the "colonization of the imaginary" in nineteenth-century California "structure[d] society and recursively inform[ed] political identity and practices of citizenship." Long after the political and economic relations of colonialism were removed through Mexican independence or replaced by U.S. conquest, the coloniality of knowledge and being (that is, identity) persisted and, in fact, was sedimented through the racialization of citizenship and the entrenchment of a racial/economic caste system. The coloniality of identity and citizenship (through colonial concepts such as gente de razón, limpieza de sangre, and vecindad) was prevalent in Mexico even in the absence of Spanish colonial administrative systems. Likewise, during and after U.S. conquest of the Southwest in the Mexican-American War, U.S. American colonial and racial logics about Manifest Destiny and ("nonwhite" or "off-white") inferior Californios and Mexicans contributed to the racialization of citizenship in the new territory. As Tomás Almaguer concludes, the same "Eurocentric binary distinctions" of coloniality "by which European settlers initially racialized the 'nonwhite' black and Indian populations they confronted in America were later used to differentiate the new cultural groups European Americans encountered during their mid-nineteenth-century expansion into the Southwest."[31] Of course, this exclusion and racialization was pervasive, but it was not felt equally, as some criollo Californios had greater ability to perform whiteness and citizenship and thus assimilate into Anglo California (admittedly, thereby embracing the coloniality of power), while other Mexican Californians such as indios and mestizos were de facto racialized and excluded from the new Anglo society. We could say more about the broader moment of racialization, coloniality, and exclusion faced by newly conquered Californios and Mexicans. However, this chapter focuses instead on the complex negotiation and contestation of borders and citizenship between Anglo-Americans and Californios. The specific moment of historical and rhetorical negotiation I focus on in this chapter is the 1849 Constitutional Convention of California. As I will explain below, the 1849 convention represents a moment of articulation and negotiation of borders and citizenship that speaks to broader historical struggles over U.S. identity and racial/cultural difference. In the 1849 California Constitutional Convention, competing Mexican and U.S. ideologies about citizenship, race, and territorial borders clashed as Californio and Anglo delegates negotiated the parameters of California's government.

I have chosen to examine the California Constitutional Convention of 1849 because it played an important role in historical constructions of race and gender, citizenship, and identity in the U.S. Southwest. Not only was it the first such explicit and legal negotiation of citizenship, race, and identity in the newly conquered territory, but as historian John F. Burns put it, the 1849 Constitutional Convention also "was the last time until the late twentieth century that a sizable number of Latino Californians had a significant role to play in state political events." Though the convention is a significant historical event in its own right, it is also emblematic of similar struggles over borders and citizenship throughout the U.S. Southwest at the time. Thus, to borrow from Linda Heidenreich, I am also focusing on the 1849 Constitutional Convention "not because it is unique or different from other spaces in Greater Mexico/the U.S. West, but because it is similar to other places in so many ways." The debates between Californios and Anglos defining the parameters of the new state provide a particularly poignant illustration of the confluent and performative construction of race, privilege, and citizenship. The vernacular discourses of Californio delegates in the 1849 Constitutional Convention are also important because they can contribute to the overall "decolonial aim" of Latina/o vernacular discourse studies, illuminating strategies of contestation and negotiation over the boundaries of belonging. The next section briefly introduces the immediate historical context of the California Constitutional Convention and the theoretical background for the subsequent rhetorical analysis of the delegates' discourses.[32]

Border Rhetoric and the California Constitutional Convention

The California Constitutional Convention was convened in Colton Hall in Monterey, California, in September of 1849. Forty-eight convention delegates—forty U.S. Americans and eight Californios—were elected by their respective regions to help form a new government. The delegates to the California Constitutional Convention included U.S. northerners and southerners, Californios, and European settlers; they had sundry occupations, such as lawyer, merchant, and farmer. Though the territory had heretofore been administered by a military government, many of the representatives hoped that the convention could quickly constitute a new state government for ratification by the U.S. Congress.[33]

The election of eight Californio delegates to the convention was in itself a significant departure from the overall trend of political and economic usurpation of Californios discussed above. Though the Californio delegates formed a sort of block in the convention, they shared many differences. Seven of the eight delegates were native Mexican Californios, born in the province before U.S. occupation. One delegate—Miguel de Pedrorena—was a Spanish-born immigrant. Some were lawyers, politicians, or soldiers, while others were traders and farmers. What they did share, however, was a prominent social and economic position among the territory's Anglo and Mexican population. The eight Californio representatives to the convention had land holdings and economic resources as well as a certain level of social distinction. Perhaps fearful that they would quickly be marginalized in the convention, when the first meeting convened, the Californio delegates "entered Colton Hall proudly decked out in traditional garb and sat at one table." According to historian Leonard Pitt, this demonstration of unity was effective since it warned the "Yankees" that if they "hurled insults or grew surly, the Californios could threaten to bolt the chamber and give the convention a black eye in the federal Congress."[34] The Californios' act of solidarity at the start of the convention could be viewed as purposefully symbolic, as a rhetorical statement about their defiance, and for my purposes it demonstrates how the convention featured a rhetorical contestation over the racial/cultural borders of U.S. citizenship.

At the same time, however, the Californio delegates, who found themselves in a precarious position in the racial and colonial logics structuring U.S. citizenship at the time, also regularly attempted to define themselves within the borders of belonging. For example, on the second day of the convention, Wednesday, September 5, 1849, Jose A. Carrillo, a Californio delegate from Los Angeles, addressed his colleagues, clamoring for recognition by his fellow delegates: "Although a gentleman belonging to this body had stated," Carrillo affirmed forcefully, that "it was not the object of the Convention to form a Constitution for the [Mexican] Californians, he begged leave to say, that he considered himself as much an American citizen as the gentleman who made the assertion." Carrillo's declaration of his newly granted U.S. citizenship could be seen as an appeal for inclusion and recognition, a rhetorical attempt to define himself within the U.S. civic imaginary in the face of racial and colonial logics that problematized his status in the new nation.[35]

These conflicting examples of the Californios' discourse from the earliest moments of the 1849 Constitutional Convention intimate the main argument I will make about their vernacular discourse of borders and of citizenship. Analyzing convention debates over a number of issues, including suffrage rights, the territorial borders of the state, and language rights, I explore how the Californios engaged in (an admittedly flawed and ultimately unsuccessful) "border thinking," or, more precisely, a border rhetoric, of U.S. citizenship. I argue that the Californios performed (and thus reified) U.S. citizenship, with all of its entanglements of race, gender, and coloniality, but also challenged these exclusionary borders of belonging. The California Constitutional Convention debates of 1849 demonstrate the rhetoricity of the border, the performance of citizenship, and the contestation of race, identity, and coloniality through vernacular discourses.

Recall that "border rhetoric" implies that bordering takes place through the reiterative rhetorical practices of both dominant groups invested in maintaining the borders of citizenship as well as by those minoritarian groups that contest (or sometimes contribute to) the borders of the nation. As I noted above, vernacular border rhetorics become avenues for constituting affirmative identity and agency from the contradictions and tensions of the borderlands and (thereby) rewrite the parameters of belonging. This is because, as Walter Mignolo argues, border thinking originates from and embraces the border(land)s of identity, race, gender, citizenship, and coloniality. In other words, border thinking entails the "disruption of dichotomies through being" (in) a dichotomy. According to Mignolo, border thinking (which is represented in a border discourse, or an "inter-epistemic communication") works from subalternized knowledges and voices and brings them into articulation with dominant logics.[36] Border rhetorics are of and from the physical and metaphorical "border[s] of [the] coloniality of power."[37] As noted in the introduction to this chapter, they arise from the point of colonial or cultural contact. Mignolo as well as a number of other scholars of coloniality trace this notion of border thinking to the work of (post)colonial and third world writers such as Anzaldúa. Drawing from her notion of the borderlands as source of division and contradiction as well as of contact and crossing, José David Saldívar describes border thinking as a "geopolitically located thinking from the borderlands of Americanity and against the new imperialism of the USA."[38] For Saldívar, Mignolo, and others, then, border discourse represents the possibility of a double movement that struggles from and transforms multiple and overlapping borders of belonging. Border rhetoric (the expression of a border thinking) is "positioned at the fissure or fault-lines of Western hegemony" and moves between colonial and subaltern knowledges and voices, articulating a position that challenges both traditions and tensions.[39]

This notion of border rhetoric as a source of "asserting subjectivity and agency,"[40] of rewriting the parameters of belonging, will help to unpack the multiple and overlapping levels of coloniality that were negotiated and contested in the 1849 Constitutional Convention. In debates about borders, race, and citizenship, Californio delegates worked from, within, and against Western / Eurocentric traditions to problematize many of the Anglos' assumptions. This border discourse helped Californios to resist internal colonialism, challenge the coloniality of Mexican and U.S. citizenship, and broaden the borders of belonging. At the same time, however, the Californios' border discourse did not sufficiently embrace the tensions of the border(lands) because they were too tethered to the racialized and colonial logics of citizenship of both the Mexican and U.S. American traditions. In this sense, the Californios' vernacular discourse did not express enough disobedience to hierarchies of race, identity, and citizenship, because it emanated from Californios' privileged position. Put simply, the Californio delegates presented an ultimately unsuccessful and incomplete border discourse that was undermined by its own "darker side" in the coloniality of power.[41]

Shaping Citizenship in the Convention Debates

Suffrage was one of the first issues concerning citizenship confronted at length in the convention. It was obviously of major concern to the Californio delegates, as they raised the issue four times before a decision on the constitutional provisions was reached. The debate on the subject began on Wednesday, September 12, only nine days into the convention, when the question of the qualifications of suffrage was posed. The provision under consideration by the delegates that day explicitly granted suffrage only to "white male citizens of the United States." However, San Francisco representative Edward Gilbert, an immigrant to California himself (from New York), offered an amendment to include into the franchise in addition "every male citizen of Mexico who shall have elected to become a citizen of the United States" (61). While he did not disagree that suffrage should be granted only to males, Gilbert argued that since the Treaty of Guadalupe Hidalgo granted Mexican citizens the rights of U.S. citizenship, Californios too should be given suffrage.

Unsurprisingly, the debate over suffrage soon devolved into anxiety about race and citizenship. In response to Gilbert's amendment to extend suffrage to "every male citizen of Mexico," Charles Botts, a forty-year-old delegate of Monterey (originally from Virginia), professed concern that Mexicans would compromise the racial traditions of citizenship practiced in the United States. In his words, he was concerned "that citizens of Mexico who had become citizens of the United States should be placed upon the same footing with ourselves." Botts feared that extending suffrage to all Mexican citizens could dilute the strict racial makeup of U.S. American identity, and he believed "that white citizens alone should be admitted to the right of suffrage" (63). Interestingly, the comments of these two native U.S. delegates—Edward Gilbert and Charles Botts—demonstrated conflicting understandings of Mexicans' place in the U.S. racial hierarchy. While the New Yorker Gilbert seemed to assume that Mexicans were worthy of suffrage because they were (close to) "white" (and because they were granted those rights through the Treaty of Guadalupe Hidalgo), Botts, the Virginian, saw the inclusion of all Mexicans as potentially polluting the ("white") makeup of citizenship. Both delegates presumed that full citizenship (represented by suffrage) was linked with whiteness, yet they differed on where Mexicans fit into that racial hierarchy.[42] As the preceding discussion should make clear, these disagreements about the racial status and franchise of conquered Mexicans stemmed from conflicting U.S. perceptions of criollos, mestizos, and indios.

Californio delegate Pablo Noriego de la Guerra rose to respond to this conflation of citizenship (suffrage) and white U.S. American identity. De la Guerra was a lawyer by training and had knowledge of Mexican law, both as a practicing attorney and as a long-serving public official under Mexican rule. He was a native Californio (from Santa Barbara) whose father was an influential Spanish immigrant (peninsular) and whose mother came from one of California's famous founding families (the Carrillos, who had emigrated to the territory in one of the first Spanish colonial expeditions). De la Guerra's family tree exemplified the complex mix of nationality, culture, and race that constituted identity in nineteenth-century California. His heritage straddled several racial and social castas, for he was a native-born criollo, with elite (white) Spanish peninsular on his father's side and Californian mestizo on his mother's side. His wealthy and prestigious parentage "gave him an influence . . . greater than he could otherwise have acquired," including a first-rate education and a string of political appointments.[43] That de la Guerra was an eminent member of Californio society both in spite of and because of his racial and class position demonstrated the differences of the racial caste/class system of Mexico. That is, the intersecting class and racial caste system of Mexican citizenship, as well as its roots in the coloniality of power, was evidenced by de la Guerra: though his family straddled multiple racial and class lines, de la Guerra's economic status, Spanish parentage, and (performance of) European identity and whiteness (through education, demeanor, and language) provided him social mobility and an elevated status in California society. The same was true for the majority of the Californio delegates to the convention, who had elite status through their families' economic power and their status as "gente de razón" (that is, European, "white," reasonable). In this respect, de la Guerra and his fellow delegates' social, economic, and racial positioning also spoke to the continued marginalization faced by most mestizos and native indios, who were entirely absent at the constitutional convention.[44]

Thus in the debate over suffrage, Pablo de la Guerra—himself a person of reason based both on his parentage and his experiences as an educated lawyer, government official, and landowner—responded to the claim that "white citizens alone should be admitted to the right of suffrage." De la Guerra began by raising the question of the terminology used by Botts and other U.S. American delegates to describe the basic racial component of citizenship; he introduced an alternative understanding of the link between race/class and citizenship, but also engaged in his own racially exclusionary discourse. I will quote de la Guerra's response in full and then discuss each significant part of the statement in turn. According to the convention proceedings,

> Mr. Noriego [Pablo Noriego de la Guerra] desired that it should be properly understood in the first place what is the true signification of the word "white." Many citizens of California have received from nature a very dark skin; nevertheless, there are among them men who have heretofore been allowed to vote, and not only that, but to fill the highest public offices. It would be very unjust to deprive them of the privileges of citizens merely because nature had not made them white. But if, by the word "white," it was intended to exclude the African race, then it was correct and satisfactory. (63)

As is evident, this passage about the racial parameters of suffrage is rich with multiple threads that both problematize and reinforce the Anglo delegates' conflation of whiteness with citizenship and suffrage. As I unpack this quotation and de la Guerra's subsequent statements during this debate (he was the main Californio delegate to contribute to conversations on suffrage), I want to focus on how de la Guerra articulated a discourse that worked "from both traditions" of citizenship—U.S. and Mexican—"and, at the same time, from neither of them."[45] In other words, de la Guerra's position on the racial parameters of suffrage straddled the borders between U.S. and Mexican racial and colonial traditions of citizenship. On the one hand, de la Guerra challenged Anglos' conflations of whiteness and citizenship; on the other hand, and as elements of the preceding quotation make clear, de la Guerra's rhetoric was dependent on and complicit with white, Eurocentric citizenship.

De la Guerra's question about "the true signification of the word 'white'" subtly highlighted the incongruence between discourses of race and citizenship. Whether because of a translational barrier or to make a larger point, de la Guerra expressed confusion concerning the applicability of "white" identity in California. He seemed to voice an alternative understanding of race and citizenship rooted in the Mexican traditions of vecindad and gente de razón, which, at least in name, recognized some room for the performativity of race and ethnicity and thus citizenship. By explicitly asking the definition of the word *white,* de la Guerra implicitly pointed to one of the privileges of whiteness, which is often defined, according to Thomas K. Nakayama and Robert L. Krizek, as a "negative," colorless, and invisible identity.[46] And yet, de la Guerra did not seem to have any doubt that he was considered a white citizen (person of reason). As I will discuss below, he would, in fact, later sue the state of California for infringing on his rights as a *white* citizen. Nevertheless, de la Guerra's simple question about "the true signification of the word 'white'" problematized the bifurcation of "white" and "Mexican" and at the same time performed white citizenship in and through his Californio identity.

After posing this question, de la Guerra argued that "many citizens of California have received from nature a very dark skin; nevertheless, there are among them men who have heretofore been allowed to vote, and not only that, but to fill the highest public offices," and that "it would be very unjust to deprive them of the privileges of citizens merely because nature had not made them white." Here de la Guerra followed on his question about whiteness by drawing on Mexican traditions to decouple the link between whiteness and citizenship. De la Guerra brought forth the experiences of mixed-race Californios and lodged it within the U.S. citizenship traditions. By drawing attention to those indigenous people and mestizos in Mexican society who could *perform* citizenship (by paying taxes, adopting European culture, owning property, and so forth), de la Guerra's comment decoupled the presumed whiteness of U.S. citizenship from the behaviors, duties, and identities of the citizen-subject. In other words, de la Guerra partially invoked a "foreign" history of Californio citizenship—one rooted in neighborliness and reasonability—into the presumed racialized logics of U.S. citizenship; his point that many Californios had "received from nature a very dark skin" and yet had "been allowed to vote . . . [and] to fill the highest public offices" subtly undermined the presumption of whiteness that was at the heart of Anglo delegates' understandings of full citizenship.

To bolster his argument concerning the citizenship rights of indios and mestizos, de la Guerra had the aid of fellow delegate Manuel Dominguez, a farmer from Angeles County and a dark-skinned, mestizo delegate, whose "face," according to Pitt, "could remind the gringo delegates of their responsibility toward the thousands of non-Caucasians in the state."[47] The presence of Dominguez in the Constitutional Convention of 1849, who (tellingly) did not himself speak during this debate over suffrage rights, embodied de la Guerra's concern for indigenous and mixed-race Californios. By deploying whiteness in his proclamation of citizenship rights, de la Guerra created what Homi K. Bhabha often refers to as "slippage" in the colonial, racial categories of U.S. citizenship.[48] In concrete terms, de la Guerra used his privileged status as a "white" Californio to question the racial makeup of U.S. citizenship. He demanded that "it should be properly understood in the first place what is the true signification of the word 'white,'" questioning the whiteness articulated by Botts and other U.S. delegates. Being criollo himself, de la Guerra was "almost white" in the Anglo-American delegates' minds. This identity as white / European in relation to the nonwhite and largely absent "others" of California society (for example, indios and mestizos) provided de la Guerra with some leeway as an "insider" to question the link between whiteness, citizenship, and suffrage forwarded by Anglo delegates. He did so by foregrounding another possibility for full citizenship, namely, one's cultural assimilation and *performance* of whiteness and Europeanization (what the Mexicans referred to as a person of reason or a good neighbor). Important to remember, however, is that even de la Guerra and his fellow Californios were racialized as "off-white," not quite white, or, at the very least, as inferior by the majority of Anglo settlers. In a sense, these ethnic and cultural differences (and those of his colleagues) served to underscore the socially constructed and exclusionary racial project of U.S. citizenship to those around de la Guerra. The other delegates would not articulate the true signification of the word *white* because de la Guerra problematized that distinction (whether intentional or unintentional, we don't know). This duality in de la Guerra's statement—his problematization of the conflation of whiteness and citizenship through a performance of white, reasonable, and European "person of reason"—intimates what I referred to above as the Californios' border discourse. That is, it represented "simultaneously an undoing and redoing"—an undoing of the racial and colonial logics of U.S. citizenship and a redoing of thinking about citizenship and subjectivity from an alternative perspective.[49]

However, what was unstated in de la Guerra's mimicry was the "darker side" of Mexican traditions of gente de razón and vecindad, which not only presumed a wild, feminized, and ignorant native who became "reasonable," but which also ignored black Mexicans and mulattos (mixed race, white and black), who were invisible in this caste system. The silence of Dominguez in the discussion demonstrates the double-edged nature of de la Guerra's discourse and the ways that it presumed coloniality even in its challenge to Anglo racializations. De la Guerra was still assuming that the keys to citizenship rested in the performance of whiteness and European identity. Furthermore, his comments merely created an exception to the (white) rule and entrenched the coloniality of the Mexican citizenship tradition discussed above. This is evident in de la Guerra's concluding statement, for though he advocated that "white" citizenship be problematized to include indigenous and mestizo Californios, "if by the word 'white,' it was intended to exclude the African race," he clarified, "then it was correct and satisfactory." In sum, de la Guerra's comment about suffrage questioned the norm of white U.S. citizenship by foregrounding an alternative and vernacular citizenship tradition while at the same time entrenching whiteness and coloniality.[50]

Despite the racism and coloniality in de la Guerra's own position, Anglo delegate Charles Botts objected to his comments and seemed to perceive them as a threat. Botts responded by shifting debate away from the meaning of "white"; Botts instead focused his remarks on redrawing the racial project by describing those categorically defined as "*non*white" and thus unworthy of citizenship. According to Botts, darker skin colors were not significant per se but only insofar as they "indicated the inferior races of mankind." Botts stated that "he would be perfectly willing to use any words which would exclude the African and Indian races" (63). Here, of course, Botts relied on white privilege to elide the question of whiteness, and he capitalized on de la Guerra's own identification with whiteness and Eurocentricity to reify a strict distinction between white and nonwhite. In effect, Botts denied de la Guerra's call to recognize the (admittedly partial) place of indio and mixed-race Californios and the performativity of race; he elided de la Guerra's questioning comments by turning the debate back to the locus of racial *essence*. Thus, Botts rearticulated racialization and coloniality by implying that only whites were worthy of citizenship (suffrage), while nonwhites should be excluded based on their inferiority no matter how much they resembled the "us." Though "the African and Indian races" could perhaps try to act more "white" to seek greater inclusion, as they did in Mexico, for Botts racial identity (based on phenotype) was ultimately the essential marker of citizenship (suffrage) and subjectivity. By turning the debate to the question of racial essence, Botts's remarks absorbed de la Guerra's challenge.[51]

De la Guerra responded to Botts's and other delegates' comments by shifting the debate to questions of law and rights. He stated that "according to Mexican law, no race of any kind is excluded from voting. . . . So far were [Indians] considered citizens" under Mexican law "that some of the first men in the Republic were of the Indian race" (63). De la Guerra's historical argument was important because, since the treaty between the United States and Mexico demanded equal citizenship rights for all Mexican citizens, if he could prove that Mexican citizenship extended to nonwhites, it would create a legal imperative for his demand. In one sense, this was an effective enthymeme because all the Anglo-American delegates knew about the treaty and were eager to uphold U.S. law so as to speed California's statehood. Thus the delegates were much more open to considering arguments about compliance with U.S. treaties, as is evidenced by several delegates who confirmed de la Guerra's assessment of Mexican citizenship. Some delegates began to consider the possibility of acknowledging the "apparent" and "mixed-blood" descendants of Indians while excluding the "real," "full-blooded" Indian, whom they viewed as truly miserable. Kimball H. Dimmick, a delegate from San Jose, stated this argument succinctly: "[W]here there was here and there a good Indian, capable of understanding our system of government, he had no objection to making such provision as would entitle him to vote" (64). William M. Gwin, a forty-four-year-old southern farmer recently immigrated to California, "did not think the descendents of Indians should be excluded, but the pure uncivilized Indians should not be permitted to vote" (65). Thus Anglo delegates debated whether "real" or "half-blooded" Indians might fall under the racial categorization of full U.S. citizenship. These discussions demonstrated that de la Guerra's appeals to Mexican traditions of vecindad and gente de razón may have provoked the U.S. American delegates to consider expanding their definitions of U.S. citizenship beyond strictly racial phenotypes.

However, in another sense, these Anglo delegates' comments about the few "civilized Indians" being allowed into citizenship merely represented a rearticulation of coloniality, through which the few "civilized" indios could be included as long as they became Europeanized. Furthermore, Anglo delegates' comments about there being "here and there a good Indian" worthy of citizenship evidenced the rhetoric of tokenism,[52] in which a few nonwhites could be recognized as evidence of the superiority and benevolence of white U.S. society. Acknowledging the descendents of indigenous people or the isolated, assimilated "good Indian" in fact entrenched dominant logics of coloniality and race. Elite Californios, such as de la Guerra, could be granted suffrage (full citizenship) on a case-by-case basis based on their assimilation into Anglo-American whiteness, while the majority of Mexicans remained nonwhite "others." This created a substratification for indigenous and mestizo Mexicans (much like the casta system of colonial New Spain), who could be acknowledged as somewhere between "white" at the top of the racial hierarchy and "black" at the bottom.

Returning to the convention debates, instead of accepting the dissociation between "good Indians" and "uncivilized Indians" created by Dimmick and Gwin,[53] de la Guerra responded with a speech in defense of full indio and mestizo suffrage that further illuminates the Californios' discourse. De la Guerra again translated an alternative tradition of citizenship and foregrounded the experience and history of indigenous Californios. In answer to J. D. Hoppe of San Jose, de la Guerra "requested that gentleman to place himself in the position of one of those Indians" and to "suppose he had to pay an equal tax with all other persons, to sustain the expenses of the State," as many indios and mestizos who owned property did. De la Guerra asked, "Would it not be most unfair to deprive him of equal privileges, when he had to bear an equal burden? . . . The gentleman, he hoped, would readily perceive the great injustice of such a provision" (70). Next, de la Guerra introduced a long narrative about the native Californio Indian that rhetorically transported the delegates back through the history of indigenous people in California, letting them bear witness to the experiences of indigenous people as a "proud and gifted race" worthy of inclusion as citizens. "It has been asserted by some members," de la Guerra argued, "that Indians are brutal and irrational. Let those gentlemen cast their eyes back for three hundred years and say who were the Indians then." Indigenous life before Spanish colonization demonstrated that indios were "capable of forming a government for themselves. If they were not so much enlightened as [we are] now, it was not for want of natural gifts, but because the lights of science were not then so bright as now, even in Europe; and they could fall but simply upon the natives of the soil." De la Guerra's remarks worked to rewrite collective memory of indios in a way that challenged conventional racist stereotypes and rhetorically constituted them as citizens/neighbors. Indios were not ignorant, foolish, or inferior; they were a "proud and gifted race," with "natural gifts" and "capable" of governance. What led to their less "enlightened" status was not an inferior essence (as some U.S. delegates had argued) but the circumstances of their location far from ("enlightened") Europe. (Furthermore, de la Guerra also subtly suggested that Europeans may have not been very "enlightened" at that time.) It was not necessary to look back three centuries, said de la Guerra. He "bid them look back but for half a century" to the Spanish colonization of California. "All the work that was seen in California, was the work of Indians led by some foreigners. If they were not cultivated and highly civilized, it was because they had been ground down and made slaves of." De la Guerra shifted responsibility for indigenous peoples' poor material conditions to Spanish colonizers, who had exploited them into squalor. He questioned the racial essentialism of Anglo delegates, for Indians "were intelligent and capable of receiving instructions, and it was the duty of the citizens to endeavor to elevate them and better their condition in everyway, instead of seeking to sink them still lower." De la Guerra concluded his impassioned speech by appealing for compromise: "[I]f it was the will of the Convention to exclude the body of Indians," he hoped exceptions would be made for those who held property and paid taxes and should therefore be offered the rights of full citizenship (305).[54]

De la Guerra's speech again exhibited the tensions of working from the borders of the coloniality of power. Mignolo claims that border thinking (for our purposes, border rhetoric) involves a "'saying against' and a 'saying for.'"[55] In this case, de la Guerra was both "saying against" Anglo racialization and dehumanization of indigenous people and "saying for" an understanding of indigenous people as honorable and worthy of inclusion. In his "saying for," de la Guerra used historical argument to prove that Native Americans were central to the building of California and to disqualify beliefs that they were inferior. Rather than accept the explicit demonization of indigenous people, he presented them as "a gifted race" that had played an integral part in California history. He showed that indigenous people were in fact worthy of attaining citizenship once they became gente de razón and that, in many ways, they had always been reasonable and neighborly people. Since *neighbor* meant *citizen* in the Mexican tradition, de la Guerra's historical narrative of indigenous contributions to California in a sense *made them* neighbors / citizens.

In this way, de la Guerra suggested that whiteness and citizenship could be performed by indigenous people and mestizos. As Mignolo describes, the colonial difference refers to "the double bind between an excessive similarity and an excessive difference." The colonizer desires that the colonized "other" imitate and thus validate his superior way of life, yet this process of imitation is fraught with uncertainty because if done too well it can unsettle the very colonial difference that distinguishes the colonizer from the colonized. De la Guerra was working from within this double bind between similarity and difference by arguing that indios and mestizos could imitate (so-called) civilized, white citizenship even though they "were not so much enlightened" as their Anglo counterparts. In a sense de la Guerra was exposing the limit of U.S. rights / citizenship discourse by showing that it extended to nonwhites who could mimic U.S. civic identity *and*, even more, by performing the civilized identity of a U.S. citizen even better than did his Anglo counterparts. Despite the fragile position the Californios held in U.S. racial and imperial logics, de la Guerra intentionally or unintentionally placed the recalcitrance of his Anglo colleagues, who refused to create exceptions to their own hierarchical and exclusionary logics of citizenship, in stark contrast to his more reasoned and fair position on suffrage rights.[56]

If in his "saying for" de la Guerra stressed that indios and mestizos were honorable and positioned citizenship as performative, in his "saying against" de la Guerra's border discourse embraced a more tenuous relationship to the colonial difference. De la Guerra's narrative of indigenous history challenged the naturalized racism of his fellow delegates by arguing that indigenous culture and history held many of the seeds of what they would consider Western culture, including self-government and reason. The supposed superiority of Anglo civilization and inferiority of Native American and Mexican peoples might not seem so self-evident once Anglo delegates took into account that native cultures and history embodied the same lofty qualities of reason, self-government, and a Protestant-like work ethic that were presumed to be the sole possession of Europeans. De la Guerra also subtly indicated that, three hundred years ago, "even in Europe" the "lights of science" may not have been "so bright as now." Perhaps, de la Guerra's speech seemed to suggest, the (colonial) difference between white and nonwhite was not essential but rather historically constructed (and a product of recent history at that) and based in power relations.

However, the ambivalence of de la Guerra's border discourse is quite obvious in his own employment of coloniality and racial logics. The Californios, represented by de la Guerra, struggled for their place in the society of the colonizer (the United States), but they took for granted coloniality perpetrated by Mexicans on indigenous people. While acknowledging that indigenous people had overcome the initial act of colonization by the Spanish, who had "ground down" the indios, de la Guerra erased the coloniality of power implicit in Mexican society after independence. In externalizing coloniality to Spain and the United States he ignored the colonizing elements of Mexican citizenship law, which forced indigenous people to make themselves in the image of the colonizer (a "person of reason") to achieve full inclusion. De la Guerra read the worth of the natives of California in their possibility for reason and self-government—that is, in their ability to imitate their criollo superiors. He measured indios' worth as a "proud and gifted race" in their ability to overcome their colonization by the Spanish and assimilate into Mexican society. De la Guerra's version of history positioned indigenous people not only as a people without reason ("not cultivated and highly civilized" and without "the lights of science") but also as a people without history, at least before the colonization of the "New World" by the Spaniards. He argued that because of their position outside of Europe, indigenous people had always been subservient to European colonizers. According to de la Guerra, Anglos should work to civilize indigenous people just as the Spaniards and Mexicans had done. Thus even the subversive elements of de la Guerra's discourse—his challenge to U.S. racial and colonial logics—were articulated from within the coloniality of power. Therefore, de la Guerra's rhetoric reified its own "darker side" of coloniality, modernity, and racialized citizenship, including his own reliance on the performance of white / European / civilized / masculine citizenship. His appeal to the "reasonableness" of indigenous Mexicans (as well as the literal invisibility of Afro-mestizos in his comments) entrenched a white, Eurocentric norm. De la Guerra had placed himself firmly in the role of white, European, and reasonable citizen, thereby protecting the sanctity of whiteness.

In the responses to de la Guerra's oration several delegates still opposed providing suffrage for even "civilized" indigenous people. Despite de la Guerra's attempts to rewrite the stereotyped memory of indigenous people as "savage," many delegates expressed fear that allowing indigenous and mestizo people to vote opened the door to manipulation by those who would take advantage of a "brute" race. Delegate Hoppe asked: "Was there a man . . . who was willing to place himself on a level with the Indian or the negro? Not he, for one. The proposed amendment [to allow suffrage for all male citizens of Mexico] was loose in the extreme. Where were those Indians who were to be admitted by this amendment? They were along the Pacific coast, populating the *ranchos*. There was not a *rancho* where you would not find fifty or a hundred buck Indians, and the owner could run these *freemen* up to the polls, and carry any measure he might desire" (306). These comments not only relied on the racial formations and stereotypes discussed above, but they also appealed to what Arjun Appadurai has called a "fear of small numbers," which refers to the anxiety that even small numbers of minorities provoke the integrity and purity of the nation-state and national culture.[57] Hoppe feared the amendment was "loose in the extreme" because it opened the door for racial minorities ("Indians") to overwhelm and corrupt the system, wrestling control from the majority. These comments also illuminated a confluence between racial and gender discourse, because Hoppe feared that the wild, impressionable, and feminized "Indians" could be taken advantage of by an unscrupulous, domineering, and manipulative (that is, masculine) white owner. Hoppe suggested that (feminized) "Indians" were not able to think for themselves; they should be the wards of their owners (men in both cases). Similar comments by other delegates illustrated the durability of these gendered racializations. De la Guerra's discourse was in one sense conciliatory, for the only thing he asked for in the end was the possibility of a few nonwhites to become people of reason; it was also apparently a threat to dominant logics of racialized citizenship and to the Anglo delegates' presumed monopoly on whiteness.

Hoppe's anxiety-filled statement about the dangers of "plac[ing] himself on a level with the Indian or the negro" also demonstrates another dimension of the colonial difference. In essence, Hoppe and his Anglo colleagues were arguing that indigenous or black citizens would capitalize on democratic institutions like free and open elections to undermine the coloniality of power. These arguments unintentionally undermined those selfsame Enlightenment ideologies of governance and their purported universality. To borrow from Homi K. Bhabha, Hoppe's fears about indigenous people exercising democracy, in a sense, "mocks [the] power" of the colonial system "to be a model, that power which supposedly makes it imitable."[58] In other words, Hoppe's response unraveled the presumed superiority of his worldview, for his fear of small numbers and his anxiety about enfranchised Native Americans and blacks scorned democracy's supposedly "imitable" and immutable "power" as a political ideology. In his obsessive concern to prevent the "tyranny" of true democracy Hoppe unintentionally uncovered the oligarchic tendencies of U.S. republicanism. Jacksonian democracy, which purported to be the most open and accessible of political systems, at the same time rested on societal repression of women and minorities and on exclusionary political and economic systems. Ironically, the champion of democracy feared the results that could come from fully carrying out its supposedly universal political and social values of equal participation.

Californios' responses to Hoppe and the other Anglo delegates did not explicitly attack their hypocrisy but rather reflected even more conciliation. De la Guerra stated that "he did not at all desire that the mass of Indians should vote, and he had expressly said so." Assuaging the "fear of small numbers," de la Guerra argued that the "Indians" owning property who would be eligible to vote were too small a number to be a threat to Anglo-Americans: "There was no fear of two hundred votes [from indigenous people] having any serious effect in a population of 60,000" (307). By quantifying the number of nonwhites to be granted suffrage, de la Guerra seemed to minimize the threat they might pose of polluting citizenship's (racial) makeup. Nevertheless, several of the U.S. delegates were still suspicious about expanding suffrage to racial and ethnic minorities. In an invocation of the idea that would be known after the Civil War as the "one-drop rule," Anglo-American delegates seemed to argue that allowing a person with even one drop of "nonwhite" blood to access full U.S. citizenship would threaten the entire franchise. Though de la Guerra assured them that granting suffrage to eligible individuals was a legal necessity and a minor inconvenience, his view did not gain traction. The measure to expand suffrage rights to indios and mestizos was defeated by only one vote.

Ultimately, the Californio delegates were unable to achieve a compromise on suffrage, and the compromise was brokered off the floor of the convention and offered up for a vote several days later on October 3. The most de la Guerra and others were able to negotiate was a proviso that suffrage could be extended to indios and mestizos on a case-by-case basis through further legislative decrees. Specifically, the constitution of 1849 stated: "Every *white* male citizen of the United States, and every *white* male citizen of Mexico, who shall have elected to become a citizen of the United States . . . shall be entitled to vote . . .: Provided, that nothing herein contained, shall be construed to prevent the Legislature, by a two thirds concurrent vote, from admitting to the right of suffrage, Indians, or the descendants of Indians, in such *special cases* as such a proportion of the legislative body may deem just and proper."[59] On one hand, the compromise achieved here created a middle ground between the strict racial makeup of U.S. citizenship and the more performative, community-based elements of the Mexican tradition. While suffrage was explicitly extended only to *white* males, the constitution acknowledged that some indigenous or mestizo men might be worthy of suffrage. Presumably these "special cases" would be judged based on how well indios or mestizos became U.S. Americans (that is, vecinos), including their movement into whiteness. On the other hand, this compromise cannot be considered much of a victory for Californios; not only did the constitution explicitly affirm the standard of white male personhood, it also implicitly reified the notion of nonwhite abjectness. Also, indios and mestizos were faced with limited options to prove their social worth. De la Guerra's presencing of nonwhite Californios performing whiteness / citizenship meant that Anglo delegates could acknowledge that "here and there a good Indian" could be included while denying the majority of indigenous people suffrage. Those who were nonwhite were excluded, while a few could possibly be "considered" citizens.

Moving on from the debate over suffrage analyzed thus far, another moment in which Californios negotiated borders and citizenship came on Wednesday, September 5, 1849, by Jose A. Carrillo. At fifty-three years old, the Californio delegate from Los Angeles was the oldest member of the convention. He was also the most experienced of the Californio delegates, in the words of Leonard Pitt, having "been in the thick of things for three decades, first as a plotter of rebellions, then as a soldier, and finally as a signatory to the treaty of Cahuenga" that ended the Mexican-American War in California. Three years earlier, in 1846, Carrillo had been fighting the U.S. Americans in defense of Mexican sovereignty. In 1848 he watched as a defeated Mexico ceded California to the United States in a treaty of peace. Now in 1849 Carrillo stood before the same U.S. Americans he had once fought against, this time as a fellow citizen of the United States and as representative of a newly conquered population. Thus Carrillo came to the convention from a particularly complex position. He had significant ethos based on his wealth and political / social prestige, but he was also a prominent leader of the resistance to the Anglo intervention in California. He was representing the Californio population but was also an elite largely separate from the "masses" of poor mestizos or indios. In terms of his position in the castas, early twentieth-century historian Hubert Howe Bancroft states that Carrillo was "pure Castillian," while contemporary historian Martha Menchaca states his heritage was "uncertain," thus exemplifying the complexities of the Mexican racial and socioeconomic system.[60]

The convention considered an important matter the day of September 5: whether to craft a constitution for a state government or a federal territory. What degree of independence in relation to the U.S. government would California have? Were Californians ready to be "Americans," or should they be a separate entity? As the delegates debated the future of the territory, Carrillo rose to contend with the Anglos' sense of Manifest Destiny. He "proposed that the country should be divided by running a line west from San Luis Obispo, so that all north of that line might have a State Government, and all south thereof a Territorial Government . . . because he believed it to be to the interest of his constituents" (22). The northern half of California, heavily populated by Anglo settlers and the site of the gold rush, could form a state government while the southern portion, sparsely populated, mostly by Californios, remained a separate territory. Carrillo presented an interesting instance of what I have termed rhetorical bordering. In the most explicit sense, Carrillo proposed rebordering the territory so that the two populations—conqueror and conquered—could remain separate and self-governing. This was a direct challenge to U.S. efforts to subsume the territory and its inhabitants.[61]

Carrillo objected to the Anglo delegates' presumptions that they should quickly establish a state constitution so as to be absorbed into the Union because he believed it was ignoring the voices of Californio citizens. He argued, "Although a gentleman belonging to this body had stated it was not the object of the Convention to form a Constitution for the [Mexican] Californians, [Carillo] begged leave to say, that he considered himself as much an American citizen as the gentleman who made the assertion" (22). In this statement, Carrillo seemed to draw himself into the boundaries of the U.S. civic imaginary by constituting himself as citizen, yet he was doing so in the service of advocating for the separation of Californios into their own territory. Carrillo's discourse, then, represented a moment of citizenship enactment in which he strove to constitute Californios as U.S. citizens, but as citizens who still preserved a distance/difference that necessitated self-governance. Like de la Guerra in debates over suffrage, Carillo was differentiating Californios from Anglos in and through his identification as U.S. citizen. Thus we could see this as another example of border rhetoric that worked at the borders of imperial Manifest Destiny. Carillo's enactment of citizenship and simultaneous demand for separatism illustrates how Californio delegates both enacted U.S. citizenship, drawing themselves into the United States, but at the same time challenged the colonial and racial boundaries of the U.S. imaginary.

Apart from the two specific cases analyzed here, Californios' vernacular discourse of borders and of citizenship was evident in other moments throughout the convention debates.[62] Their border rhetoric negotiated multiple positions and contributed both to resistance and reification of coloniality and white supremacy, for the Californios' discourse was complicated by their blindness to their own coloniality of power. Their rhetoric not only entrenched the epistemic and material marginalization of indigenous people and mestizos, it also undermined the effectivity of the Californios' appeals for accommodation. In this case, while Anglo delegates praised Carrillo's identification with U.S. citizenship, they rejected his call for separatism and instead interpreted his (strategic) identification as a warrant for assimilation. Since Carrillo and the Californios sought to be "as much American citizen[s]" as Anglos, their particular rights could be sacrificed to the greater (white / Anglo) society. Carrillo's measure to split California in half was defeated, and the delegates voted overwhelmingly (29–8) to craft a state constitution. As delegate Stephen Foster responded to Carrillo, since the Californios wanted to be equal citizens, "they would prefer to bear their share of the burden of a State Government rather than divide the country" (23).

Carrillo's border discourse was co-opted by Anglo delegates as identification with and justification for the superiority of U.S. logics of citizenship and identity. This inclusion of Californios into the U.S. project of citizenship and statehood maintained the colonial relations of power despite assurances of inclusion. As Mignolo writes, "Those who propose inclusion do not reflect critically on the fact that those who are welcomed to be included may not necessarily want to play the game generously offered by those who open their arms to the inclusion of the difference."[63] Foster's assumption that Californios wanted to be included and would be "bear[ing] their share of the burden" by assimilating belied the dual reality that some Californios did not want to share this burden and, even more, that Californios would continue to be colonial subjects after statehood despite assurances to the contrary.

The Californio delegates "helped mold" many other key provisions of the 1849 constitution besides those considered here.[64] Nonetheless, the debates I have analyzed represent moments within the broader constitutional convention in which Californios were compelled to negotiate the terms of their newly imposed U.S. citizenship. What would it mean to be a U.S. American in this new state? How did their old political and cultural identity translate? What were the rights that Mexican Americans would be able to exercise as citizens? In the debates over suffrage and territorial borders I have considered here, the Californios crafted a border discourse that worked "from both traditions" of citizenship—U.S. and Mexican. De la Guerra tried to present an alternative voice and history that located indigenous people as members of the California community, to constitute indios and mestizos as worthy of suffrage, and to subtly challenge America's racial project of citizenship. Meanwhile, Carillo "work[ed] . . . from the double bind between assimilation . . . and marginalization," demanding inclusion and difference / separation for Californio citizens.[65] This analysis also demonstrates the pitfalls and weaknesses within Californios' discourse—that is, the ways in which their rhetoric did not provide enough epistemic disobedience to coloniality and thus was easily co-opted by entrenched exclusive logics of citizenship. In the conclusion I elaborate on the effectivity of Californios' rhetoric and the lessons it provides for the larger study of Latina / o vernacular discourses, borders, and citizenship.

Conclusion

It may seem, based on where the debates over citizenship and suffrage ended in the Constitutional Convention of 1849, that the Californios' vernacular discourse was a failure. After all, the compromises reached on suffrage and state borders were not much of a compromise at all: the Anglo delegates largely won their way in both cases. However, I have shown throughout the preceding analysis that the process was more subtle and complex. Though it certainly was not a dialogue between equals, the negotiation of citizenship rights and borders in the Constitutional Convention of 1849 more broadly expressed an interplay between dominant and vernacular appeals. Beyond who could vote or the state's territorial boundaries, the debates in the convention were about what it meant to be a U.S. citizen, what it meant to be "white," "Indian," or "mixed race," and where the borders between those identities would be drawn.

Californios' vernacular rhetorics of citizenship were structured through a border discourse that embraced the duality and contradiction of their position at the newly formed U.S.-Mexico border. They performed a simultaneous enactment and problematization of citizenship. Bringing forth the experiences of citizenship under Mexican rule and constituting themselves as citizens/neighbors, the Californio delegates enacted U.S. citizenship but also weakened links between whiteness, coloniality, and citizenship. The Californio delegates in the 1849 California Constitutional Convention enacted a border discourse that was in/at the intersection of multiple forms of coloniality—Spanish, Mexican, and U.S. American. Through rhetoric of citizenship, Californios translated "both ways" across the coloniality of power/knowledge. In one sense, the delegates translated knowledges about Mexican citizenship and indigenous people to the Anglo/U.S. context as a means to challenge U.S. ideologies of race, identity, and citizenship. In another sense, the delegates worked to translate the Anglo and U.S. ideologies of race, identity, and citizenship to the Mexican and indigenous context, appealing to those logics to craft a space for indigenous and mestizo peoples within U.S. national imaginaries. Particularly in debates over the question of suffrage and the state's territorial boundaries, border discourse took shape through the conflicting coexistence of and speaking through multiple languages and traditions "in conflictive and tense relations."[66]

However, it is important to remember that, as Walter Mignolo writes, in order to be a truly radical challenge, border thinking or border discourse must emerge as "a double critique," a "think[ing] from both [dominant *and* subaltern] traditions and, at the same time, from neither of them." In this case, though the Californios' border discourse worked from the interstices between Mexican and U.S. traditions of citizenship, it was not sufficiently "critical of both" traditions. De la Guerra's and

Carillo's border discourse could not mount enough disobedience to coloniality and racial thinking because the Californios were themselves constituted within the coloniality of power. Californio delegates like Carrillo and de la Guerra surrendered to the coloniality of the Spanish/Mexican caste system as well as to U.S. logics of Manifest Destiny, whiteness, and citizenship. De la Guerra's "dominant vernacular" appeals on behalf of indios and mestizos rested on his deployment of privilege—whiteness, masculinity, social class, and Eurocentricity—that other Californios could do nothing more than mimic. Dominant vernacular discourses are those rhetorics not entirely or even primarily liberatory, even though they emanate from vernacular positions.[67] Though de la Guerra's and Carrillo's rhetoric emanated from a marginalized position (relative to Anglo delegates) and voiced an alternative tradition of race and citizenship, their discourses nevertheless entrenched whiteness and heteropatriarchy in many ways. Similarly, while the Californio delegates sought to represent their "people" in the convention, in truth they were part of an elite class that had participated in the stratification of Mexican society and the marginalization of indios, mestizos, blacks, and women. In fact, one could read the Californio delegates as embodying the position of protectors and advocates for indios and mestizos by shepherding their passage (that is, conversion) into "reasonable," "white" U.S. citizenship. In this way, Californio delegates both challenged the conflation of whiteness and U.S. citizenship and also reified it. The practical failure of most of the compromises Californios attempted to craft in 1849 demonstrates the inherent limitations of their vernacular rhetoric. The Californio delegates' compromised and circumscribed border rhetoric at most was able to achieve a partial challenge to coloniality and dominant logics of citizenship. In a sense, by identifying with and deploying whiteness and U.S. citizenship, Californios were able at most to achieve only a provisional recognition. The privileged Californio delegates enacting their newly attained U.S. citizenship reaffirmed the colonial difference (the colonizer's belief that the colonized wants to be just like him) and entrenched racial, cultural, and colonial logics of superiority.

Considering the developments in the latter half of the nineteenth century that reversed many of the minor concessions guaranteed to Californios in the 1849 Constitution demonstrates that the most the Californios might have been able to achieve was some degree of legal recognition for the select few who could adequately perform their citizenship. In fact, one of the first acts of the inaugural California legislature was to affirm that suffrage applied only to white citizens, despite their constitutional power to allow nonwhite Californios to vote on a select basis. As Heidenreich concludes, after the 1849 Constitutional Convention, "Californios pursued a white identity—and a small number, a very small number, were able to achieve it. The price for doing so was high; such families became 'gringoized' . . . as romantic characters in the white imagination." This paradox became clear to Pablo de la Guerra in

1868; despite his service in the constitutional convention and in the California state government, he was prosecuted by the state of California for his efforts to exercise citizens' rights to hold office after the state judged that de la Guerra was not white. De la Guerra's case was ultimately decided by the California Supreme Court, which both upheld the state's constitutional racial restrictions on citizenship and ruled that de la Guerra was white and therefore a citizen. Despite de la Guerra's isolated victory, his case would become one of many such justifications for decades of racialization and segregation of Mexican Americans.[68]

The inclusion of Californio elites in the Constitutional Convention of 1849 signaled that, at the very least, they enjoyed a place of relative worth and respect in the newly conquered society, a position that justified accommodation. However, the demographic and economic changes taking shape in California after the ratification of the 1849 constitution and the territory's acceptance into statehood would soon undermine Californios' tenuous position. Immigration to California ballooned in the late nineteenth century, as Anglos came west and Mexicans and Asians migrated looking for work. By the 1870s, these demographic shifts created intense social and economic pressure. As Anglos grew in number and social/economic position, they emphasized what Pitt called a narrative of "clash of cultures" between Californios and U.S. settlers. Competition for land and resources as well as political and social power increased, resulting in nativism and racism against Mexicans and Chinese immigrants. The demand to address these economic and social challenges provided the impetus for a new Constitutional Convention in 1879, a brief consideration of which can help us draw conclusions about the effectivity of Californios' vernacular discourse just thirty years earlier.[69]

All the delegates to the 1879 California Constitutional Convention were Anglo-Americans, and the physical absence of Californios illustrates most concretely a shift in the social role of Mexican Americans in just thirty years. The debates of the 1879 convention also demonstrated a shift with regard to citizenship rights for those considered nonwhites. The contrasts with the 1849 constitution and convention were marked. While the 1849 constitution mandated Spanish translation of government documents and proceedings, in 1879 the delegates quickly agreed upon an English-only provision. The 1849 constitution provided for, as we discussed above, at least provisional inclusion of nonwhite men to suffrage in "special cases." In contrast, the 1879 constitution barred all nonwhites from any access to citizenship rights (especially suffrage). Racism against Chinese immigrants was also virulently expressed and codified in the 1879 constitution. Anglo delegates to the 1879 convention classified all Spanish speakers as illegal immigrants (in light of recent increases in immigration from Mexico), ignoring the provisions and guarantees of the Treaty of Guadalupe Hidalgo and infringing on Californios' citizenship rights. The Californios were conflated with Mexican immigrants and seen as no different and no better than other "usurpers." As delegate John West (himself an Irish immigrant to California) argued during the 1879 convention, if thirty years had not assimilated these "foreigners," "bandits, cutthroats, and robbers" into U.S. American society, perhaps "we had better send missionaries" to do the job. In fact, historian Albert Camarillo notes that the 1879 Constitutional Convention demonstrated an increasing conflation of Mexican immigrants with Mexican Americans that has become prevalent today.[70] The presumption that all Mexican-looking or Spanish-speaking people were foreigners or immigrants (rather than citizens) contributed to the marginalization of Californios as well as immigrants. In just thirty years, Mexicans had been conquered and colonized, forcibly made citizens, and then had lost their rights and property despite legal guarantees. Now, Mexican Americans became foreigners in their own land.

This brief description of the 1879 California constitutional debates demonstrates how in just thirty years the politics of citizenship and borders changed drastically in the state. Not only did Californios not participate formally in the 1879 Constitutional Convention, the new constitution itself reversed many of the rights and concessions won by Californios in 1849. This mirrored a broader process of political/economic marginalization and exclusion for Mexican Americans in California in the late nineteenth century. As Californios were weakened politically and economically, Anglo settlers capitalized on these changes to solidify their control of the new state. Threats to U.S. citizenship such as immigration and racial/cultural diversity created border anxiety that justified Mexican Americans' increasing exclusion and usurpation.[71]

This historical moment, therefore, demonstrates the evolution of the U.S.-Mexico border and of rhetorical and material bordering of U.S. citizenship. The struggle of the Californios elucidates one of the first moments in which Latinos (specifically, Mexicanos) negotiated and enacted U.S. citizenship through vernacular rhetoric. As Bancroft dramatically summarizes, "Never in the history of the world did a similar convention come together. They were there to form a state out of . . . territory only lately wrested from a subjugated people, who were elected to assist in framing a constitution in conformity with the political views of the conquerors." As subjugated people but also as subjugators from a privileged status, the Californio delegates became "the representatives of their class, in order to avert as much as possible the evils they foreboded."[72]

Given this precarious position in relationship to the coloniality of power, the Californios' efforts to achieve recognition as political subjects worked alongside their entrenchment of logics of marginalization. The coloniality of power, knowledge, and being stemming from U.S. racialized traditions of citizenship worked as a form of subjectification of Californio elites, constituting them as "off-white" and thus inferior to their Anglo-American counterparts. At the same time, the coloniality of the

Spanish/Mexican traditions positioned the Californio delegates to the 1849 convention, for the most part, as superior to other, nonwhite Californios. This allowed the Californios a certain degree of subjectivity and agency in constituting themselves as equal citizen-subjects to their Anglo counterparts. In this way, Californio delegates demonstrated their embrace of coloniality by assimilating to Anglo/U.S. conventions.

By foregrounding alternative traditions of race, language, and political tradition and working at the intersection of coloniality, Californio delegates in the 1849 convention enacted their citizenship but also created slippage in the strict, exclusionary dynamics of belonging. Their vernacular discourse challenged coloniality and the racial and cultural contours of U.S. citizenship. At the same time, the disruptive potential of their border rhetoric was undermined by the Californio delegates' deployment of coloniality and white privilege. The border crossed Californios both literally and figurally, and through vernacular rhetorics of citizenship and U.S. identity they contested but also reified those dominant logics. This same dynamic between exclusion and assimilation endemic to the border would contribute to the Californios' marginalization in the late nineteenth century and throughout the early twentieth century.

The next chapter focuses on a moment a little over a century after this first instance of the border's crossing and the crossing of borders. Demographic and societal changes contributed to a very different position for Mexican Americans in the Southwest during the mid-twentieth century, and in the radical climate of the time, these citizens looked critically at their legal, social, and political position in the United States and began to clamor for recognition and voice. Chicana/os again contended with the physical and figurative borders of U.S. citizenship through vernacular discourse. Specifically, the struggles of one particular group of Chicana/o citizens during the 1960s and 1970s for political and social recognition—La Alianza Federal de Mercedes and its leader Reies López Tijerina—will serve as the case study to further examine vernacular rhetorics of borders, citizenship, and Latina/o identities.

Inhabiting the Border

Radical Rhetoric and Social Movement in 1960s New Mexico

Right now we look like a cricket. What is a cricket? King of the insects; a little tiny animal. All the cricket can do is just "cricket, cricket, cricket." Just a noise, that's all. But you know, if that cricket gets in the eye and the ear of the lion and scratches the inside, there is nothing the lion can do. . . . We are a cricket, but we are too deep inside of this continent, of this country.

—*Reies López Tijerina*

The Alianza Federal de Mercedes (Federal Alliance of Land Grants) was organized in 1963 to lobby for the return of Mexican and Spanish land grants to their original heirs (the same land grants guaranteed by the Treaty of Guadalupe Hidalgo), but by 1967 its mission and influence had expanded and its tactics had become more confrontational, leading to increased government surveillance and persecution. The Alianza was planning a large-scale convention to be held in the small town of Coyote, New Mexico, on June 3, 1967, which would be one of several national conventions publicizing the Alianza's cause, coordinating future actions, and building relationships with other activist organizations. However, before it could convene, and because rumors circulated that the Alianza would be coordinating violent resistance at this meeting, New Mexico district attorney Alfonso Sanchez shut down the meeting by arresting several of the aliancistas (Alianza members). Sanchez's aggressive and preemptive crackdown on the Alianza's planned convention on June 3 in Coyote was part of an escalating contest between the movement and law enforcement, and, unbeknownst to anyone, these events would lead to the Alianza's most (in)famous action.

On Saturday night, June 3, 1967, the night of Sanchez's arrests, seventy-five members of the Alianza held a meeting "in the back room of an old adobe building" to discuss their response. Later, the group's leader, Reies López Tijerina, would tell one of his biographers that the aliancistas who congregated there "were furious like never before." After all, or so they reasoned, the Alianza had intended to meet only to demand the return of their ancestral, communal lands and to protest the violation of their cultural and civil rights. They viewed Sanchez's action as a gross abuse of power. In its anger, the group decided to make a "citizens' arrest" of Sanchez for "tampering [with] and abusing" their "constitutional rights" of assembly.[1] As a result, a group of activists including Tijerina and his daughter Rose raided the federal courthouse in Tierra Amarilla, New Mexico, two days later, on Monday morning, June 5, with the goal of freeing the jailed aliancistas who were being held there and arresting Sanchez. Though the group had decided to refrain from violence during the citizens' arrest, the armed aliancistas immediately clashed with law enforcement. They were unable to free the prisoners or arrest Sanchez, neither of whom were in the courthouse as expected. Instead, the raid provoked a shootout with police in which two policemen were wounded and two individuals were taken hostage in the Alianza's escape. The events at Tierra Amarilla and the federal search that led to the participants' arrest garnered national attention and catapulted the group to the forefront of the then still nascent Chicano movement(s).[2]

The events at Tierra Amarilla on June 5, 1967, which have come to be known as the "courthouse raid," present a peculiar case in our exploration of Latina/o discourses of citizenship, particularly in comparison to the preceding chapter. In contrast to reasoned debate about citizenship rights and duties, the Alianza's radical activism seemed to stand against citizenship, as an act of revolution or separatism rather than civic identification. Paradoxically, an armed and violent raid on government agents was purportedly performed, according to the Alianza, as an expression of Mexican Americans' citizenship (as a citizens' arrest). As I will show in this chapter, not only the courthouse raid but the Alianza's rhetoric and activism in general struck a tenuous balance between citizenship and separatism, from Tijerina's speeches to the group's demonstrations. The tension in the Alianza's discourse—between enacting U.S. citizenship and challenging its very boundaries—forms the locus of this chapter. I argue that the Alianza demonstrated an unstable model of performing citizenship based on the liminality of the border itself; its vernacular border rhetoric straddled the divide between citizen and separatist.

The last chapter explored how Californios' rhetoric negotiated the border(s) between Mexican and U.S. concepts of citizenship, between white, criollo, mestizo, and indio racial identity, and between cultural and linguistic traditions. Through their vernacular rhetoric, Californios navigated the borders of belonging and the material bordering of the U.S.-Mexico frontier. At the same time, the chapter showed that vernacular border rhetorics may also contribute to the building of new borders of belonging. Sometimes these border rhetorics can reify the exclusionary boundaries of the civic imaginary, even as they seek to undermine it, when they do not fully embrace the contradictions and dualities of the borderlands. Thus vernacular rhetoric may challenge borders and help provide agency and voice for those voices and agents that have been "subalternized," but in order to do so it must embrace a "double critique" that is "critical of" and "think[s] from both traditions and, at the same time, from neither of them."[3]

Here I consider the Alianza's discourse as another form of border rhetoric, one that engaged such a double critique as a strategy for enacting citizenship and negotiating agency. Analyzing several rhetorical moments that revolved around the time of the 1967 courthouse raid, I show that the Alianza's vernacular discourse paradoxically performed citizenship in tandem with its condemnation. The Alianza appealed for redress from the government, met with state officials, and talked of rights, the Constitution, and U.S. citizenship, yet its members also condemned the United States and publicly eschewed citizenship identification, advocating forcible takeover and armed revolt. At the center of this contradictory activism was a fundamental struggle with the tensions of exclusion and inclusion that by the 1960s had already characterized Mexican Americans' (and Latina/os') lives within the United States for over a century.

In essence, the Alianza's discourse migrated across the precarious borders of belonging as its adherents straddled the line between radical revolutionaries and civil rights activists. The Alianza's vernacular discourse of citizenship did not adhere to a forced choice between assimilation and exclusion but rather oscillated between these and held in tension appeals to citizenship and foreignness. As an example of what Chela Sandoval calls differential social movement, the Alianza (partially) embraced a "*tactical subjectivity*" that deployed citizenship and border logics but also displaced those logics to "de- and recenter . . . the forms of power." The Alianza's border rhetoric, "like the clutch of an automobile, . . . select[ed], engage[d], and disengage[d]" with the dominant borders of citizenship to allow "for the transmission of power," identity, and agency to Mexican Americans.[4] The movement's vernacular discourse both claimed and challenged the bounds of belonging and was betwixt and between the recognized traditions of race, identity, and citizenship we have considered thus far. As a result, the Alianza's border rhetoric was more unstable but also presented more of a challenge to the borders of the civic imaginary than did the Californios' compromise discourse. Nevertheless, this vernacular rhetoric, too, was partly undermined by its own reliance on dominant logics of race and gender. To unpack this argument, I first contextualize the analysis by briefly reviewing early and mid-twentieth-century debates about borders and Latina/o citizenship and by narrating the Alianza's history. Then, the chapter turns to Tijerina and the Alianza's verbal, embodied, and performative rhetorics, which provide insights into the broader Chicano and Mexican American politics of the 1960s–70s as well as to the broader study of Latina/o vernacular discourses.

From Mexican American to Chicana/o

At the turn of the century, the realities of citizenship and race that structured the lives of Californios extended to Mexicans and Mexican Americans throughout the Southwest. Though Mexican Americans were officially citizens of the United States, they still often lived on the borders of belonging based on exclusive norms of racial and cultural identity. Mexicans and Mexican Americans were often seen as neither black nor white, as "off-white" or "mongrel," at best as white on an individual basis, and as foreign. Thus the majority of Mexican Americans remained excluded from full citizenship. Treaty guarantees were ignored or usurped by state governments, and other legal protections, such as the Fourteenth Amendment, were interpreted to exclude Mexican Americans, Asians, or American Indians from their promise of citizenship rights.[5]

These logics of borders and citizenship contributed to a complicated tension for Mexican Americans between assimilation and exclusion. Striving for civic belonging entailed a difficult choice between assimilating into dominant logics of "Americanness" with the hope of being recognized as a citizen, or facing exclusion based on one's status as nonwhite and therefore foreign. Throughout the early twentieth century, the choice between assimilation through sameness or exclusion based on difference had the effect of entrenching the exclusivity of U.S. citizenship that kept Mexican Americans, women, blacks, eastern European immigrants, Irish immigrants, and other groups deemed different, as at best second-class citizens. To say that assimilation was a choice, however, is also to overstate in many cases the degree of agency that Mexican Americans and other minorities had in the dominant logics of U.S. citizenship at the turn of the twentieth century. Mobility was available only to a small minority of advantaged elites, and it was achieved only through distancing from poorer and more racialized Mexican Americans and immigrants.[6]

Take, for example, Mexican Americans' struggles with segregation, which was institutionalized as the norm in the Southwest by the turn of the twentieth century. In schools, public facilities, businesses, and government, segregation was justified through a variety of arguments about race/whiteness and cultural inferiority. Even light-skinned Tejano or Californio students, who were seen as "white" in some contexts, were often segregated into "Mexican schools" despite their parents' protestations. As Gregory Rodriguez writes, "While Mexicans had once been perceived as diverse, they were now more likely to be viewed as a monolithic, subordinate class."[7] When lawsuits were filed to challenge segregation on a case-by-case basis, plaintiffs usually appealed to their presumptive whiteness to contest their segregation. In some cases Mexican Americans assimilated through whiteness, while in other cases even those who could perform whiteness were seen as "foreign" based on their language, culture, or ethnic background.

A similar binary between assimilation and exclusion structured Mexican American civic organizations in the early twentieth century. Many of these groups organized for Mexican American rights and greater social and economic mobility. For example, the League of United Latin American Citizens (LULAC) and the American G.I. Forum—the two most successful Mexican American civil rights organizations of the first half of the century—both strived for the integration (that is, "Americanization") of Mexican Americans within the nation. Both LULAC and the American G.I. Forum demonstrated the tendency of activists during the early twentieth century to define Mexican Americans as assimilated citizens worthy of inclusion. Faced with dominant logics of belonging and a tension between foreignness and assimilation, these Mexican American activists tried to negotiate entry through identification with U.S. citizenship, a strategy that was evident in the organizations' terminology ("Latin American," "Mexican American," or "Spanish American" replaced "Mexican") as well as in their emphasis on patriotism, economic mobility, and military service. Both groups argued that Mexican Americans had served their country in both World Wars and were active, hard working, and assimilated members of their communities and thus deserving of full citizenship.[8]

A central issue for many Mexican American activists during the first half of the twentieth century was the increasing number of Mexican immigrants entering the United States. Mexican migration in the three decades leading up to the Great Depression more than doubled the size of the Mexican population in the United States. Fueled by political and economic upheaval in their native country and enticed by a demand for migrant labor, one-tenth of Mexico's population migrated to the United States during the first half of the twentieth century. As I noted in the introduction, those migrants were seen as both necessary and unwelcome. Thus during this time Mexican migrants were subject to a migratory circuit that locked Mexican migrants into poorly paid, backbreaking labor with few protections or benefits. For example, the Bracero Program, which began in 1942 as a wartime temporary guest worker program meant to meet U.S. labor shortages, worked from this very idea of Mexican migrants as an exploitable and hardworking but ultimately racialized and undesirable population. The Bracero Program continued long after the end of the war and eventually cemented the image of the Mexican as migrant stoop laborer.[9]

Many Mexican American activist organizations resisted Mexican immigration and ignored the exploitation of migrant workers because they feared that Mexican migration would weaken their already tenuous position as second-class members of the nation. Mexican Americans saw opposition to Mexican migration as a way to express their patriotic Americanism and assimilation. In essence, the exclusion of Mexican migrants (and other Latin American immigrants) became an avenue for Mexican Americans to perform Americanness. Here again was the catch-22 of assimilation or exclusion. Both LULAC and the American G.I. Forum feared that anxiety about braceros would fuel racialization of Mexican Americans. Their fears were partly justified, for the "threat" of Mexican migrants did increasingly fuel an "anti-Mexican hysteria" in the mid-twentieth century.[10] This hysteria spilled over onto the Mexican American community, which was increasingly marginalized as "alien" despite its legal status. A cycle of enticement of Mexican labor and then crackdown of forced repatriations characterized immigration and labor policies throughout the first half of the century. The Bracero Program, for example, was followed ten years later by Operation Wetback, which saw the deportation of almost one million Mexican migrants, legal residents, and Mexican American citizens presumed to be migrants.[11] Caught in the binary between assimilation and exclusion, Mexican American civil rights organizations sought to enact their citizenship and demonstrate their suitability for inclusion into the national community. "Mexican Americanization," argues Francisco Rosales, "was in large part dominated by middle-class reformers who advocated assimilation and working within the system."[12] The same was true for other Latina/os settling in the United States in the mid-twentieth century, from Puerto Ricans to Dominicans, who struggled with similar pressures of assimilation into or exclusion from the U.S. racial/civic imaginary.

I have chosen to focus on the Alianza Federal de Mercedes in this chapter precisely because it was active from the early 1960s, during the tail end of the "Mexican American" era, to the 1970s, the era of "Chicanismo." If the 1940s and 1950s can be characterized as the "Mexican American" generation, then the late 1960s and 1970s can be seen as the "Chicano" era, in which activists reappropriated racial stereotypes (such as the term *Chicano*) into positive racial and cultural identifiers and as a grounding for ethnic nationalism. Most Chicano activists embraced a politics of difference and rejected conventional rhetorics of assimilation, belonging, or the "liberal agenda" of citizenship that characterized Mexican American civic organizations.[13] Instead, as Fernando Delgado summarizes, "Chicanismo reconceived Mexican Americans as radicals, populists, and nationalists."[14] The Alianza is significant because it inspired many of the most enduring themes of the Chicano movement(s) and served as a bridge between the Mexican American movements of the 1940s and 1950s and the Chicano movement(s) of the late 1960s. The Alianza's discourse remains an understudied dimension of this broader historical and rhetorical moment in Mexican

American, Chicana/o, and Latina/o history. Therefore, in the next section I briefly trace the group's history and trajectory.[15]

The Alianza Federal de Mercedes

With its founding in New Mexico in 1963, the Federal Alliance of Land Grants revived a century-long struggle to retake lost Spanish and Mexican lands. Its founder, Reies López Tijerina, a former migrant laborer and Pentecostal minister, had toured the Southwest as an itinerant preacher in the 1950s learning from poor farmers about the land that had belonged to their families since before the Mexican-American War. These ancestral lands belonging to colonized Mexicans (lands that Mexicans had themselves wrested from Native Americans) were guaranteed through Spanish or Mexican government grants (or sometimes through tradition) to individuals and communities, and protection of Spanish and Mexican land grants was guaranteed in the Treaty of Guadalupe Hidalgo. Nevertheless, many of the lands were taken by corporations and wealthy Anglo farmers over the course of several decades through a combination of trickery, legal maneuvering, and outright violence. The U.S. government also converted many of the lands that had once been used for livestock, which were seen as underused, into national forests throughout the early twentieth century.[16]

Thus Tijerina founded the Alianza, in collaboration with existing land activists in New Mexico, as an advocate for these poor, dispossessed, rural New Mexican "Hispanos."[17] Its slogan became "Justice Is Our Creed and the Land Is Our Heritage."[18] The organization argued that the ancestral land grants had been stolen from Mexican Americans in violation of both treaty rights and federal and state laws. The Alianza demanded that state and local governments investigate the land grants and enact restitution for those Mexican American families who still held title to their stolen ancestral lands. Fueled by a multimedia rhetorical campaign that consisted of public speeches, newspaper columns, local radio programs, letters to state and national government officials, and even trips to Mexico to promote the organization, the Alianza grew to over ten thousand members in a few short years, energizing previous land rights organizations and infusing the struggle with new life.

The Alianza's most well-known activism took place in the late 1960s in a climate ripe with social movement agitation—including the founding of the Black Panther Party, the rhetoric of "black power," Dr. Martin Luther King Jr.'s increasing antiwar activism, and the confrontation of antiwar and student activists.[19] The group's protests, marches, and confrontations with state and federal law enforcement at the time reached front pages and TV screens across the country. In July 1966, for example, the Alianza held a march from Albuquerque to the state capital, Santa Fe, demanding a meeting with the governor.[20] The organization's members had grown tired of petitioning state and federal officials through conventional means, and thus the "spectacular march or demonstration," in Tijerina's words, became a way to publicize the organization and force officials to listen to the Alianza's demands. The sixty-three-mile, three-day march drew media attention to the movement, as did the aliancistas' protests and encampments at the state capitol until the governor met with them.[21]

The march from Albuquerque to Santa Fe became the first of several protests and increasingly radical acts by the Alianza. Later that year, in October 1966, the group stormed Echo Amphitheater Park—part of a Spanish land grant that had been absorbed into the Carson National Forest—and occupied the land for two consecutive weekends as a form of protest.[22] Tijerina justified the occupation because "the U.S. government has ignored all pleas and petitions relative to these land grants."[23] The Alianza camped on the land, forcibly expelled federal Forest Service officials, and "revived" and defended the ancient land grant from Anglo "incursion" until they were forced to abandon their encampment by law enforcement and the courts.

As I discussed above, perhaps the most famous action of the Alianza during this time period was the courthouse raid of June 5, 1967, a spur-of-the-moment response to preemptive crackdowns by state law enforcement. The events at Tierra Amarilla catapulted the Alianza's regional land grant movement onto the national stage. The feeling at the time among other activists, as José Angel Gutiérrez later wrote, was that Tijerina and the Alianza "did what Malcolm X and the Black Panthers only talked about. [They] waged war against the state of New Mexico and the United States government."[24] The courthouse raid attracted a larger and more diverse group of followers to the movement and spurred collaboration with other organizations. The Alianza continued to publicize land and rights claims through a national speaking tour by Tijerina and participation in the Poor People's March on Washington in the summer of 1968. Tijerina also met with Dr. Martin Luther King Jr., Maulana Ron Karenga of US Organization, Ralph Featherstone of the Student Nonviolent Coordinating Committee, Hopi tribal leaders, members of the Black Panther Party, and a variety of Chicano leaders. With this increasing influence also came the heightened surveillance of law enforcement, including the FBI, and legal prosecution of Alianza members, ultimately leading to Tijerina's imprisonment in 1969.[25]

The Alianza's activism has been described in contradictory terms in both scholarly and biographical circles. At once, the movement is seen as radical, rebellious, even revolutionary and as conservative and reformist. For some, the Alianza represented the "radical wing" of the Chicano movement(s): "aggressive," "dramatic," and "audacious," characterized by "militancy," even "separatism"; a "rebellion" that was "at odds with the majority."[26] For others, even the Alianza's most "radical" actions were seen as aberrations, or, at most, instruments to draw attention to the organization's reformist, civil rights message, a message that "reflected . . . conservative values" and was "more traditional than radical."[27] Along these lines, Manuel Gonzales argues that Chicano activism "could be divided into those associations that sought to work through the system and those that called for a major restructuring of the system, the moderate and the radical wings of the movement respectively."[28] Yet the conflicting assessments of the scope and meaning of Tijerina and the Alianza's activism as well as their long rhetorical trajectory suggests that they will provide fruitful cases for exploring the tensions, exigencies, and resonances of Chicana/o vernacular rhetoric.

The Alianza and Tijerina bridged the "Mexican American" and "Chicano" generations and integrated the "moderate" and "radical" strands of Chicano activism, as I will argue below. For Tijerina and the Alianza, petitions, letter-writing campaigns, and civil suits were just as common as protests, vandalism, and physical confrontation. The Alianza worked to integrate the tensions of inclusion and exclusion and the themes of civil rights and nationalism. Instead of negotiating the borders of citizenship and civic identity, the Alianza straddled them and used border rhetoric to unravel dominant binaries of citizenship and democracy. The Alianza married radical and confrontational appeals to ethnic nationalism with legal and moral appeals for the civil rights of Mexican American and other Latin Americans. In fact, the Alianza integrated these tensions into a complex identity that I trace through several of the movement's discourses. The Alianza's activism stretched throughout the decade of the 1960s and evolved with the times, but analysis of the group's rhetoric and activism illustrates a vernacular rhetoric of citizenship and Latina/o identity that broke with the dominant binaries of either assimilation or exclusion, a border rhetoric whose power lay in the migration between these dichotomies.

The following rhetorical analysis of Tijerina and the Alianza's vernacular discourse centers on the time period of their most well-known activism, from 1966 to 1969. I focus on several rhetorical moments in the broader movement to develop an understanding of how Tijerina and the Alianza crafted border rhetoric, a discourse that transgressed the boundary between inside and outside (citizen and alien, assimilation and exclusion) and resided in this middle space. The Alianza at times performed U.S. citizenship, clamoring for rights and protections, and in other moments performed the position of outsiders, critiquing the evils of U.S. society and articulating a call for an ethno-nationalist identity. First I focus on Tijerina's rhetoric, particularly his 1967 speech "The Land Grant Question" and two public letters written from prison in 1969. Then, I turn to the Alianza's activism, discussing the Echo Amphitheater takeover of 1966 and the Tierra Amarilla raid of 1967. Together, these discourses demonstrate that the Alianza's border rhetoric moved between separatism and citizenship. In this way, its vernacular discourse evinces "an other thinking" in, from, and through the border(s) of citizenship as a way of negotiating civic identity.[29]

The Rhetoric of "King Tiger"

Reies Tijerina has long been recognized as a "fiery and effective speaker," a "golden-tongued Spanish-speaking leader of the landless" known for his "oratorical flair." Therefore, beginning our analysis with Tijerina's rhetoric provides an entry point into the Alianza's broader strategy of vernacular discourse. Though a number of biographers and scholars have mined Tijerina's rhetoric for its basic themes and for his underlying motivations, this section focuses instead on the leader's discourse as example of the group's broader rhetorical strategy.[30]

Tierra Amarilla had thrust the Alianza to the forefront of the burgeoning Chicano movement, and it also presented a number of challenges as Tijerina toured the country speaking about the cause. The group's leader had to continually address criticisms of the movement, justify the courthouse raid, and clarify its purpose. This was the task Tijerina faced as he gave the speech known as "The Land Grant Question" on November 26, 1967 (just five months after the courthouse raid). It was delivered at the University of Colorado at Denver to a mostly Anglo student audience during a national speaking tour. The speech is emblematic of much of Tijerina's public address during the time, and as a result it has been anthologized as a representative example of Tijerina's rhetoric. For our purposes, the speech is worthy of analysis because it integrated the tensions and contrasting arguments of the Alianza's border rhetoric.[31]

Validating those who claimed his rhetoric was separatist and militant, one of Tijerina's arguments in the speech constituted a relationship of opposition between Anglos and Mexican Americans. Tijerina argued that Mexican Americans were a separate race and nation (a "new breed"), legally sovereign in their own right, and thus demanded sovereignty. However, another argument he made in the same speech enacted full citizenship, situating Mexican Americans not as a "new breed" but as "true Americans." Tijerina at times called for U.S. society to be faithful to its promises of rights and inclusion for Mexican Americans, while at other times he called for the new breed to come together and struggle against "evil" Anglo society. Tijerina sometimes constituted the Alianza (and Latina/os more broadly) in an ethno-nationalist identity, and at other times as "American citizens," as "true Americans" seeking full citizenship.[32] Rather than, on one hand, eschewing cultural and racial difference to achieve inclusion or, on the other, rejecting inclusion for the sake of separatism, the speech featured a back-and-forth rhetoric filled with tensions and contradictions that both enacted and problematized U.S. citizenship.

Let us consider in more detail an example of these contrasting arguments in Tijerina's speech:

> Right now we [the Alianza] look like a cricket. . . . King of the insects. . . . All the cricket can do is just "cricket, cricket, cricket." Just a noise, that's all. But you know, if that cricket gets in the eye and the ear of the lion and scratches the inside, there is nothing the lion can do. There is nothing . . . the lion can use . . . to destroy the cricket because . . . he's way deep in the structure inside. The more the lion scratches himself the more deeper [*sic*] the cricket goes inside and scratches. We are a cricket, but we are too deep inside of this continent, of this country. . . . And the lion, the greatest giant ever built by taxpayers, Uncle Sam. There's nothing he can do to destroy us. Let's face it.[33]

Tijerina's metaphor here served in the context of his long speech to explain the Alianza's mission and identity to his audience. Though it represents only a small portion of the text, analyzing the different implications of his argument in this passage demonstrates the double movement of the broader speech.

On one hand, the metaphor of the cricket and the lion supported the identification of the Alianza as U.S. citizens "way deep in the structure" of the nation. Tijerina was performing the Alianza's status as "American citizens" or "true Americans" who sought inclusion and integration into the national fabric. The cricket (Mexican Americans) was crying out for rights and inclusion, though it sounded like a small noise to the great lion. The lion could scratch at (persecute) the cricket, as it had done for centuries, but it would only push the cricket "deeper" into the structure and intensify its demand for recognition. Ostensibly, the Alianza and Mexican Americans were not aiming to destroy this great lion (the United States) or to separate from it, but demanding that the lion come to terms with the cricket, to reach symbiosis. As Tijerina put it in another part of the speech, "I only stand as a citizen, as an American citizen, for those rights that truthfully, constitutionally belongs [*sic*] to the Spanish American." "We are not asking for something that does not belong to us legally, constitutionally," he stated. "The land grant question is part . . . of the Constitution." Thus Tijerina refuted the "narrow and stupid opinions" that the Alianza members were "rebels," identifying them instead, as previous Mexican American movements had characterized their adherents, as American citizens. His appeal to the Constitution and to citizenship as well as the metaphor of the lion and the cricket created identification with U.S. Americans, demanded recognition, and drew the Alianza into the bounds of the U.S. civic imaginary.[34]

On the other hand, the polysemy of the above metaphor is indicative of the border quality of the broader speech. That is, the metaphor not only enacted citizenship and inclusion but performed confrontation and ethnic separatism. The cricket, "king of the insects," antagonized the lion (the great imperial power) though it was small. Try as it might, "there is nothing . . . the lion can use . . . to destroy the cricket." The more it was persecuted, the more the cricket buried itself in the lion, "scratch[ing]" at the great beast. This interpretation of antagonism rather than symbiosis—of revolution from within—was buttressed by the final line of the quotation, where Tijerina clarified that "there's nothing he [the lion, "Uncle Sam"] can do to destroy us. Let's face it," a conclusion that rang with the tone of defiance rather than deference. This activation of the metaphor represented Tijerina's ethno-nationalist and confrontational discourse in "The Land Grant Question." Rather than perform the persona of the citizen and position the movement as integrationist, Tijerina constituted the Alianza as representatives of a separate race and nation of Latina/os (a "new breed") who were fighting to free themselves from the colonial yoke of an imperial power. As he put it earlier, "There is a hidden side . . . a dark side of the history of the United States"; the U.S. was responsible for "violence" and colonization across the globe, which demonstrated that it was a society steeped in "evil." In this strand of his rhetoric, hope rested not in reform of the present system or in the promise of citizenship but rather in the leveling justice of a coming "chain reaction" against Anglo racism. Tijerina argued, "This is the era of justice and claims": the "Indian" and "black man" were clamoring for justice, as was the Mexican American, and "small nations [were] getting independence, such as [in] Africa." Though these diverse groups struggling for freedom did not "use atom bombs to secure their independence," he stated, "the pressure of justice" seemed no less fateful. By analogizing revolutionary struggles at home and abroad to the Alianza movement, and by constituting Mexican Americans not as citizens but as a separate race and nation (a "new breed"), Tijerina constructed a different persona and position for the movement. Instead of calling for Anglo recognition, he constructed a relationship of confrontation and opposition, for "the pressure of humanity and the pressure of mankind will deliver . . . [and] liberate these land grants." In these moments, Tijerina seemed to draw on the tenor of the courthouse raid to construct a confrontational and almost revolutionary agency for his supporters, one that barred collaboration with "evil" Anglos. As he put the relationship in its clearest form, "with power you cannot reason."[35]

Therefore, Tijerina enacted both citizenship and confrontational ethnic nationalism. "The Land Grant Question" actually moved back and forth across this boundary between reformist civil rights discourse and radical ethno-nationalist discourse throughout the speech.[36] Tijerina offered an identity for the movement and for Mexican Americans (and Latin Americans more broadly) that broke down binaries between integration and separation.[37] By migrating between contradictory modes of identification, Tijerina critiqued dominant logics but also strategically appropriated them; he constituted Mexican Americans as first-class citizens but subverted and challenged racial hierarchies of U.S. identity. Tijerina channeled the radical energy of Tierra Amarilla into a consummatory moment that threatened "Anglo" society but at the same time squelched threats that the organization was too radical or communistic by identifying as "American citizen." This bordering rhetoric provided a complex and conflicting mode of belonging for Mexican Americans that I consider in more detail below.

Turning to Tijerina's letters from prison, written in 1969, can further illuminate this rhetorical strategy. Surveillance of the Alianza by state and federal law enforcement increased after the courthouse raid, putting a strain on Alianza members, especially Reies, his wife, Patsy, and their family.[38] Nevertheless, in spite of fire bombings and other attacks perpetrated against Alianza members, and in between legal struggles, the group's activism continued. On June 8, 1969, the Alianza confronted forest rangers and state police during the symbolic destruction of federal government forestry signs. After Patsy Tijerina burned the signs in protest of the theft of land grants, law enforcement agents, who were observing the activists, surrounded Alianza members. A scuffle between police and the aliancistas resulted in a standoff, as both sides drew their firearms. Finally, Reies and Patsy Tijerina and several other Alianza members surrendered to arrest. Because Reies Tijerina had been released on bond from charges related to the takeover of Echo Amphitheater, he was imprisoned shortly thereafter. Ultimately, Tijerina would remain incarcerated for twenty-one months.[39]

On August 15–17, 1969, Tijerina wrote a letter to the Alianza, which was published on September 26, 1969, in *El Grito del Norte*, an unofficial northern New Mexico newspaper for the Chicano movement(s) that had been cofounded in 1968 by Elizabeth "Betita" Martinez and Beverly Axelrod. Tijerina's public letter reiterated the radical, confrontational, and ethno-nationalist strands that I identified in "The Land Grant Question." He maligned the U.S. government, Anglos, and American society as racist and rooted in violence, and he called on Latina/os and Alianza supporters to rally together as a separate race/nation against the Anglo threat. The "Letter from Santa Fe Jail," as it was dubbed in an echo of Rev. Dr. Martin Luther King's "Letter from Birmingham Jail," has been described by scholar Rudy Busto as "angry." An analysis of Tijerina's text certainly supports this interpretation because the letter called for the unity of a global "Indo-Hispano" people, for the continued struggle against the violence and racism of Anglos, and for the sovereignty of the "new breed."[40]

Tijerina addressed his audience at the beginning of the letter as "my people, the

Indo-Hispanos," and "the entire Indo-Hispano world—'Latin America.'"[41] This identification as "Indo-Hispanos" rather than Mexican Americans, Spanish Americans, or Hispanos, is significant. Tijerina coined the term "Indo-Hispano" and used it often to represent the racial/ethnic nationalism of Mexican Americans and Latina/os. Along with his reference to Latina/os as a "new breed" or race (similar to the notion of a Raza Cósmica),[42] Tijerina's term "Indo-Hispano" positioned Latina/os as a mestizo race and nation made up of the indigenous (indio or Native American) and the Spanish ("Hispano" or "Spanish"). Referring to Mexican Americans and all of Latin America as "Indo-Hispano" exemplified Tijerina's position that Latina/os embodied a common history, racial/ethnic heritage, and culture that could serve as a point of unity through nationalism. In other words, Tijerina claimed that the new breed was united not only by historical and legal ties but also literally by mixed blood, which provided the impetus for political solidarity. Wrote Tijerina, "I pray to God that all the Indo-Hispano people will awake to the need for unity," for "times have changed and the spirit of the blood is no longer limited by national or continental boundaries."[43] Here Tijerina made multiple references to his "people," furthering his construction of a collective of supporters united by their common racial, linguistic, and cultural ties. Tijerina invited consubstantiality between Mexican Americans, other Latina/os, and Latin American people throughout the world.[44]

Further, this presumed racial heritage as a "new breed" also provided a basis for claims to national sovereignty because "Indo-Hispanos" were a colonized race separate from Anglo society. According to Tijerina's letter, Latina/os everywhere were united through the "spirit of the blood" to fight against Anglo society. Like the ethnonationalist strands of "The Land Grant Question," Tijerina's letter from prison focused on decrying the injustices of the U.S. government in an indignant and accusatory tone: "I write to you as one of the clearest victims of the madness and racism in the hearts of our present-day politicians and rulers." Tijerina's personal struggles became a stepping-stone for constructing a wide-ranging critique of Anglo racism and imperialism against Latina/os, "all those who do not want anybody to speak out for the poor, all those who do not want Reies Lopez [*sic*] Tijerina to stand in their way as they continue to rob the poor people, all those many rich people from outside the state with their summer homes and ranches here whose pursuit of happiness depends on thievery, all those who have robbed the people of their land and culture for 120 years." It was the "madness and racism" of Anglo society that was responsible not only for his imprisonment but for the plight of all Mexican Americans in the Southwest and of all Latina/os throughout the hemisphere. Later Tijerina called this a "criminal conspiracy against the Indo-Hispano in New Mexico," and compared the historical persecution of the Indo-Hispano to that of Jewish people. According to his analogy, one made often in Tijerina's rhetoric, both groups were a race and nation, recognized through international law and history, that had been subject to violence, racism, and historical persecution. Presumably, the Indo-Hispanos, like the Jewish people, held a claim to nationalism and sovereignty because of this racial/national legacy. Thus Tijerina not only constituted an ethno-nationalist identity for Mexican Americans (and Latina/os), he also constructed an "oppositional" rhetoric that stood against the dominant culture. The oppositional identity implicit in this separate race/nation was evident in a subtle language of threat, for Tijerina promised that the Indo-Hispanos were "keeping a record" of all of the violations and oppression wrought against them for a future reckoning.[45]

While Tijerina's public letter from prison, published on September 26, 1969, fell short of calling for violent revolution (though his language of threat was suggestive), neither did it call on his supporters to be good citizens or to demand inclusion. Instead Tijerina framed the solution as a meeting of equals in which the "Anglo" United States could finally return the land and honor the sovereignty of the "Indo-Hispano world." Certainly, then, Tijerina's "Letter from Santa Fe Jail" could be classified as an ethno-nationalist rhetoric that did not demand citizenship but rather performed separateness as a form of political identity and agency. Along with those similar moments in "The Land Grant Question," this strand of Tijerina's discourse represented what Fernando Delgado called the Chicano movement's "rhetoric of otherness," which affirmed a common and separate identity, critiqued dominant society, and issued a call to collective action.[46]

However, this rhetoric stands in stark contrast to Tijerina's second letter from prison written on October 13, 1969, from the State Penitentiary in Albuquerque, to which he was transferred after his conviction on charges relating to the Echo Amphitheater takeover. This second letter was published two years later in 1971 in an anthology of Chicana/o activist writings. While Busto characterized Tijerina's August letter as "angry," he described the October letter from the state penitentiary as "celebratory" and a "parade" of "legal texts" in the service of a "moral high ground." Busto wrote, "Here there is no mention of . . . [a] vendetta," and "his call for justice" is not drawn along "racial lines." While Tijerina's August letter presented an ethno-nationalist and oppositional critique of U.S. citizenship, his October letter presented a reasoned appeal for civil rights and a performance of citizenship.[47]

Strikingly, in this second letter Tijerina outlined his purpose as to "inform" the general "public" of the Alianza's cause. Whereas in his August letter he addressed supporters (the "Indo-Hispanos" throughout the world) and maligned his enemies (the "agents" of the federal government and Anglo society), here Tijerina addressed "the public" without distinction or delineation and wrote to "inform" rather than to "condemn." Rather than portray the Alianza or Mexican Americans and Latin Americans as a separate race and nation struggling for sovereignty, Tijerina here argued that they were advocating for rights and recognition. "For the rights of my people," wrote Tijerina, "I am held captive. Because of the rights of my blood brothers to their property, their culture, and their inheritance, I suffer imprisonment. And I shall suffer it again if necessary. . . . For the land, culture, and inheritance of my people I am ready not only to suffer imprisonment, but I would, with pleasure and pride, sacrifice my life to bring about the justice which is so much deserved by my people—the Spanish American people."[48] The tone in this passage was neither indignant nor accusatory but rather that of a righteous defender of his people. Their cause was just and worthy of the ultimate sacrifice. Rather than employing a language of opposition (of "madness and racism," "evil," and "conspiracy"), Tijerina emphasized rights, justice, and the duty to "inform" and convince the general public. Likewise, Tijerina's "people," those whom he fought for and who supported him, were the "Spanish American people" rather than the "Indo-Hispano" people. Through his choice of terminology, Tijerina constituted his supporters not as an independent racial and ethnic nation but as a constituent part of American society ("Spanish" modifying "American," that is, citizen).

Unlike in the earlier letter, where Tijerina's struggle was defined in racial and ethnic terms, here he claimed, "The desire for justice knows no boundaries of race or culture. I think that if another race were the victim of oppression, I would defend it as I now defend my people." Tijerina's struggle was not an ethnic or racial call for separation but a movement for "rights" and "justice." Tijerina wrote that he was a "little perturbed by what my critics say against me," because "they are ignorant of the documents, accumulated with great expenditure of time and money, to prove my people's claims to their land grants." The tone and attitude Tijerina presented toward his critics was remarkably different in this second letter, for gone were the references to their "madness and racism." Instead, Tijerina's detractors were simply "ignorant" of the facts. Tijerina stated that these critics would "someday also come to support" his struggle for "justice."[49] Rather than criticizing U.S. society for its complicity in racial oppression, Tijerina purported to educate U.S. Americans under the assumption that he could change their minds to support the Alianza's cause for justice and civil rights.

Not only was Tijerina's tone and purpose drastically different—that is, deliberative, conciliatory, and didactic—but the dominant theme of "justice" was unique to his October letter from prison. While in his first letter Tijerina emphasized themes of crime, conspiracy, persecution, and the need for unity and resistance, here he relied on the implicit belief that reason, "documents," and evidence would lead to mutual understanding. The bulk of the letter, in fact, constructed a detailed and evidence-based case for restitution of Mexican land grants based on the U.S. Constitution and state and federal laws. Tijerina's October letter from the Albuquerque state penitentiary exhibited an "obsession with text-based authority."[50] Through the frequent citation of federal and state constitutions, international law, and historical sources, Tijerina built a logos-based argument for the restitution of Spanish/Mexican land grants. If we could analogize his first letter to the confrontational and nationalist rhetoric of black leaders such as Malcolm X, this letter echoes the themes of legal equality and justice of the Southern Christian Leadership Conference (SCLC) and the early rhetoric of Rev. Dr. Martin Luther King Jr.[51] Here, Tijerina made a case for the Alianza's cause that could win the support of Anglos in the movement's struggles for justice. "We are determined to ask for, to demand, and to struggle for justice until the world gives it to us," he concluded.[52] Tijerina was "critical of his white audience but not alienated from it," and he spoke with "restrained energy" that "encourage[d] the white audience to reaffirm its basic values" (that is, justice) and reevaluate its understanding of the Alianza and its cause.[53] As Tijerina put it, "[W]e do not want to destroy the culture of the Anglo; we only ask that our culture also be protected by the law, just as the law reads." Tijerina did not condemn all Anglo-Americans for collaborating in his and his people's persecution but appealed to them to support the movement for justice.[54]

Thus in Tijerina's speech "The Land Grant Question" as well as his two public letters from prison we see the two distinct dimensions of the Alianza's border discourse: a radical and confrontational discourse grounded in Mexican American and Latina/o racial nationalism and a discourse of civil rights and inclusion. Tijerina critiqued U.S. institutions and American society and called the "Indo-Hispano" people to unite based on blood and cultural ties to secure their own power and recognition. Fueled by legal arguments and textual authority, Tijerina also enacted full citizenship for "Spanish Americans," drawing them into the U.S. civic imaginary. These contrasting arguments as well as their mediation and presence within a single speech, and even within a single metaphor such as that of the cricket, demonstrate the complex vernacular rhetoric that Tijerina constructed. Put simply, Tijerina's rhetoric inhabited the borders between citizenship and ethnic nationalism by demanding both integration and separateness. In doing so, his rhetoric seemed to problematize these borders. Tijerina portrayed himself and the movement as rebels fighting the system and as U.S. citizens demanding inclusion. Mexican Americans were at times and at once a separate race and nation struggling for its independence and ordinary Americans demanding protection. Tijerina both indicted America as evil and promised a return to America's basic foundations. Though it seemed inconsistent, his discourse worked within, from, and through these contradictions, emphasizing reformist civil rights discourse and a revolutionary ethno-nationalism.

Recall that border discourse moves between and across demarcations (such as the distinction between citizen and other). It is unsettled because it sits at the place of contact and contradiction. But, for this reason, vernacular border rhetoric can also negotiate a powerful position to enact and remake the parameters of belonging. We saw one strategy of unsuccessful border rhetoric take shape in the previous chapter, yet in contrast Tijerina and the Alianza in many ways inhabited the binary between inclusion through assimilation or exclusion based on difference. They crafted a border rhetoric that held in tension citizenship and foreignness, civil rights and separatism. Before considering these implications in more detail, I will show in the next section that this strategy was evident not only in Tijerina's rhetoric but in the Alianza's activism as well.

Border Rhetoric and the Alianza Federal de Mercedes

In October 1966, before the speeches and letters considered in the previous section and prior to the infamous courthouse raid, the Alianza reached notoriety when the group decided to dramatize the land grant struggle by taking over a piece of the Carson National Forest known as Echo Amphitheater.[55] The Alianza argued that this national forest had been created from a Spanish and Mexican land grant whose heirs were Alianza members and maintained title to the land. On Saturday, October 15, after publicizing these claims, over 350 members of the Alianza stormed and took possession of Echo Amphitheater, "reviving" an independent land grant town called La Republica de San Joaquin del Rio de Chama created by the Spanish in 1806.[56] Since they claimed the land grant was unjustly stolen from its rightful heir, the Alianza members advanced their right to reestablish its proper ownership and governance. Later, the Alianza would abandon Echo Amphitheater, but for several weeks the group's separatist rhetoric, takeover of federal land, and confrontations with police made headlines. The press called the group "armed," "militant," and ready for a "showdown."[57] The takeover of Echo Amphitheater, as a rhetorical act, evinces the Alianza's unique vernacular discourse.

After taking over the territory on October 15, aliancistas proclaimed a revival of the old nation and a restitution of its independent powers. As a show of its sovereignty, they chose the heir to the land grant as the town's rightful mayor. They also elected town officials and a court, and they deputized fifty armed soldiers to protect the new republic. The Alianza was "fully resolved to exercise all their lawful rights to their lands," Tijerina claimed, and the new town officials "dared authorities to try and move them out."[58] On the following Saturday, October 22, the group returned to the land with over one hundred settlers, food, building materials, and the signs and flags of a new nation.

A caravan of cars turned into the campground at around 11 a.m. that Saturday, horns blaring. Forest Service and state police had set up at the entrance to the park, where they planned to force the group to pay for camping permits. Instead, the caravan sped through the gate, almost running over the government officials guarding it. As the aliancistas left their cars, tensions with Forest Service and state police escalated. An angry crowd began to form around the three officials—forest rangers Phil Smith and Walt Taylor and New Mexico policeman Ernesto Vigil. As sociologist and Alianza sympathizer Clark Knowlton described the scene: "Hot words were exchanged. People left their cars and . . . grabbed the rangers. There were cries in Spanish of 'Lynch them,' 'Kill them,' and 'Now it is our turn'" (a reference to the lynching and killings of Mexicans practiced for decades in the Southwest).[59] The aliancistas dragged Smith and Taylor to the new Republic of San Joaquin's three-man court, which convened at a picnic table. There the rangers were tried and convicted of trespassing and public nuisance (Vigil, a Mexican American, was not tried). Their sentences were suspended, their vehicles impounded, and the two rangers were escorted from the territory.

After establishing order, the Alianza set out armed guards who forcibly turned away vehicles filled with tourists coming to visit the campground. "We are here to stay," said Tijerina, and the group made clear its intention to build settlements.[60] The aliancistas covered over or removed federal Forest Service signs and replaced them with the flag of the new republic (gold letters on a blue background spelling out the nation's name). A sign at the campground entrance proclaimed in part, "IN THE NAME OF GOD ALMIGHTY, KNOW ALL MEN BY THESE PRESENTS [*sic*], that the Pueblo Republic of San Joaquin del Rio de Chama, does hereby proclaim that it has resumed all of its rights and authorities vested in it August 1, 1806."[61] The sign not only proclaimed the reconstitution of the republic, it also outlined the boundaries of the new nation. The Alianza began developing the settlement by constructing temporary residences and "converting" Forest Service property for the use of the republic, including vehicles and radios. Aliancistas cut down trees, built fires, began cooking, and that evening held a rally celebrating the reconstitution of the Republic of San Joaquin.[62]

Despite these laborious efforts, the group ended its campout and turned over the land four days later (eleven days into the occupation), on Wednesday, October 26, when a federal court issued an injunction against the Alianza. Reasserting the U.S. claim to the land, district court judge H. Vearle Payne said the Alianza did not "have the right to establish a town, make arrests, incite violence, and do other things in violation of U.S. law."[63] Eventually, Tijerina and several other aliancistas would face charges for their actions at Echo Amphitheater, and Tijerina would even be imprisoned. In the immediate aftermath, however, the Alianza's actions gained significant attention. The takeover was covered in newspapers throughout the Southwest and even into Mexico. It energized the group's escalating activism and began to draw support for the Alianza from other activists and movements.

According to one view of these events, the Alianza's takeover of Echo Amphitheater served as a spectacle to highlight the plight of Mexican Americans in New Mexico and to publicize the group's cause. In this sense, the takeover was a deliberate tactic meant to draw media and public attention to the Alianza's message.[64] Another view, summarized by historian Manuel Gonzales, stated that the takeover of Echo Amphitheater was an irrational act of "desperation"—an extra-rhetorical, revolutionary outburst in an otherwise intelligible movement for reform.[65] In between these two extremes—one viewing the events as deliberate and the other as spontaneous—some biographers and scholars argued that Echo Amphitheater marked the Alianza's conscious movement into revolutionary nationalism (and thus heralded the coming of Chicanismo).[66] Like the broader estimations of the Alianza, contradictory portrayals of the Echo Amphitheater raid persist. Was it an extra-rhetorical and irrational act of desperation, a public spectacle staged for media attention, or an act of revolutionary nationalism and separatism?

True to the movement's border rhetoric, the Echo Amphitheater takeover legitimized all of these diverse interpretations. In fact, the Alianza's actions at Echo Amphitheater represented a performative blurring of this very border between citizenship rhetoric and radical separatism. In one sense, the armed takeover of land, the arrest and trial of federal officials, the harassment of Anglo tourists and hunters, and the reconstitution of a separate Indo-Hispano nation all performed a rejection of citizenship and an affirmation of a separate racial and national identity. In effect, the Echo Amphitheater takeover critiqued the theft of land, exclusion, and state violence experienced by Alianza members and other Mexican Americans throughout history by reenacting and perpetrating that very theft and exclusion on Anglo-Americans. Aliancistas carried loaded rifles and used them to take over government property and vandalize it, and they physically confronted police and federal forest rangers, arresting two and ejecting them from the park. After delineating the boundaries of the new republic, the Alianza immediately armed and deputized men and boys to protect them from intrusion or attack. Tijerina stated that the Alianza would "arrest anyone who interfered . . . including the U.S. Forest Rangers."[67] Aliancistas were more than willing to "shed blood for their new nation," one member insisted.[68] They threatened citizens who encroached on the land, whether they were campers or hunters. The takeover was "a military matter," said Tijerina, in response to objections over the armed guards. Tijerina warned the public to "beware the wrath" of the aliancistas, and his brother Anselmo threatened, "[I]f there is going to be bloodshed . . . it will be because of those who want to destroy the rights of the pueblo."[69] By arresting and trying Forest Service rangers for trespass and public nuisance, and later turning away tourists and hunters with threats and harassment, the Alianza highlighted the very real violence and exclusion conducted against Mexican Americans over time. As Tijerina stated to one journalist, the aliancistas arrested Anglo forest rangers "so they could find out how it feels to be arrested."[70] After a reporter saw one of the armed guards turn away a group of tourists who had arrived to take pictures, he asked if anyone was allowed to enter. "As long as they're Spanish [that is, Hispano]," the Alianza guard replied.[71] This same exclusion was evidenced in the unequal treatment given by the republic's court to the government officials on October 22, two of whom (both Anglo-Americans) were arrested, tried, and sentenced, while the Mexican American official was spared. By explicitly enacting racial profiling and racial exclusion as means of policing their new nation, the Alianza mocked U.S. racism and rejected any hope in institutional redress of their grievances.

Read in this way, the Echo Amphitheater takeover represented the eschewal of citizenship and an embrace of radical separatism. The group "revived" the Republic of San Joaquin del Rio de Chama, an independent nation and government established "August 1, 1806 by the High and Mighty Prince Don Carlos IV," king of Spain.[72] Tijerina's comments to reporters dovetailed with this interpretation, for "if our children are facing death and giving their blood to defend U.S. principals in Vietnam," he noted, "I don't see anything wrong in their facing any kind of danger" to defend "*our* rights," the rights of Mexican Americans "in the [1848] Treaty of Guadalupe-Hidalgo."[73] The treaty rights between the United States and Mexico underlying the Alianza's claim to the land demonstrated the degree to which the group disassociated from U.S. citizenship both through its use of confrontation and in its verbal appeals. For over three years the aliancistas had been petitioning at city, state, and federal levels concerning the loss of Mexican American land at the hands of Anglos, the cultural violence they had experienced, and discrimination against Mexican Americans and Chicanos in the workplace, in schools, and from police. Now at Echo Amphitheater the Alianza seemed to reject the path of citizenship and choose a different avenue for cultural and political power. The Alianza aimed to "re-conquer" stolen land, one supporter wrote.[74] "Our case is not based on the laws of the United States," clarified Tijerina, but on international laws and treaties between nations.[75]

As I noted above, some have argued that the Alianza's takeover of Echo Amphitheater was just a symbolic action meant to draw attention to the movement's more conventional message. This interpretation is based on the Alianza's ultimate surrendering of the land, for when the group was met with a restraining order, it eventually left Echo Amphitheater and capitulated to authorities. Instead, Tijerina argued the Alianza would "fight in the courts," for "now the burden of proof is on [the federal government]"; "it's a moral victory."[76] Yet this view refuses to take the Alianza members at their word and deed at the time of the takeover and instead views their actions and statements at the time as duplicitous, strategically hyperbolic, or at the very least misguided. Instead, if we interpret the Alianza's takeover of Echo Amphitheater on its own terms we see that it represented, in one sense, an act of dissent that rejected U.S. citizenship as a framework for identification.[77] However, this is not to say that the Alianza was rejecting citizenship altogether. In another sense, the Alianza's actions at Echo Amphitheater betrayed this radical message and demonstrated the degree to which radical rhetoric that eschewed identification as citizen could paradoxically coexist with appeals to reform, civil rights, and citizenship. That is, the Alianza's use of force to establish a Mexican American nation was followed by capitulation to authority; revolution gave way to appeals to civil rights and law. Tijerina's statement that despite abandoning the republic the Alianza had achieved a "moral victory" and would shift its strategy to the courts demonstrates how the organization blurred this boundary between performing citizenship and rejecting it. The illegal takeover of Echo Amphitheater could work in concert with a strategy of legal redress.

A similar claim can be made about the 1967 courthouse raid in Tierra Amarilla. The courthouse raid was performed in response to district attorney Sanchez's preemptive arrest of aliancistas on June 3, yet the Alianza had been facing heightened persecution and surveillance for months. In 1967 the group had officially disbanded and reconstituted itself as the Alianza Federal de Pueblos Libres (Federal Alliance of Free City-States) in an attempt to avoid a court order to turn over the names of its members. Nevertheless, state and federal officials continued their pursuit. The Alianza meeting planned for June 3 in Coyote, New Mexico, had been the subject of press coverage and publicity for several weeks beforehand. Many speculated that the Alianza would stage another takeover. For example, a story in the *Albuquerque Journal* on May 28, 1967, entitled "Former Alliance Grant May Try to Takeover Vast Southwest Area" expressed concern that the land grant organization would seek to forcibly retake even more territory this time, and it quoted Tijerina as stating that June 3 would be "showdown day" for the Alianza. Rumors grew (and were fed by the Alianza) that the group would take over five hundred thousand acres of land to reestablish a nation, and that this time the Alianza would be less willing to abandon the land when pressed.[78] Thus law enforcement shut down the meeting based on this speculation, arresting Alianza members and accusing the group of a "Communist" plot.[79]

The day after Sanchez's arrests, June 4, the Alianza composed a scathing press release signed by Tijerina that condemned the district attorney's actions. The press release stated that the arrests were the most recent example in a "hundred years of fraud, perjury and terrorism" perpetrated against Mexican Americans and that the Alianza was "willing to meet force with force, terrorism with terrorism." The Alianza represented "free city-states [that were] political entities outside the territorial jurisdiction of the U.S.," and thus, the arrests were "an act of terrorism against the citizenry of these free city-states." The statement portended the next day's violent confrontation, as it hearkened back to "the good old days," when in response to government interference into their lives, Mexicanos "called out the militia" and "ran the governor and his henchmen" out of town.[80] Both the Alianza's opponents and its supporters read this message in light of the next day's events as proof of the Alianza's abandonment of constructive negotiation and its embrace of revolution.

The Alianza's response to Sanchez's preemptive crackdown on June 5, which I discussed in the introduction to this chapter, is now famous. The group decided that evening to lead a raid on the courthouse the following Monday with a small number of Alianza members. Even state sheriff Benny Naranjo, who was present at the raid, stated afterward that the aliancistas had not intended to engage in a shootout with police.[81] The group was after Sanchez and intended to free the jailed aliancistas. Nonetheless, the raid escalated, and the ensuing violence reached national attention and quickly galvanized opinion against the Alianza. The federal and state response to the Alianza was swift and decisive, including arrests and persecution of any and all Alianza members, even those uninvolved in the raid. After the fact, Spanish-language corridos or ballads throughout the Southwest celebrated the Alianza and Tijerina and framed the event as a valiant revolution against Anglo racism and persecution.[82] At the same time, the Alianza claimed that the courthouse raid was intended to perform a citizens' arrest on Sanchez for his unjustified arrest of Alianza members who were simply intending to exercise their right of assembly. As a result of these conflicting characterizations, Chicano scholar Lee Bebout writes that the courthouse raid "has been described across the spectrum from a mere citizen's arrest to an insurrection."[83] As with the other discourse I have examined here, the Alianza justified both interpretations and, in a sense, worked between them.

The day after the courthouse raid the *Albuquerque Tribune* noted there was only one word for the Alianza's actions: "revolution." A reporter for the *Denver Post* referred to the day's events as the Alianza's "reign of terror."[84] As these reactions indicate, those who saw the courthouse raid as the Alianza's attempt at revolution against Anglo society were justified in their interpretation, based not only on the violent actions of the aliancistas but also on the rhetoric that surrounded the courthouse raid. According to this view, the violent elements of the courthouse raid represented not a moment of speaking truth to power but the sea change in Chicano politics toward revolution. The aliancistas took justice into their own hands and circumvented the process of law and citizenship; instead they used violence to resolve their complaints. Their rhetoric before the fact suggested that the courthouse raid was a declaration of war. While many Alianza supporters celebrated this revolutionary event, as evidenced by the many corridos, others lamented the movement's shift away from constructive activism. For example, Knowlton noted that "if either state or federal governments had investigated the Alianza claims [earlier], most of the subsequent violence could have been avoided."[85] In this sense, both the group's detractors and supporters presumed that there was a critical border between revolution and rhetoric that the Alianza had crossed, for good or ill. As Celeste Condit and John Louis Lucaites explain this distinction, "A dissenter can 'talk' revolution right up to the point of violence, but violence is antithetical to all ideas—indeed, it is the very abrogation of ideas. The ultimate act of dissent thus stands in fundamental opposition to the crafting of a constructive rhetoric." Viewed in this light, the events at Tierra Amarilla crossed the boundary between rhetoric and revolution; they represented the "abrogation of ideas"—of identification or citizenship—and the embrace of separatism, violence, and revolution.[86]

However, as it did with its other expressions of activism, the Alianza straddled, stretched, and traversed this border between constructive rhetoric and revolution. The courthouse raid did not abrogate "ideas" but, in contrast, was enacted with a clear rhetorical message in mind, a message of citizenship at that (a citizens' arrest). On one hand, the Alianza took up arms against the state government and thus performed a paradigmatic act of revolution, and its rhetoric of ethnic separatism and nationalism supported this interpretation. However, the group members also framed the courthouse raid as an expression of their citizenship rights as U.S. Americans. Sanchez had infringed on their rights to peaceably assemble and to speak freely, which was just one in a long chain of violations. The only response to this tyranny was to exercise their rights as citizens and challenge the government's extralegal use of power. It was these abuses, as Tijerina would later put it, that justified the Alianza's actions at Tierra Amarilla:

> Todo esto fue lo que obligo al pueblo manso y humilde a tomar un paso historico, y estableser un ejemplo nunca antes establesido en Nuevo Mexico. Alfonso Sanchez obligo al pueblo a inforzar los derechos que la policia del Estado no inforza. Esto fue un caso unico en la historia de Nuevo Mexico y posible en todo el Sud-Oeste, en el cual, el pueblo fue obligado a corregir y enderesar la Justicia que los politicos han torcido. . . . Que Tierra Amarilla sea un buen ejemplo para todos los que juegan con los derechos del pueblo para tods los politicos ladiados.
> [All of this was what forced the calm and humble people [pueblo]

> to take a historic step, and establish an example never before established in New Mexico. Alfonso Sanchez forced the people to enforce the rights that the state police do not enforce. This was a unique case in the history of New Mexico and possibly in all of the Southwest in which the people were forced to correct and straighten out [a] Justice that the politicians had made crooked. . . . May Tierra Amarilla be a good example for all of those who gamble with the rights of the people, for all of those crooked politicians.][87]

Tijerina here echoed an argument made by other Alianza members that the group had been forced to engage in the courthouse raid to take back the rights that had been denied them by the government. Because of the failure of the government to protect Mexican Americans' (the pueblos') citizenship rights, the Alianza was forced to engage in the courthouse raid. Tijerina appealed to some of the themes we saw above—the focus on "Justice" and "rights" rather than nationalism, and the scapegoating of a few "crooked" politicians rather than the entirety of Anglo society. By displacing responsibility for the raid onto those who abused power, the Alianza seemed to draw Tierra Amarilla back into the bounds of acceptability and into the mythical fight against tyrannical government. Furthermore, by emphasizing its singularity ("a unique case in the history of New Mexico and possibly in all of the Southwest"), Tijerina emphasized that this was an aberration in the group's overall appeal to citizenship and belonging.

As with the takeover of Echo Amphitheater and Tijerina's rhetoric, the courthouse raid can be seen as an event that both embraced citizenship and challenged its conventional (racialized and exclusionary) borders. The Alianza's actions subverted a conventional split between appeals to integration or separation, citizenship or foreignness, constructive rhetoric or revolution. Racial nationalism and separatism ultimately participated, along with more conventional appeals to law and citizenship. In fact, in the courthouse raid they were intertwined as the act of revolutionary violence was also a performance of citizenship (a citizens' arrest). Daniel Brouwer argues that social movements oscillate "between spheres and fora"—between oppositional discourses like protest and institutionalized forms of discourse like congressional hearings. But in this case oscillation could describe how the Alianza moved back and forth across the border between acceptable citizenship discourse and a radical discourse that shunned U.S. citizenship. The group's oscillation between these strands even within the same text or rhetorical act problematized the commonly accepted borders of belonging. This unique border rhetoric entails significant consequences for our notions of borders, citizenship, and agency.[88]

Conclusion

Through examination of various texts from the movement, including speeches, radio show transcripts, protests, and radical acts of confrontation, this chapter has provided a picture of the broader vernacular discourse of the Alianza Federal de Mercedes. The Alianza crafted a vernacular discourse that was at times *"a part of"* and at other times *"apart from"* the "dominant culture" of U.S. citizenship, one that straddled the choice of assimilation or exclusion, citizenship or (Mexican, racialized) foreignness.[89] Tijerina and the Alianza represented Mexican Americans who were legally recognized citizens but who faced various types of exclusion nevertheless. Mexican Americans in particular (as well as other U.S. Latina/os) were legal citizens yet displaced from their land, stripped of their economic livelihood, and refused the full rights and dimensions of their citizenship. Those who struggled with and at the borders of U.S. citizenship often faced a difficult choice between assimilating into (white) norms of U.S. identity as a condition for provisional inclusion or facing second-class status because of their racial and cultural difference. Not members of the institutional spheres of power like the Californio delegates considered in chapter 1, the Alianza and its members had to rely on a vernacular discourse that straddled and stretched these boundaries rather than subtly negotiating them.

The Alianza's rhetoric was unique because it worked from and within some of the contradictions of the borders of belonging. The Alianza's rhetoric "occupie[d] the periphery" but also constituted itself within "a contextually determined center."[90] The group performed citizenship but at the same time embraced separatism, radicalism, and ethnic nationalism. In order to hold these conflicting discourses in tension, the movement moved across borders of citizenship, engaging in a "series of multiple border crossings and multilayered transitions."[91] In other words, because they faced not only institutional barriers but also cultural and historical antagonism and outright persecution, the aliancistas deployed a tactical subjectivity as both citizens-subjects and noncitizen radicals. This border rhetoric oscillated between enacting citizenship through civil rights discourse and reformist appeals and performing a separate identity through ethno-nationalist discourse and radical activism. The Alianza moved between and within these discourses of citizenship in different moments and seemed to integrate or at least hold in tension conflicting strands to construct a differential social movement.

As I mentioned above, I draw this concept from *Methodology of the Oppressed*, in which Chela Sandoval traces the recurring forms of "oppositional consciousness" enacted by U.S. social movements (with a focus on the feminist movement) throughout the twentieth century, which include demands for equal rights as well as calls for revolution, supremacy, or separatism. Sandoval reviews these modes of oppositional ideology and forwards a "differential" mode of consciousness as an alternative to conventional social movement strategies. This differential mode of social movement, which Sandoval grounds in U.S. third-world feminism, "can be thought of as mobile—not nomadic, but rather cinematographic: a kinetic motion that maneuvers, poetically transfigures, and orchestrates" different ideologies, modes of activism, and subject positions. Differential social movement is a "mobile, flexible, diasporic force that migrates between contending ideological systems." In fact, Sandoval's positioning of this differential social movement within the ideas of U.S. feminists of color such as Anzaldúa speaks to the connection between differential social movement and the idea of border rhetoric. In essence, border rhetoric describes the type of rhetorical strategy that "enables movement 'between and among' ideological positionings . . . in order to disclose the distinctions among them." For this reason, a differential social movement inhabits the dichotomies of citizenship and subjectivity and embraces multiple forms of oppositional ideology, including calls for equal rights and demands for separatism. Unlike movements that remain trapped within particular ideologies of consciousness and activism that can themselves become hegemonic, Sandoval advocates for a differential social movement that is flexible, that can shift and move between different subject positions, identities, and modes of activism, choosing those that can best engage, challenge, and remake dominant conditions.[92]

Following this idea of a differential and flexible form of social movement helps us to understand how the Alianza strategically (but ultimately unsuccessfully) moved between and integrated these conflicting identities and forms of agency. The Alianza enacted a rhetoric of difference through ethnic nationalism and radical rhetoric, thereby challenging the very borders of citizenship. The group also performed citizenship and inclusion, which represented a rhetoric of sameness articulated alongside or in tandem with the eschewal of citizenship. A rhetoric of difference alone risked further marginalization while a rhetoric of sameness could lead to co-optation or assimilation.[93] Therefore, the Alianza used border rhetoric to engage in and shift between these different subject positions in relation to the U.S. civic imaginary, "like the clutch of an automobile." At times the aliancistas constituted themselves within dominant traditions of U.S. citizenship, emphasizing identification as citizens. At other times, they critiqued traditions of U.S. citizenship and performed a separate, radical ethnonationalist identity. In a way, these discourses were in tension with one another, but at the same time they represented a performative identity that was tactically ambivalent and ambiguous. By migrating between antagonistic modes of identity, both within and outside of citizenship, it navigated the tensions of and inhabited the border.

The agency enacted in the Alianza's border rhetoric is also worth considering. At times, Tijerina and the Alianza constructed rhetorics of inclusion by making a legal and moral case for their political and social citizenship. They appropriated the "master's tools"—America's laws and founding documents, civil rights and justice—to expand the borders of U.S. citizenship. At other times, the Alianza's rhetoric and activism implied that the tensions of citizenship could not be reconciled. Standing on the outside of U.S. citizenship, the Alianza sought to destroy the borders of the "master's house" and to construct an oppositional national identity. Instead of negotiating with the racial project of U.S. citizenship as the Californios did, the Alianza called for its reform and at other times enacted its rejection. By integrating and challenging the positions of citizen and radical revolutionary, U.S. American and Indo-Hispano, the Alianza crafted an agency that moved between different recognized traditions. The group's vernacular discourse privileged the ability to adapt in response to racism and the flexibility to appeal to multiple constituents and purposes. This discourse is closer to what the last chapter called "border thinking" or border rhetoric, a speaking from and to the condition of the border, including the coloniality of power and boundaries of racial, cultural, and national belonging. More than the examples in the last chapter, the Alianza "work[ed] . . . from the double bind between assimilation . . . and marginalization" to embrace a complex identity and agency.[94] The aliancistas embraced, challenged, and integrated (though oftentimes unsuccessfully) the contradictions of the multiple words they were torn between.[95]

The Alianza served as a bridge between the "Mexican American" generation, which largely sought integration into U.S. citizenship, and the "Chicano" generation, which reacted to these integrationist movements by rejecting citizenship. Returning to the contradictory scholarly and biographical portrayals of the Alianza as both "conservative" and "militant," it is difficult to classify the Alianza's vernacular discourse in relation to this accepted binary, for, to borrow from Victor Turner, it was "neither one thing nor another"—it was both.[96] Many scholars and biographers have sought to reconcile Tijerina's and the Alianza's conflicting tensions. Yet trying to smooth out the conflicting dimensions of their rhetoric is an unnecessary endeavor, for its dichotomies represent a fundamental quality of the movement's rhetoric. The Alianza refused to be painted into one side or another of this binary and instead oscillated between inclusion and separation, citizenship and foreignness. Tijerina and the Alianza seemed adapted to the borders of belonging by enacting a conflictual relationship with U.S. citizenship. The Alianza embraced and performed a unique mode of citizenship and agency for Latina/os struggling with belonging.

However, the drastic rise of Tijerina and the Alianza after the courthouse raid in 1967 was accompanied by an equally dramatic fall. Though the Alianza continued its activism after Tijerina's arrest, the group and its founder parted ways after Tijerina's release from prison in 1971. By the mid-1970s the Alianza was weakened by government persecution, imprisonment, societal backlash, and internal conflicts.[97] Thus it is important to recognize the shortcomings of the group's rhetoric as well as its strengths. Border discourse may be at times too foreign to challenge dominant logics. A discourse that is betwixt and between evades easy categorization—both its bane and its boon. Thus in spite or perhaps because of its contradictory rhetoric, the Alianza was framed as radical or as having a mixed message, which fueled its increasing marginalization in the public eye.

Furthermore, the Alianza's vernacular rhetoric itself contained some of the strands of its own undermining. First, the Alianza's ethno-nationalist notion of Mexican American and Latina/o racial identity (that is, Indo-Hispano) rested on troubling gendered and racialized assumptions. The idea of a "new breed" combining Spanish and European with Indian and Native American elements, which was at the core of the idea of Latina/os as a separate race and nation, rested on the presumption that the "feminine," "dark" Indian was "domesticated" by the "masculine" and "white" Spaniard, their miscegenation producing a new racial hybrid. These notions would later and rightly come under criticism, especially by Chicana feminists, for their patriarchal and racial ascriptions.[98] When the Alianza proclaimed it represented a "new breed," it seemed to valorize indigenous ethnicity and culture over links to Spanish culture, which, on one hand, celebrated an indigenous past that was often erased from collective memory but, on the other hand, did so in a romanticized and fetishized manner. Second, the Alianza's regular conflation of race, culture, and nation problematically rooted common identity and agency in potentially exclusive characteristics and risked collapsing differences between Mexican Americans and Latina/os. Put simply, with an identity still tied to the links between land, race, nation-state, and citizenship, the Alianza's ability to subvert bordering logics was limited.

Though the Alianza's radical activism helped ignite a broad movement, it also influenced the language and strategy of Chicano ideology in exclusionary ways. The celebration of the Alianza's actions at Tierra Amarilla, for example, contributed to a patriarchal vision of Mexican American identity and valorized a hyper-masculine, confrontational form of activism. The Alianza's notion of racial unity and nationalism influenced and helped to fuel Chicano ideas about La Raza, an even more rigid, nationalistic, and patriarchal vision of racial and cultural solidarity. Women were prominent members and leaders in the movement, such as Patsy Tijerina, who played a prominent role in the Alianza's activism, and Elizabeth "Betita" Martínez, who founded the first Chicano movement publication. Yet the role of individual women in the Alianza notwithstanding, the problematic gender politics of the Alianza's modes of ethno-nationalism and masculinity contributed to the marginalization of these women in the movement. These problems indicate that the Alianza's vernacular discourse straddled some borders while entrenching others. The Alianza movement was not a truly differential social movement because it embraced a tactical subjectivity on only some axes while ignoring others. These observations remind us that vernacular rhetorics are not always or even primarily liberatory, but rather that the relationship between resistance to and reification of dominant logics is tenuous. Though the Alianza's border rhetoric featured some strategic tensions, the group also was unable to embrace a fully inclusive identity.[99]

However, that the Alianza ultimately failed in bridging diverse audiences and achieving its stated goals, and that the movement presented a flawed example of border rhetoric, does not and should not discount its significance. Evaluating the rhetorical and political impact of a social movement based on its success in appealing to dominant power brokers has always been the quickest way to marginalize all but the smallest group of activists. The Alianza's collaboration with other prominent movements of the time, including civil rights, black power, and Native American movements, and its recognized impact on the development of Chicana/o activism suggests it had a lasting rhetorical impact despite its fate. Furthermore, despite the pitfalls of its vernacular discourse and its own constraining dimensions, the Alianza's rhetoric helps us to understand the relationship between borders and citizenship and especially between enacting belonging and challenging the parameters of the national and cultural community.

The Alianza presented a critique of the politics of citizenship and U.S. identity, highlighting the exclusion of Latina/os from U.S. belonging and exposing the assimilation and racialization forced onto Latina/os (in this case, Chicana/os) as an entry point into U.S. citizenship. The Alianza performed a mode of citizenship and U.S. identity that was troubling to dominant society but that also contained the dimensions of its own dissolution as well as its own "darker side" in relation to coloniality, race, and gender. The aliancistas illuminate some of the contradictions and conflicts of borders and citizenship. In the next chapter I explore how border anxiety and exclusionary logics of citizenship have persisted into contemporary society, morphing into new and more diffuse expressions. More important, I trace the contours of a Latina/o vernacular discourse that challenges bordering logics and national imaginaries rather than negotiating or inhabiting the borders of citizenship. By embracing hybrid discourses of borders and citizenship, contemporary immigrant social movements reborder community in more expansive ways.

Rebordering the Nation

Hybrid Rhetoric in the Immigrant Marches of 2006

Latina/o immigrants remain in(sub)ordinate, both because that space of in-between-ness that Latina/o immigrants occupy is always subaltern*ised* and other-*ified*. But also, and herein lies the promising menace of that space, as the makers of in(sub)ordinate speech.

—Nathaniel I. "Nacho" Córdova

Between March and May of 2006, several million people, mostly documented and undocumented immigrants, engaged in organized protests of proposed federal immigration legislation in cities throughout the country. In Chicago, for example, one hundred thousand people marched, while in Washington, DC, forty thousand protestors gathered outside the capitol. Demonstrators in Milwaukee numbered almost fifteen thousand, while in Denver and Detroit nearly fifty thousand congregated. In Los Angeles, on March 25, 2006, almost a million people filled the streets in one of the largest demonstrations of recent history. One of the first and most influential of these nationwide protests, La Gran Marcha in Los Angeles spurred demonstrations in cities across the country for close to two months. In towns large and small, from Des Moines, Iowa, to New York City, protestors organized by the thousands, demanding that immigrants be granted rights, protections, and a clear path to nationalization.[1]

These recent protests, and the anti-immigrant and restrictive legislation that spurred them, typify the contestation over borders and citizenship traced throughout this book as well as the enduring tension between exclusion and inclusion that structures the nation's civic imaginary. Renewed attempts to police the boundaries of U.S. citizenship and strengthen the borders of the nation in the form of anti-immigrant laws and vigilante border policing constitute contemporary moments of rhetorical and material bordering. Though some of the motivations for these bordering practices remain the same, the border also moves and materializes in response to a number of new challenges, including neoliberal economics, globalization, and new waves of transnational migration. In this context, contemporary immigrant rights demonstrations represent moments of vernacular rhetoric through which Latina/os and immigrants have cooperated with and contested borders, articulating renewed and reimagined visions of U.S. citizenship. These vernacular rhetorics, however, are not without their own problems, for modern movements often mobilize against nativist policies only to reify the very exclusivity of U.S. citizenship.

In this chapter I unpack these arguments by analyzing the protests and demonstrations over immigration policy that took place throughout 2006. In particular, I focus on La Gran Marcha because it was one of the earliest, largest, and most influential of the nationwide protests. This particular demonstration highlights a vernacular rhetorical strategy through which Latina/o and immigrant movements contested borders and performed U.S. citizenship. I argue that contemporary protest movements evince the emergence of a hybrid Latina/o citizenship discourse that fuses multiple national traditions, diverse cultures and languages, different political identities, and various constituents. Rather than negotiating assimilation or articulating a border discourse that moved between and held in tension belonging and alienness, some contemporary Latina/o vernacular discourses, evidenced in the 2006 pro-immigrant demonstrations, can be understood as crafting a hybrid, transnational vision of the national imaginary. Rather than performing inclusion or straddling the borders of citizenship, the vernacular discourses I examine in this chapter transcend these options to create something new that challenges the preeminence of race, legality, culture, and single-state national identity. Before exploring these vernacular rhetorics of hybridity and citizenship in more detail, this chapter first discusses the contexts of contemporary immigrant mobilizations and evolving politics of borders and immigration, and then I explain my use of the term *hybridity* and how it helps to contextualize the vernacular performances of citizenship by immigrant and Latina/o social movements, which are examined in the third section of the chapter.

Bordering Contemporary Immigration

Scholars and political pundits who write about the contemporary challenges to borders and citizenship have increasingly noted a broad set of transformations in the civic imaginary. They argue that twentieth-century economic, demographic, and cultural changes brought on by globalization have rearranged the terrain of borders and citizenship.[2] In particular, one of the oft-repeated claims is that the integration of the global economy, communication networks, relations of governance, and the greater flow of people across national borders demonstrates how the strictly national paradigms of citizenship and borders fall short. Observations concerning the evolving transnational dimensions of borders and citizenship in light of globalization are now commonplace among scholars and political commentators. According to this view, the challenges wrought by globalization, in particular transnational migration, create a "fundamental contradiction" in traditions of citizenship.[3] Those "border" groups, such as migrants or refugees—who are the casualties of neoliberal globalization and exist betwixt and between already recognized territorial, political, and cultural boundaries—challenge the fundamental assumption of single-nation-state, territorial belonging.[4] These changes have given rise to a number of concepts used by scholars and cultural critics to make sense of contemporary postnational citizenship and transnational political activity in the era of globalization, including "cultural citizenship," "transnational citizenship," "nomadic citizenship," and "flexible citizenship." One of the things these very different ideas have in common is the assumption that globalization forced changes in the expressions and dimensions of national belonging beyond its conventional, statist logic.[5]

Yet claims concerning the end, decline, or transformation of citizenship notwithstanding, anxiety about the future of citizenship and national identity persists and, in fact, has heightened in intensity in recent decades. Despite or perhaps because of globalization's challenges to citizenship, there seems to be an intense need by both political actors and citizens to shore up the boundaries of the civic imaginary. In the United States, for example, the last three decades have seen renewed levels of anti-immigrant legislation at the federal and local level and heightened debates about the decline of American culture in the face of a "foreign" element. Past anti-immigrant and nativist initiatives are almost too numerous to mention but include the controversial California Proposition 187 outlawing social services for immigrants, California Proposition 227 outlawing bilingual education, national campaigns for English-only amendments, the Illegal Immigration Reform and Immigrant Responsibility Act of 1996, which contributed significantly to the criminalization of unauthorized immigration, and the Personal Responsibility and Work Opportunity Act of 1996, federal welfare reform that also restricted immigrants' access to federal support. Increasing immigration from Latin America not only fueled nativist campaigns throughout the country but also resulted in armed patrols, surveillance, the building of border fences, and a number of other efforts to militarize and "secure" the U.S.-Mexico border.[6] These debates about immigration and border security rose to national attention once again during the fall of 2005 in a renewed climate of anti-immigrant fear and border anxiety, and this context is especially important to outline here because it served as the immediate reason for the Latina/o and immigrant protests of 2006 that form the main focus of this chapter.

Media coverage and public discussion had intensified around immigration and border security for months in 2005, spurred on by the spectacle of border vigilantism. As I discussed in the introduction, the Minuteman Project and the Minutemen Civil Defense Corps, two citizen groups that organized in response to what they perceived as a vacuum of federal attention to border security and immigration enforcement, coalesced that year and began to take border policing into their own hands. These Minutemen's main effort consisted of patrolling a "high-traffic" stretch of the Arizona-Mexico border. The Minutemen aimed to detect and report illegal crossings to federal authorities, persecute suspected immigrants for violating immigration laws, and deter future border "violators." In the wake of the September 11 attacks and concerns about homeland security, the actions of these border vigilantes drew significant media attention, so much so that many have argued the Minutemen aimed at nothing more than public spectacle. Their true motivations notwithstanding, the Minutemen contributed to a heightened debate about immigration and border enforcement, most of which operated from the presumption that there was a border problem, linked to terrorism, that demanded federal attention.[7]

At the same time, throughout 2005, public debate about immigration and borders contributed to congressional efforts to secure "comprehensive" immigration reform. The Republican-controlled House of Representatives introduced HR 4437, formally titled the Border Protection, Anti-terrorism and Illegal Immigration Control Act of 2005, in December. The Sensenbrenner bill, as it was commonly known after its sponsor James Sensenbrenner (R-WI), professed to be a wide-ranging approach to immigration and border policy. Its aim was clearly to address perceptions of a deficit of federal attention to border security and to answer public calls for immigration enforcement. President Bush toured southwestern states throughout the fall to tout this immigration reform proposal, which successfully passed the House of Representatives on December 16. Though the legislation ultimately failed to pass the Senate, a number of its restrictive immigration provisions were enacted into law.[8]

The Sensenbrenner bill and the debate over immigration that took shape during 2005 illustrated the virtually unquestioned status of criminalization and border militarization as the dominant logics of immigration policy. Leo Chavez argues that HR 4437 was crafted as a clear "exercise of exclusion," and the legislation's many provisions certainly supported that interpretation. Among these, HR 4437 included the mandating of over seven hundred miles of border fence along the U.S.-Mexico border, increased penalties for a number of immigration violations, intensified surveillance of potential terrorism on the borders, and termination of the "catch and release" policy of releasing apprehended undocumented immigrants. Not only did the law propose to make a person's first undocumented entry a felony crime with a minimum prison sentence of three years (as opposed to a civil crime punished by a fine), the legislation also contained a controversial "Good Samaritan" clause that made it a felony crime for anyone to "assist" an undocumented immigrant. Martha Menchaca writes that this specific change would have been "of historic proportions, since people who were found to have offered shelter, transportation, and medical assistance to undocumented aliens could now be arrested and converted into aggravated felons." The attempt to punish not only undocumented immigrants but also those who harbored them—as if immigrants were terrorists or enemies of war—was also matched by the bill's focus on border enforcement to the exclusion of any reform of naturalization laws. HR 4437 precluded the possibility of belonging in any form for the millions of undocumented individuals and families living in the United States. With no provisions for a path to legalization or naturalization for undocumented immigrants, the legislation marked the codification of an exclusive criminalization and securitization framework of immigration policy, an approach fueled by border anxiety and the presumption that immigrants were a threat.[9]

In addition to the legislation itself, media coverage of the actions of the Minutemen condensed a number of unique and problematic ascriptions about immigration and Latina/o identity. For example, the debate over HR 4437 further codified the association of Latina/os with "Mexican illegality" and terrorism, entrenching the presumption that all Mexican-looking people were presumed to be illegal immigrants and terrorists. Largely because of September 11, the figure of the (Latina/o-Mexican) immigrant and the (Middle Eastern) terrorist—both purportedly dangerous and threatening foreigners—increasingly merged in public discourse to encapsulate the (supposedly) problematic porousness of the nation's borders. Thus the Minutemen justified their border vigilantism in part through the purported threat of illegal immigrant terrorists. Similarly, HR 4437 sought to expand the role of Homeland Security in immigration enforcement in the face of public concern that the U.S.-Mexico border might provide the ideal place for terrorists to infiltrate the nation. This association of "illegal immigrants" with "Mexicans" and "terrorists" is evident in the legislation's title: the Border Protection, Anti-terrorism and Illegal Immigration Control Act, an association that admittedly contributed to fears about racial profiling among the legislation's critics. Thus, regardless of the ultimate success or failure of HR 4437, a point to which I return in more detail below, the legislation was significant as an act of rhetorical and material bordering. The anti-immigrant legislation and anti-immigrant sentiment of 2005 represented a broader moment of nativist anxiety about the status of U.S. borders and the integrity of U.S. citizenship.[10]

This review of recent anti-immigrant legislation and public discourse demonstrates that the supposed "decline" or fragmentation of citizenship, much heralded by scholars and cultural critics, has actually resulted in a renewal of border anxiety and efforts to protect the sanctity of the U.S. nation. Proclamations about the globalization of society stand in stark contrast to persistent, militaristic, and exclusionary border rhetorics such as HR 4437 and the Minutemen. In fact, we could even see the efforts to secure the borders, both physical and figurative, as reactions to the increasing challenges supposedly posed to citizenship by globalization and transnational migration. The heightened border anxiety and militarization of immigration policy witnessed over the last several decades is connected to the "crisis" of globalization identified by so many cultural critics. On this point, Anne T. Demo explains that "border enforcement formalizes the relationship between citizens, outsiders, and the state . . . [and] play[s] a significant role in both cultivating a view of the nation and legitimating state designations and practices that delimit the space of belonging." Thus it is in part the very challenges to citizenship and nation-state sovereignty such as transnational migration and globalization that breed heightened border anxiety and renewed attempts to solidify the borders of the nation. Efforts to rearticulate the borders and the space of citizenship, as Demo notes, serve to shore up national sovereignty and the exclusivity of the civic imaginary.[11]

These contemporary border rhetorics, as I explore below, spurred a wave of social protest and contestation. The 2006 nationwide immigrant rights demonstrations that materialized in response to HR 4437 are examples of a renewed struggle with the bordering logics of the U.S. civic imaginary. Dominant logics of citizenship present a contradictory picture of immigrants and their role in the nation. Immigrants are conceived of as physically within our borders yet not within our people, necessary but threatening. The concept of hybridity, discussed in the next section, describes the "troublesome" ambivalence and ambiguity of the Latina/o immigrant as a transnational subject. There is a "deep ambivalence" about immigrants' role in U.S. society and a conflicting view of immigration.[12] This "troublesome both/and" of migrants—as necessary yet unwelcome, "visible and invisible, . . . acknowledged and ignored"—constitutes, I argue below, a productive tension that contemporary Latina/o and immigrant social movements put to use through vernacular performances of hybrid citizenship.[13] Rather than trace some evolving but underlying structure of citizenship in the era of transnational globalization, as many previous scholars have done, my goal in this chapter is to describe a particular rhetorical and performative strategy of enacting and challenging citizenship that takes shape in the discourse of contemporary immigrant rights protests. The vernacular rhetorics of the 2006 protests demonstrate the possibility of hybrid performativity to resist and rewrite dominant representations of the ideal U.S. citizen and to push citizenship into new directions.

Hybridity and Citizenship

The concept of hybridity has received significant attention from scholars in cultural and postcolonial studies precisely because it speaks to the fragmentation and fusion of culture and identity in the conditions of globalization. Contrary to its essentialist racial and biological legacy, critical appropriations of hybridity as a cultural theory start from the presumption that all culture and identity is hybrid—a recombinant amalgamation of traditions—and therefore there is no authentic or essentially "pure" identity. In this sense, the concept is descriptive of both cultural exchange / fusion in general and the forms of identity that are produced through these globalized exchanges. For these scholars, hybridity debunks the idea of a prior and pure culture by recognizing the inherent mixture and fusion that characterize all cultures and identities.[14]

More important for my purposes here, hybridity also represents a trope for understanding particular identities that take shape in the interstices of colonialism and/or the modern nation-state. Hybridity, then, is both a discursive formation and a discourse of identity; it represents a form of cultural fusion and a strategy of identification in relation to discourses of power. As Angharad Valdivia summarizes, hybridity "opens up the space for the study of cultural negotiations, conflicts, and struggles against the backdrop of contemporary globalization." Though rooted in racist and essentialist historical notions, hybridity now represents an anti-essentialist theory of culture and identity. Hybridity has come to challenge those very essentialist ideologies in its description of identity under globalization and the possibility to deploy cultural fusion and colonial interstices as modes of agency and subjectivity.[15]

The concept of hybridity has also received its fair share of criticisms as essentialist, as all too easily embraced by corporate consumer capitalism, or as an example of armchair theorizing. While these critiques are insightful, I tend to agree with Marwan M. Kraidy's argument that they are the result of excessive theorizing about *hybridity* without adequate attention to the *hybridities* that are negotiated and articulated in everyday discourses. In fact, Kraidy argues that, as "the cultural logic of globalization," hybridity is truly everywhere, from the identities of émigrées and migrants to the cultural productions of consumer capitalism. Yet because hybridity is a fact of contemporary identity and culture, it represents both a technology of governance and a potential mode of cultural appropriation and agency. "Our attention," concludes Kraidy, "needs to be directed from debating the political and theoretical usefulness of hybridity, to analyzing how structures and discourses . . . shape different hybridities, and how, in turn, hybrid cultural forms . . . reflect at once the presence of hegemony and its limitations."[16]

In the analysis of contemporary immigrant and Latina/o activism that follows,

I argue that immigrant protests functioned as vernacular performances of hybrid citizenship. For me, hybridity represents a particular form of vernacular discourse, a performative strategy of identity negotiation. The discourse of hybridity represents the possibility of resistance by migrants, refugees, and/or certain racial/ethnic minorities to the homogenizing tendencies of coloniality and the nation-state. Because of the dual nature of hybridity—as both the cultural logic of globalization and a discourse of identity and resistance to globalized capitalism—it "needs to be understood," Kraidy states, "as a communicative practice constitutive of, and constituted by, sociopolitical and economic arrangements" that are "complex, processual, and dynamic." As a strategic and contingent rhetoric, hybridity arises out of specific contexts and is imbricated in complex relationships between structure and agency, coloniality and the nation-state.[17]

Immigrants are interpellated into an "ambiguous positionality" of hybridity—in terms of race, ethnicity, and culture—as not quite like us, as both "necessary and unwelcome" in the civic imaginary. In fact, it is this hybrid and troublesome position that often compels bordering practices and efforts to police, prosecute, and exclude migrants.[18] As Sara Ahmed explains, hybrid immigrants "come to embody the threat of loss: lost jobs, lost money, lost land. They signify the danger of impurity, or the mixing or taking of blood. They threaten to violate the pure bodies." This explains why the rise of "cultural globalization" and the heightened public struggles of transnational migrants have gone hand in hand with the acceleration of border policing and the militaristic demarcation of national borders. In fact, discourses of hybridity, ambivalence, and troublesome ambiguity of the migrant continually fuel the material efforts of the federal government, including the Border Patrol, to militarize the border and prosecute suspected immigrants.[19]

A similar discursive formation of hybridity can often serve to marginalize Latina/os as racially and culturally in between. Latina/o individuals or groups have often been framed in mass media and political discourse as "mongrel" or "hybrid," a gendered racialization as mixed and therefore less than fit for belonging. Even in contemporary popular culture, Latina/o icons and Latina/o culture (in a homogenized way) are often seen as "spicy" and "exotic" because they are understood as rooted in excess, ethnic mixture, and a syncretism of cultural elements.[20] The hybridity of many migrants and minorities—their status as "both us . . . and not us"—fuels "a deep anxiety about the national project."[21] We saw this gendered racialization of Mexican Americans and Latina/os in the nineteenth-century debates over Californio citizenship as well as in the Alianza's struggles over citizenship and civil rights in the mid-twentieth century.

However, the construction of immigrants and Latina/os (and other minorities) as "hybrid" creates anxiety because of the very power of hybrid performativity (of migrants and Latina/os) to problematize borders and lay bare the otherization endemic to citizenship. While critics are correct that hybridity is often articulated as a hegemonic discourse of consumerism, globalization, race, or colonialism, it can also be negotiated as a discourse of resistance, identity, or citizenship. This echoes my broader argument that border rhetorics contributing to the marginalization of supposedly hybrid "others" (who do not belong because of their in betweenness) can sometimes be appropriated strategically as discourses of subjectivity and can be deployed to challenge conditions of marginalization and exclusion. Specifically, while migrants and minorities create increasing anxiety about the boundaries of the nation-state, there is also a radical potential in the tenuous condition of migration that contributes both to anxiety and concurrently to the agency of migrants and Latina/os (and many other such minorities) to reformulate national belonging. Hybridity is both a form of subjectification of migrants and Latina/os as "other" (and therefore outside the bounds of belonging), and it constitutes a mode of subjectivity for these groups to challenge the boundaries of the civic imaginary.

This is the point made by Córdova in the epigraph of this chapter. Latina/o immigrants are often positioned as hybrid and in between and thus as "in(sub)ordinate," often marginalizing them within the U.S. civic imaginary. But, at the same time, Córdova notes that this position of in betweenness, this "in(sub)ordinate" space, provides the opportunity to subvert the boundaries of the civic imaginary and to create insubordinate speech. Shane T. Moreman similarly writes, though it is "borne out of deterministic discourse," hybridity "becomes discursive strategy." The strategic deployment or performance of hybridity (through vernacular rhetoric) may operate differently than the dominant, stereotypic discourses of hybridity in mainstream media. This rhetorical view of hybridity suggests that it is the performative position(ing) of migrants and minorities as outside the bounds of belonging yet integral to it that challenges the nation-state logic of citizenship. Migrants and formerly colonized people, Homi K. Bhabha once wrote, "deploy the cultural hybridity of their borderline conditions to 'translate', and therefore reinscribe, the social imaginary of both metropolis and modernity." Thus, whereas past vernaculars may have worked to stretch or migrate over the boundaries of citizenship, hybridity suggests the possibility of blurring and (re)making the parameters of belonging, of inhabiting the border as "an intervening" and transformative space.[22]

In the remainder of this chapter, I examine the nationwide immigrant protests in 2006, in particular La Gran Marcha of Los Angeles held on March 25, through a number of textual "fragments," including video recordings (from both news media and participants) as well as photographs, protestors' accounts, and news media coverage.[23] Collectively, this rhetoric provides a picture of La Gran Marcha and the broader immigrant mobilizations as hybrid performances of citizenship. My argument builds on the work of other scholars who have identified similar strategies in the 2006 pro-immigrant demonstrations. For example, in his discussion of *Nuestro Himno*, the Spanish-language version of the U.S. national anthem produced in May 2006 during the height of the protests, Córdova recognizes some of the hybrid elements of the 2006 protests, though he ultimately argues that this was a "self-defeating" rhetorical strategy. Likewise, in their provocative analysis of the flag waving of the 2006 protests, Richard Pineda and Stacey Sowards identify a liminality and "tension" evident in the protestors' rhetoric.[24] Extending this analysis, I contend that the Latina/o and immigrant vernaculars in the protests of 2006 are hybrid in at least two senses. First, they constructed a hybrid rhetoric that fused multiple citizenship traditions and varied forms of discourse into a new, more expansive vision of the U.S. civic imaginary. In other words, as the use of foreign flags, languages, and political traditions demonstrated, contemporary mobilizations not only enacted U.S. citizenship and belonging but did so in and through racial, cultural, and national difference. Second, these movements went beyond demands for U.S. citizenship or expressions of identity politics by transcending conventions of single-nation-state belonging and embracing transnational solidarity. The hybrid performance(s) of citizenship during the 2006 demonstrations had a complex reception, demonstrating both the possibilities and limitations of this hybrid performativity.

La Gran Marcha and the Immigrant Marches of 2006

On March 25, 2006, a massive group of immigrants and Latina/os marched through the streets of downtown Los Angeles. Starting at the corner of Olympic and Broadway, the protest moved over a mile through the city on its way to LA's city hall. Dubbed "La Gran Marcha" by protest organizers, the march of March 25, even at conservative estimates, involved over half a million people in one of the largest demonstrations of recent history.[25] More important for my purposes here, La Gran Marcha was one of the earliest protests of 2006, and it spurred a wave of marches across the country over the next two months. In the conventional opinions expressed by news media and political pundits, the protest was either an "alien" discourse or an "American" call for inclusion.[26] According to the former view, immigrants who took to the streets justified their exclusion from U.S. citizenship by embodying their foreignness, criminality, and threat to the nation.[27] In the latter view, La Gran Marcha and the other immigrant marches of 2006 represented conventional discourses in which immigrants presented themselves as assimilated, "good" members of the nation deserving full "inclusion."[28] These contrasting estimations of La Gran Marcha begin to intimate how the immigrant protests of 2006 channeled the ambivalence of hybridity into a productive though inherently problematic challenge to bordering logics.

As I discussed above, La Gran Marcha and the immigrant movements of 2006 were mobilized—in the most immediate sense—in opposition to HR 4437 and the anti-immigrant, anti-Latina/o discourses surrounding this initiative in the popular media. As a result of these exigencies, a diverse group of organizations and groups were mobilized, including activists and community leaders, documented and undocumented immigrants, and second- and third-generation Latina/os. A series of summits were held throughout the country organized by grassroots groups and aimed at responding to the Minutemen and to anti-immigrant legislation. These organizations ranged from Latina/o and immigrant activist groups, like the Hermandad Mexicana Nacional and the National Alliance for Human Rights, to larger labor groups, like the Service Employees International Union (SEIU) and the United Farm Workers (UFW). As Matt Barreto et al. argue, "There was a history of consciousness and viable mobilizing structures that proved instrumental in facilitating the logistics and in forming the necessary frames" of the protests.[29]

After organizing the basic elements of La Gran Marcha, activists reached out to Latina/o media and Catholic churches to promote the march and spur discussion about HR 4437. Radio DJs in particular played a key role in mobilizing popular support and participation. A half dozen or so protests in February and early March (organized by many of the same groups and activists) provided impetus for La Gran Marcha and the latter wave of nationwide protests. Though the demonstrations would swell in early April and then again on May 1 (May Day), La Gran Marcha exceeded all expectations of protest organizers and remains one of the largest demonstrations of the last thirty years (only surpassed by the later LA May Day March). As Alfonso Gonzales argues, anti-immigrant forces saw the march as "proof of [immigrants' and Latina/os'] unwillingness to assimilate," while "migrants and their allies" saw it as "a national wakeup call to action." La Gran Marcha became a galvanizing event that helped spark a nationwide protest movement.[30]

By coming out in public and staging a multidiscursive performance of U.S. citizenship, the protestors enacted U.S. citizenship and civic identity. Yet by flouting their violations of citizenship laws (their violations of the border), celebrating transnational political and cultural traditions, and embodying racial difference, the protestors problematized citizenship, creating a hybrid "discursive space."[31] In other words, the protest was simultaneously an act of position (that is, citizenship) and an act of opposition to dominant logics of immigration, belonging, and Latina/o and immigrant identity. Even more significant, La Gran Marcha did not just oscillate between these extremes, but rather the protestors' verbal, visual, and embodied argument integrated these extremes and created something new. Instead of viewing the protests of 2006 as wholly "alien," as conceived of by anti-immigrant forces, or as purely "American," as an attempt for inclusion, I see La Gran Marcha and other such mobilizations as hybrid performances of citizenship that fused the alien and the American to (re)border the civic imaginary.

The Vernacular Rhetoric of La Gran Marcha

That La Gran Marcha was a performance of citizenship is evident in much of its verbal rhetoric, including its signs and chants, which featured a variety of messages that served to perform citizenship for immigrant marchers. For example, "Amnistía [Amnesty]! Full rights for all immigrants," read one of the prominent signs carried by protestors.[32] Other common signs included: "The USA is MADE by IMMIGRANTS . . . and that's it," "Ya basta de abusar a los migrantes" (Enough with abusing immigrants), and "We are not the enemy—we are part of the solution." These rhetorical slogans pronounced inclusion into the national body. Immigrant protestors appropriated a common cultural myth, that the United States is a "nation of immigrants," into a new context. These protestors proclaimed their place firmly within the American civic imaginary. In a sense, these signs constructed an enthymeme that drew on the historical narratives surrounding immigration: these immigrants were contributing to the "nation of immigrants," and thus they too were part of the tired, poor, and huddled masses yearning to breathe free.

Yet the appropriation of common myths of immigration, such as the notion that the United States is a "nation of immigrants," was only part of the verbal rhetoric of La Gran Marcha. In their chants and signs, protestors not only enacted belonging but also used political slogans and chants from Latina/o and Latin American history, reframing these diverse ethnic and national traditions into a performance of U.S. citizenship. With chants such as "Sí, se puede" (Yes, it can be done), "Palante" (Onward, Forward), "El pueblo unido jamás será vencido" (A united people will never be conquered), and "La *Tierra* Es De Quien *La Trabaja* [The *land* belongs to those who *work it*], No HR 4437," protestors in La Gran Marcha forged links with Latina/o and Latin American protest movements. They translated these discourses simultaneously into demands for citizenship and into challenges to the exclusionary dimensions of U.S. civic identity.

For example, a chant like "Sí, se puede," which was prevalent throughout the immigrant mobilizations of 2006, evidences the hybrid nature of the protestors' verbal rhetoric. In one sense, it could be read as "Yes, it [full recognition/belonging] can be done." Yet considering the origin and legacy of this simple chant problematizes this interpretation. "Sí, se puede," was created by Dolores Huerta and deployed in the context of boycotts and strikes by Huerta, César Chavez, and the UFW for wages and other economic rights.[33] The chant was not merely a call for rights and recognition, but an enactment of solidarity and identity for the marginalized. Similarly, "Palante" (from "Para alante"), a rallying cry of the Puerto Rican Young Lords, also presumes the radical rhetoric of Latina/o social movements. The Young Lords, a self-professed radical socialist organization, used confrontational tactics throughout the 1960s and 1970s to oppose racism and segregation.[34] The Farm Workers and the Young Lords represent not movements for assimilation but confrontational social movements struggling to contest dominant traditions of U.S. identity and that identity's implicit racial and class dimensions. While each group struggled under different circumstances, both critiqued traditions of U.S. citizenship; neither wholeheartedly embraced a conventional belief in inclusion. Furthermore, appropriation of slogans such as "Sí, se puede" and "Palante" served an ego function for the protestors in La Gran Marcha by constructing a narrative history that situated the protest in a long line of (Latina/o) struggles for social inclusion. As Michael McGee notes, constructing a "people" demands producing a "vision of the collective life." This collective life involves both a picture of the past and a plan for the future. Therefore, by drawing on the rhetorical legacies of past protest movements, protestors worked to construct a mythic basis as a movement. Through these diverse discourses, La Gran Marcha fused a Latina/o-immigrant people.[35]

To a large degree, the explicit connections made in the protestors' verbal rhetoric between contemporary and historical Latina/o struggles with citizenship are natural characteristics of social protest movements, which aim to establish a degree of continuity and connection to the past even as they radically challenge the present. Yet protestors in La Gran Marcha, as well as those in other demonstrations of 2006, also struck transnational links between their demands for citizenship and the struggles of Latin Americans across the hemisphere. Reaching across national borders, their verbal rhetoric fused multiple nationalities, political traditions, and identities into, paradoxically, a demand for U.S. national belonging.

For example, protestors in La Gran Marcha used a number of variations on the well-known Spanish chant "El pueblo unido jamás será vencido." Some of the adaptations substituted "Latinos," "Familias," and "Migrantes" for "El pueblo." This chant, though connected to a variety of South American radical resistance groups, was popularized by Chilean musical groups who used the slogan as a rallying song against Augusto Pinochet's authoritarian government.[36] Drawing on this chant as a rhetorical resource, protestors again spoke to multiple audiences. First, the chant constituted protestors outwardly as a united "people" with agency in the American public sphere. Second, it framed a more targeted message directed at Latina/os and immigrants, one that portrayed U.S. immigration and citizenship policy as an authoritarian system and immigrants and Latina/os as defenders of freedom and justice. Third, the deployment of terms such as Latinos, familias, and migrantes for "the people" created an equivalence between these groups and constituted solidarity between the diverse constituents of La Gran Marcha (a point to which I return below). Through the simple appropriation and variation of this slogan, protestors multiply rewrote the narrative of immigration, situating immigrants as political actors, as a community of families, as a united ethnic people, and as insurgents defending freedom and justice against an authoritarian regime. The use of this popular Spanish-language chant constructed both a public enthymeme and an analogy for protestors to understand their struggles and their adversary.

Perhaps the clearest example of this hybrid citizenship discourse in the protestor's verbal rhetoric is evident in the common slogan "La *Tierra* Es De Quien La *Trabaja*. No H.R. 4437," which appeared on a number of signs and banners throughout the demonstrations. In one sense, the explicit reference to congressional immigration legislation frames this statement as a repudiation of the Sensenbrenner bill. Yet in a second sense, protestors translated an alien political slogan into a radical type of standing for their claims to inclusion. The first sentence of this slogan is drawn from the rhetoric of Emiliano Zapata and continues to be a popular saying of the Zapatistas' struggle for land rights, indigenous sovereignty, and cultural recognition in southern Mexico. For some, Zapata remains a legendary political figure who fought against an authoritarian regime for the rights and liberties of ordinary mestizo and indigenous Mexicans.[37] Zapata's notion that Mexicans should be guaranteed their "land and liberty" was used by protestors as a rhetorical analogy to the struggles of immigrants for practical recognition by the United States. Protestors argued that their physical and economic presence in the country served as a type of (literal and rhetorical) grounds that should grant them citizenship. Taken in another sense, by drawing on the Zapatistas' equation of land and liberty, the protestors did not necessarily simply demand a place within the United States—they also challenged the very ownership of that land. They were "calling for a citizenship . . . based on *presence* and *residency*, as opposed to formal and explicit admission."[38] For some in the Latina/o immigrant audience, including many protestors themselves, this slogan implicitly severed the link between nationalism, citizenship, and territorial sovereignty by highlighting the United States' violent theft of the Chicana/o homeland (as well as U.S. imperialism in Puerto Rico, Cuba, and Central America). While nativist groups literally and figuratively policed the national border to supposedly protect the land from terrorism and contamination, Latina/o and immigrant protestors were squatting on that land and signaling that they had long been there.

The fusion of these diverse meanings and traditions implicit in just a few of the prominent slogans used in La Gran Marcha and throughout the immigrant protests of 2006 attests to the unconventional citizenship enacted therein. At once protestors proclaimed themselves citizens, constituted themselves as a movement, and critiqued structures of exclusion endemic to U.S. identity. "The USA is MADE by IMMIGRANTS . . . and that's it," became a hybrid proclamation both drawing upon and subverting the myth of a nation of immigrants. Of course, this hybrid verbal rhetoric is nowhere more evident than in the bilingual nature of the protest. By speaking Spanish in their enactments of U.S. belonging, protestors presented a challenge to the conventional expectations of immigrants in the United States that they speak English in the public sphere. The textured nature of these language strategies and appeals represents the hybrid function of the event (as civic performance, political demand, cultural solidarity, and radical critique) and its multiple audiences (the American public, Latina/os and immigrants, and the protestors themselves). In spite of or perhaps because Anglos may not have understood the Spanish chants or slogans, the deployment of these discourses explicitly marked the protest as a "troublesome both/and." For Latina/o immigrants, the verbal rhetoric and the use of Spanish constituted rhetorical and political agency even when situated outside the formal legal channels of recognition.

Turning to the use of visual rhetoric, in La Gran Marcha, as in the nationwide mobilizations, protestors used flag waving to construct a similar hybrid enactment of national belonging. We know that flags are symbols of national identity and can form part of a discursive enactment of public values and culture. Civic participation is often communicated through flag waving and flying flags outside one's home. In these cases, public use of the flag becomes a "figural enactment of national identity."[39] In contemporary immigrant protests, the flag likewise becomes a discourse of civic identification. In tandem with the performance of U.S. citizenship evident in their signs and chants, the waving of American flags by protestors functioned as a rhetorical enactment of U.S. citizenship. In fact, the use of American flags in the protests was an intentional choice meant to foreground the protestors' self-identification as members of the American national community.

Yet the rhetorical use of flag waving also demonstrates the discursive appropriation of multiple citizenship traditions that took shape. Though civic participation is often communicated through flag waving, flags are also used in moments of discursive resistance to dominant society (for example, flag burning). Certainly protestors waved American flags in performance of U.S. civic identity, but they also prominently displayed Mexican, Guatemalan, or Salvadoran flags, pronouncing their dual national identities and their unique transnational agency. Many spectators wondered how under conventional understandings of citizenship a group could demand protection as a member of the U.S. national community but also profess allegiance to another flag.[40] Even some Latina/o organizers lamented the inclusion of foreign flags because it contributed to stereotypes of immigrants as "Mexicans" or "foreigners" rather than Americans; "If we want to live here," said radio DJ Eddie "Piolin" Sotelo, "we want to demonstrate that we love this country and we love the American flag."[41]

Others saw the flying of these foreign flags merely as a cultural expression, akin to the display of shamrocks on St. Patrick's Day. Viewed in tandem with the protestors' verbal rhetoric, however, the use of multiple national flags was more than an appeal to cultural tradition. Instead, by appropriating multiple national symbols and transnational traditions, the protest challenged the implicit border logic that demarcates citizen from alien and demands single-nation-state identification as part of the compact of citizenship. In their visual rhetoric of flag waving, protestors both evoked and erased the nation's "totalizing boundaries."[42] Protestors proclaimed their national belonging because they were flying the Stars and Stripes, yet by flying both the U.S. flag and Mexican and other Latin American flags, protestors in La Gran Marcha enacted belonging in multiple national communities. As with their use of the Spanish language and foreign political traditions, by flying foreign flags in the American public square, protestors appropriated dominant stereotypes concerning unassimilable "aliens" in the service of challenging border logics. They created a civic imaginary that could hold in tension allegiance both to the United States and to other nations.

The verbal and visual rhetoric of the protestors I have discussed above—communicated through signs, chants, and flags—operated in tandem with the protests' embodied elements. By taking up public space and coming together as a collective body politic, protestors also fused a hybrid performance of citizenship. In the most basic sense, immigrants became visible and marked as bodies out in the open, an unusual circumstance for a group of people whose main goal is to blend indistinguishably into society. The immigrant is conceived in popular society as an ambiguous and sometimes threatening "other" who is "fundamentally outside the national body."[43] As such, undocumented immigrants, by virtue of their legal and social status, are absent from the public sphere. Yet in the case of La Gran Marcha, for example, by marching a little over a mile through downtown Los Angeles, immigrant protestors physically and visibly took up space in the public square and embodied their role as members of the national community. Since "the capacity to make oneself visible," argues Anne Norton, "is a prerogative, and hence a sign, of power," through their physical presence, the protestors performed public belonging.[44] Like earlier protest movements, immigrant demonstrators in La Gran Marcha performed their civic belonging through a "coming out" in public.[45] Their embodied rhetoric worked in tandem with their verbal and visual performances of U.S. citizenship; for example, many of the protestors intentionally wore a quintessentially American outfit consisting of blue jeans and a white T-shirt.[46] In one sense, by making themselves visible as "Americans," immigrant protestors constructed a performance of belonging.

However, La Gran Marcha was not merely a performance of Americanness. Protestors also embodied conventional racial stereotypes of immigrants as abject and threatening, using them in the service of challenging alienization. As DeChaine writes, attempts to solidify the border often "find a scapegoat" in minorities because of "the threats their racial, financial, linguistic, and cultural border-blurrings pose." Therefore, the nonwhite bodies of some Latina/o and immigrant protestors challenged these conventional racial presumptions of citizenship, performing national belonging in and through racial difference.[47] Racially and ethnically marked bodies took to the streets in numbers, shouting and waving signs in foreign languages, marching to foreign music. Latina/o immigrants in particular drove through the streets blaring Tejano or salsa music and honking their car horns. In LA, protestors congregated on green space as they marched through the streets to converse in Spanish, some even shouting, "México, México!"[48] Their embodied performances were infused with what José Esteban Muñoz calls "affective excess." In contrast to the "white middle-class subjectivity" that structures U.S. citizenship and its "national affect," protestors in La Gran Marcha appropriated the Latina/o/immigrant affect of a troublesome and hybrid figure. In a second sense, then, beyond merely coming out of the shadows to demand inclusion, the protestors' rowdy and racialized "coming out" flouted the racial components of U.S. citizenship and demanded recognition of the specifically Latina/o-immigrant citizen. Immigrants enacted citizenship in and through their racially and ethnically marked bodies rather than trying to erase those differences exclusively through performances of assimilation.[49]

Furthermore, as I discussed in the introduction, in popular discourses of immigration and Latina/o identity in the United States, Latina/os are often presumed to be Mexican and illegal immigrants: racial and ethnic markers become stand-ins for legal and political status. In response to this conflation of race and nation, La Gran Marcha and other immigrant demonstrations of 2006 featured the physical co-presence of citizens, residents, documented immigrants, and undocumented immigrants. Together these groups were fused into a hybrid "body of protestors" chanting and marching together. The diversity of protestors was easy to overlook, since in both their explicit and implicit messages the protestors were marching for the rights and recognition of undocumented immigrants. Though surveys indicate that, overall, second- and even third-generation Latina/os were just as likely to participate as immigrants in the nationwide marches of 2006, it is impossible to tell how many of the protestors even in La Gran Marcha, for example, were citizens and how many were undocumented.[50] More to the point, the voices of citizens and documented immigrants became intertwined with the struggles of undocumented immigrants for rights and recognition. Physically speaking, citizens and noncitizens stood next to one another, together enacting their hybrid citizenship. By protesting with undocumented immigrants, Latina/o citizens and documented immigrants put themselves at risk of societal stigma through association with "Mexican illegality" and also at material risk of physical violence or legal prosecution. Yet in the case of La Gran Marcha, the trope of Mexican illegality was appropriated as a "strategic" and subversive "performative logic," challenging the preeminence of that stereotype and undermining the racialized logics of citizenship that have long structured the lives of immigrants.[51]

Finally, the embodied rhetoric of protestors appropriated the "fear of small numbers" that minority populations, and immigrants in particular, pose to the nation-state. As I discussed in chapter 1, this anxiety surrounds the supposed threat that small numbers of minorities pose to the national imaginary. Thus in their physical presence on streets, sidewalks, and public parks, immigrant protestors in La Gran Marcha embodied the sense of uncertainty brought on by racial, ethnic, and cultural minorities, the same anxiety that propels bordering rhetoric. When protestors performed U.S. citizenship through Spanish-language chants, waving diverse national flags, appealing to foreign political traditions, and often physically flaunting national immigration laws, they "disperse[d] the homogeneous" traditions of U.S. national identity that impose these types of difference as conditions for exclusion.[52] Protestors demanded an acknowledgment of their *il*legal U.S. citizenship. They took over public space and symbols of American identity, as all the while they celebrated other traditions and cultures. The impact of La Gran Marcha in particular on the fear of minority numbers was evident in the contest over the size of the protest, for while LA police claimed that "500,000 plus" marched, organizers and activists countered that there were "2 million people" present.[53] Thus there was rhetorical power in both amplifying and minimizing the size of La Gran Marcha because it communicated that the "sleeping giant" was larger/smaller than expected. As part of a vernacular discourse of borders and belonging, the protestors' takeover of public space flaunted the fear of numbers that often propels exclusion or assimilation of migrants.

In its embodied rhetoric, as in its verbal and visual elements, La Gran Marcha, and the nationwide wave of social protest it helped to ignite, turned the process of alienization endemic to nationalism on its head to challenge the boundaries between "us" and "them." Protestors physically enacted inclusion into the U.S. civic imaginary, yet by appropriating stereotypes of immigrants as an ever-growing threat to the nation, protestors magnified the differences that would normally exclude them from belonging in the service of performing citizenship. La Gran Marcha, as representative of these mobilizations, featured a hybrid position for immigrants as simultaneously both citizens and others. What was the embodied "social (dis)ease of the U.S. border problem" became a body of hybrid citizens denaturalizing the borders of the nation.[54] In essence, by embodying and appropriating dominant logics of immigration in a hybrid performance of citizenship, protestors—Latina/o, immigrant, and otherwise—demonstrated the impossibility of discerning citizens from aliens, exposing the rhetorically constructed roots of U.S. citizenship. In the next section I will broaden this argument beyond La Gran Marcha and to the national protests of

2006, and I will unpack the strategy of hybridity as a Latina/o vernacular rhetoric, including its relationship to those of the previous chapters.

Hybrid Citizenship in the Immigrant Marches of 2006

Though the preceding analysis has focused primarily on La Gran Marcha of March 25, 2006, this protest was so large and central to the broader immigrant rights demonstrations of the entire year that it represents a key point of analysis in the broader Latina/o and immigrant vernacular discourses. For example, La Gran Marcha's immediate impact can be read in the wave of social protest throughout the country that it helped to galvanize. The march of March 25 directly spurred student walkouts as well as a wave of social protest across the country held on April 10–11, 2006.[55] These protests took place in cities from Atlanta to Seattle and not only "captured the nation's attention" but also "were remarkable . . . for their scale [and] also their reach," according to Ted Wang and Robert Winn. The mobilizations continued into the early summer, with an even larger wave of nationwide demonstrations and organized boycotts on May Day, representing to many the "high-water mark" of the summer demonstrations. The May Day march in Los Angeles was the largest of the year's demonstrations and shared many similarities with La Gran Marcha. These examples demonstrate that La Gran Marcha and other early protests acted as a proving ground for the organizational constituents and strategies of the year's immigrant rights movement, strategies that were translated into other locales through collaboration and emulation.[56]

In this analysis, I argued that La Gran Marcha represented a hybrid discourse of U.S. American citizenship in which migrants fused competing traditions of citizenship in the construction of a broader national identity. In a sense, the popular understandings of La Gran Marcha reflect this view. Though some interpreted the protests through conventional bordering logics, viewing them as "alien" discourses, others saw a celebration of the United States as a nation of immigrants. In effect, both of these interpretations are justified based on the analysis I offered above. In fact, they were fused together in the immigrant protests of 2006, which were both demands for inclusion and claims for separation. More precisely, and different from the Alianza's activism, protests like La Gran Marcha constructed a hybrid citizenship that fused the alien and the American to (re)border the civic imaginary and challenge conventional demarcations between citizen and alien. The Alianza migrated between reasonable public rhetoric and radical public address but was unable to transcend or integrate this binary into a new mode of belonging. In contrast, La Gran Marcha exhibited a hybrid rhetoric that created a unique rhetorical space. Precisely because of the tendency to marginalize or exclude Latina/o immigrants because of their supposed racial, cultural, and national hybridity, La Gran Marcha can be understood as appropriating this dominant discourse into a vernacular performance of citizenship.

Responding to the bordering logics circulating at the time, La Gran Marcha and the broader wave of immigrant protests of 2006 acted as a rebordering of their own. Protestors performed citizenship, though they did so through a discourse of hybridity, blurring and expanding the U.S. civic imaginary rather than accepting its already defined logics and demarcations. Immigrant protestors appropriated conventional discourses of national identity in the service of constructing a more expansive U.S. citizenship, one that expressed multiple forms of belonging, that held in tension various political and cultural traditions, and that eschewed the binary between assimilation and exclusion. In particular, we should consider La Gran Marcha and the larger wave of social protest it engendered hybrid vernacular rhetorics because they expressed hybridity in both rhetorical form and content.

First, the metaphor of hybridity describes the multiform nature of this vernacular discourse of citizenship and immigrant rights. Through their radical democratic performance, protestors challenged the conventional model of the disembodied "good citizen," who conventionally expresses "himself" as an informed, rational, and eloquent speaker. This "ideal" model of democratic discourse works hand in hand with discourses of alienization to regularly exclude and silence immigrants and minorities based on their legal, racial, gender, and cultural differences. As D. Robert DeChaine writes, the public sphere "proscribes conditions for citizenship enactment and the voices that are to be included in and excluded from deliberation."[57] While Californio rhetoric represented an attempt at border discourse and the Alianza migrated between reasonable public rhetoric (or civic rights) and radical public address (or ethnic separatism), La Gran Marcha and the broader immigrant protests exhibited a hybrid rhetorical form in which visual, verbal, aural, and material modes of discourse "intersect[ed] organically to create something challenging" to conventions of the civic imaginary as well as "norms of textual boundedness."[58] In opposition to conventional understandings of the "eloquent citizen," protestors in La Gran Marcha enacted citizenship in a rowdy confluence of signs, symbols, public speech, performance, and corporeal rhetoric. As evidence of its hybrid form, it is difficult to identify a discrete text even in La Gran Marcha (such as a speech), let alone the broader movement, because the various discourses fused into an organic whole. Protestors' enactments of U.S. citizenship—their attempts to create space and have a voice—radically contested these exclusionary logics.

More important, immigrant protestors, particularly as we saw in La Gran Marcha, constructed a hybrid vernacular rhetoric in their rhetorical content. Their performance of citizenship transcended conventional logics, though admittedly only partially and imperfectly. The citizenship staged in La Gran Marcha was literally "transnational" for it enacted civic identity through a host of foreign cultural/political traditions and it demanded national belonging without exclusive national identification or assimilation. In La Gran Marcha, Latina/o and immigrant protestors asserted national allegiance without adhering to conventions of single-nation-state identification or cultural assimilation. They embodied the possibility of belonging without legal recognition or formal dimensions of citizenship.

Culture and citizenship are often seen as independent spheres. Citizenship is understood as a universal identity without cultural markers, while expressions of unique cultural identity are deemed "differences" outside of citizenship.[59] Contractual conventions of citizenship presume exclusive allegiance to a nation-state in exchange for social and political rights. Despite these logics, Latina/o and immigrant protestors celebrated cultural difference, multiple national identities, and pragmatic linkages with other political and social movements, all the while explicitly demanding recognition as U.S. citizens. By enacting legal, political, and social belonging, protestors in La Gran Marcha demanded citizenship under conventional contractual terms: they performed their national belonging and demanded the rights that flowed from citizenship. But by warranting such proclamations through their cultural difference, Latina/o and immigrant protestors also challenged these conventional dimensions of citizenship with a hybrid enactment of national belonging. The 2006 protests demonstrate that Latina/os and immigrants articulated their citizenship as, in Bhabha's words, "a right to difference-in-equality." That is, they enacted national belonging without eschewing the markers of difference that made them "other" to begin with—a citizenship that affirmed difference rather than sameness. Put differently, the protestors de-linked the rights and recognition included in the conventional contract of citizenship from the other end of the bargain—their promise to assimilate into U.S. society. Walter Mignolo describes "de-linking" as a process of "chang[ing] the terms and not just the content of the conversation." In other words, de-linking is "the reverse of 'assimilation,'" which presupposes "that you do not belong yet to what you are assimilating," because de-linking means a disentangling from the presumption of the exclusivity of belonging. In this case, the protestors in La Gran Marcha and other demonstrations of 2006 were de-linking from the modern/colonial "imaginary" of citizenship, articulating a hybrid mode of belonging that integrated and transcended the national contract. In the face of a choice between assimilation and exclusion, these protestors chose neither, and instead enacted hybrid citizenship, which involved inclusion coupled with acknowledgment of their national and cultural differences.[60]

This hybrid citizenship performance enacted a subversion of (or de-linking from) bordering logics of U.S. citizenship. Concretely, Latina/o immigrants announced they were U.S. Americans even though they violated the formal and implicit laws (borders) of illegal entry and residence that structure U.S. citizenship. They enacted their national belonging without adhering to demands for racial, cultural, and political assimilation. In the words of one protest organizer, "Together we march to victory! Today we march for amnesty, tomorrow for citizenship, and after that, to gain the right to govern civilly along with the rest of the honest workers of this country, so that there can be justice in this country and in all the world!"[61] Justice and citizenship could not be achieved by integrating seamlessly into the melting pot. Unlike the Californios, the compromise these protestors struck was not made through integration into American citizenship. The onus of compromise rested with U.S. culture and institutions. Rather than move between the tension of inclusion or exclusion that structures U.S. citizenship, protestors demanded that they be included in spite of their differences. The citizenship protestors in La Gran Marcha enacted was hybrid in form as well as content, for it affirmed multiple national identities and cultural traditions—it created a new and more expansive civic imaginary.

Unlike the Alianza, La Gran Marcha appropriated but also challenged and subverted a strictly ethno-national and modernist imaginary. They deployed but also seemed to undermine the link between nation, people, and territory. Even more, they enacted a broader and transnational civic imaginary. Protestors paradoxically staged a citizenship that subverted the very logics of national belonging. Their demands for citizenship extended beyond inclusion and equal rights. Instead, protestors in La Gran Marcha fused a hybrid citizenship where dual national identity and transnational political mobilization were possible. This "both-and" citizenship represented a challenge to conventional meanings of citizenship expressed through "nationality and patriotism, love of country, loyalties, and allegiance to a single state."[62] The hybrid citizenship Latina/o and immigrant protestors enacted subverted bordering logics by flaunting border violations and denaturalizing the borders of citizenship and nation. Reminding us that the land belongs to those who work it and, as a corollary, that "we didn't cross the border, the border crossed us," immigrant protestors challenged the borders of belonging as well as the U.S.-Mexico border. Instead, the hybrid performance imagined the possibility of a citizenship that affirmed dual national identity, legal membership without patriotism, multiple national allegiances, and loyalty to country without assimilation. This performance of national belonging through "difference" problematized the conventional dimensions of American citizenship, but this vernacular discourse also entailed constraining dimensions. In another sense, as I consider below, protestors in La Gran Marcha and other similar immigrant rights protests of 2006 merely rebordered the civic imaginary in a more complex and multilayered but also limiting way.

Conclusion

Despite the nationwide scope of the protests and the radical potential I have identified in them to redraw visions of civic identity, most still view the 2006 immigrant demonstrations with, at best, timorous skepticism and, at worst, outright hostility. Ultimately, its critics (and even many supporters) argue that the protests of 2006 are difficult to call a "movement" because they lacked many of the long-term, organized, and sustained coalitional politics of collective movements. After all, despite record-breaking spring protests in cities throughout the country, by the late summer organizers had shifted their focus elsewhere, and efforts to re-create the demonstrations in the fall of 2006 failed to garner participation, support, or media attention. Also, the 2006 protests failed in their ultimate goal of securing progressive congressional immigration reform. Though public scrutiny of Congress resulting from the protests contributed to the defeat of HR 4437, congressional inaction meant the militaristic and securitized framework of status quo immigration and border policy would continue. Despite the failure of HR 4437 as a comprehensive piece of legislation, some of its anti-immigrant measures succeeded as stand-alone laws.

Moreover, the very hybridity of the protests represented, for many, a troubling vacillation in message. The demonstrations were too hybrid, too troubling, too "in between"—according to this view—to be truly successful. A related argument some skeptics have leveled is that the 2006 protests were ultimately too rooted in the politics of difference and in Latina/o politics specifically for the movement to really gain broader public and political support. "Our preliminary conclusion," write political scientists Irene Bloemraad, Kim Voss, and Taeku Lee, "is that the most successful framing of the movement centered on American values of family and work." In fact, they argue that elements of the protest that "hinted at foreignness" not only found "limited traction" but ultimately faced a degree of opposition from the public and mass media.[63] What many perceive to be the very limited success of the 2006 immigrant and Latina/o protests, then, is often laid squarely on the lack of a clear and consistent message of assimilation and inclusion.

Criticisms of La Gran Marcha and the immigrant protests of 2006 are buttressed when considering the backlash the protest fueled both in popular attitudes about immigration and in government policy. In fact, the societal hostility and physical violence faced just a year later by protestors in Los Angeles who tried to re-create La Gran Marcha supports this interpretation that the border-crossing hybridity of immigrants just as easily created renewed pressures for alienization as it problematized bordering logics.[64] Scholars have rigorously documented the hardening of public opinion against immigrants in the wake of the protests as well as the institutional crackdown and the swathe of anti-immigrant initiatives that passed in the protests' wake. According to Louis DeSipio, "[T]he protests spurred more rigid positions on all sides of the debate" and eliminated any chances for truly "comprehensive" immigration reform.[65] Even worse, as I discuss in the next chapter, some argue that the 2006 protests created greater border anxiety and resulted in escalation of the last decade's anti-immigrant policy and border militarization. At the very least, these developments make it possible to read La Gran Marcha and the immigrant demonstrations of 2006 as nothing more than an episodic intervention into a larger process of alienization and exclusion that continues to grow in its aggressiveness. Hybridity theorists remind us that hybrid rhetorics can serve the interests of those who wish to keep citizenship an exclusive category as well as those who wish to expand its bounds.

These conflicting estimations of the immigration protests highlight the give-and-take of vernacular rhetorics of borders and citizenship. Vernacular enactments of citizenship are always momentary and confluent; vernaculars are neither wholly liberatory nor constraining but enact complex relationships of agency and identity. The mixed success and failure of the 2006 protests demonstrates that enacting citizenship is always a process of rebordering the civic imaginary, of drawing new boundaries of belonging. The marches fused participation and protest, acculturation and cultural difference, "belonging" and "alienness." As Córdova observed, "[S]eeking that unity between being and belonging, yet also distinctness, was somewhat utopian in its assumption of being able to disrupt the hermeticism of the national symbolic from a space that could effectively hold all the threads."[66] The protests were enactments of transnational and hybrid citizenship, and in this way they demonstrated a utopian vision of belonging. Therefore, it is not surprising that they were met with backlash and had limited instrumental success. And yet for this very reason, La Gran Marcha and the immigrant protests of 2006 also had the potential to disrupt sedimented understandings of national belonging and logics of citizenship through an embodied enactment of multiple and more affirming possibilities. As a utopian (but also heterotopic) moment of vernacular citizenship enactment, the protests always had more power to unsettle and disrupt conventions of belonging than they did to forward a concrete program for political change. Evaluating the protests' lasting impact is difficult not only because of the diffuse rhetorical ends of the protests themselves but also because of the complexity of evaluating any protest's rhetorical effectivity in concrete terms.

For this reason, the protests of 2006 are most significant for giving rise to form(s) of (Latina/o) vernacular rhetoric and agency. Though in one sense they were momentary convergences of diverse groups in opposition to a common enemy (mainly, anti-immigrant legislation), these protests point to an evolving vernacular discourse of borders and citizenship that integrates and subverts the tensions and exclusions of the U.S. national imaginary. Evidence suggests that the 2006 immigration protests contributed to greater solidarity among Latina/o and immigrant activists/organizations, energized Latina/o voters, and motivated a momentary uptick in naturalization applications.[67] A single protest does not a movement make, nor can it promise to redefine the legacy of anti-immigrant rhetoric. Yet rather than thinking of the 2006 immigration demonstrations as episodic interruptions in the rhetorical and physical policing of U.S. identity, I have argued throughout this chapter that they represent part of the contingent and ongoing process of constituting U.S. national identity and, more important, they represent the crystallization of vernacular rhetoric through which Latina/o and immigrant groups struggle with the borders of U.S. citizenship. Furthermore, La Gran Marcha and the protests of 2006 were anything but episodic, as the boycotts and demonstrations in 2010 following Arizona's SB 1070 demonstrate. In this sense, the protests of 2006 were radically constitutive not only of alternative visions of citizenship outside of the dominant, accepted logics of belonging, they were also radically constitutive of agency for protestors (most of whom were Latina/os and immigrants). It is the problems and possibilities, the enduring significance of this evolving hybrid vernacular discourse, that I explore in the next chapter.

Beyond Borders?

Citizenship and Contemporary Latina/o and Immigrant Social Movements

The paradigm of the border involves us in an ontological question: What kinds of world or worlds are we in?

—*José David Saldívar*

I stood in Copley Square in Boston on Saturday, July 10, 2010, on a stunningly bright summer morning. Lining the cement path that ran along the small, grassy park were a number of small folding tables featuring an assortment of buttons, books, pamphlets, and newspapers from various activist organizations. Meanwhile, a makeshift covered stage was assembled on the bed of a pickup truck parked at the front of the square in the shadows of the stone-faced, nineteenth-century Trinity Church. I could feel an energy crackling in the air as we congregated in the open green space in front of the platform. People bubbled up from subway tunnels and streamed around street corners, while organizers passed out placards and directed protestors to the center of the square.

Most of us were assembling for an organized political protest against anti-immigrant legislation and anti-Latina/o sentiment. The protest was one of dozens of nationwide demonstrations throughout the summer of 2010, spurred on most directly by the anti-immigrant Arizona Senate Bill 1070 (the Support Our Law Enforcement and Safe Neighborhoods Act), signed into law on April 28, 2010, by Arizona's republican governor Jan Brewer. At this gathering, nearly three months after the passage of SB 1070, a coalition of student groups, labor unions, immigrant and Latina/o organizations from throughout New England and New York, and approximately a thousand demonstrators protested as Governor Brewer attended the National Governors' Association (NGA) meeting in Boston. Organizations as diverse as the Service Employees International Union, the ANSWER Coalition (Act Now to Stop War and End Racism), the International Socialist Organization (ISO), and local immigrant rights groups (Proyecto Hondureño and Unidad Latina en Acción) participated in the protest, and demonstrators came from Boston, New York, New Jersey, and throughout New England.

I approached the protest in Boston with a strange mix of the scholar's impassioned interest and the activist's nervous excitement. This was my chance to study the immigrant movement in my own backyard. More important, I could stand in solidarity with protestors and lend my voice and body to the cause. Taking inspiration from what Dwight Conquergood identifies as the "affinities" between rhetoric, performance, and ethnography, I approached the protest as an opportunity to explore vernacular voices, to unsettle truths about Latina/os and immigrants, and to bear witness as protestors brought the margin to the center. As Conquergood writes, letting go of the scholar's (supposed) objectivity and embracing the performative dimensions of ethnographic participation "alters the power relationship of the fieldwork and changes the hierarchy of observer and observed into more of a partnership." The intersection of ethnographic participation with a rhetorical/performative perspective provides the opportunity to "locate counterpublics" in their enactment "and listen for and think about 'voice over domination.'"[1] Thus as the protestors milled around Copley Square in preparation for the demonstration, I struggled to find the appropriate balance between excitement and detachment—to participate in the evolution of the immigrant rights movement, to see Latina/o vernaculars take shape, and to join my voice with others.

Though the protest was organized under a unified theme of opposition to restrictive and racist immigration legislation, the discourses of the protest—verbal, visual, and embodied—touched on a variety of topics including labor rights of the undocumented, neoliberal global economic policy, educational availability for immigrant youth, racism in law enforcement, and partisan criticisms of Republican politics. In spite of the eclecticism of the constituents and organizers, the protest was unified as a form of confrontational rhetoric against Arizona SB 1070.[2] Moreover, the "raucous" protest provided me a personal entry point into the ongoing contestation over borders, citizenship, and immigration, particularly by Latina/o groups.[3] I was no longer merely an academic observer; the demonstration constituted me as part of the movement itself through my sign waving, chanting, and marching, and the nervous surveillance of police and anti-immigrant demonstrators, both of whom hovered around the protest and followed as it moved through downtown, interpellated us as part of a disorderly, unruly, and potentially un-American group that needed to be monitored and contained.

This chapter extends the preceding analysis of immigrant mobilizations and demonstrations of 2006. Through their organizational exigencies and tactics, the nationwide movement for immigrant rights of the last several years demonstrates an evolving Latina/o and immigrant vernacular rhetoric. Like the demonstrations of 2006, including La Gran Marcha, contemporary movements exhibit a hybrid performativity in their discourses of citizenship as well as in the confluence of movement constituents and goals. The July 10, 2010, Boston protest is my point of entry to discuss the larger targeted protests and boycotts of 2010 and contemporary Latina/o-immigrant vernaculars of hybrid citizenship. As I will argue, these movements performatively enacted the possibility of belonging without citizenship, of recognition without eschewing racial, cultural, and national difference, and the impossibility of determining legality from illegality.

While the last chapter outlined some of the contours of contemporary mobilizations, this chapter explores these vernacular rhetorics in more detail, considering their consequences and lessons for our understandings of borders and citizenship. First, the chapter discusses the intervening contexts of contemporary mobilizations, then it narrates the broader movement for Latina/o and immigrant rights, including activism for the federal DREAM Act and the protests and boycotts surrounding Arizona's anti-immigrant SB 1070. Then, a critical ethnographic analysis of the Boston protest—in the context of broader, nationwide activism—illuminates a vernacular rhetoric that exemplified three unique challenges to bordering practices: (1) *hybrid performativity* to contest the affective economies of contemporary anti-immigrant legislation (such as SB 1070); (2) *coalitional politics* through collaboration between diverse organizational constituents and various political goals (labor reform, neocolonial economic policies, neoliberalism, immigration reform, and racial profiling); and (3) performance of vernacular *cosmopolitanism* as a form of belonging. Though my analysis focuses on the protest in Boston, I use it much as I did La Gran Marcha, as an entrée into the broader vernaculars of the 2010 mobilizations.

Border Anxiety and the Ever-Encroaching Border

If the immigrant marches of 2006 can be understood as organizing multiple constituencies in opposition to restrictive immigration legislation, as argued in the last chapter, then the more recent mobilizations—from protests in Arizona to student movements for the DREAM Act—are in many ways extensions or continuations of the immigrant activism of 2006. Just as La Gran Marcha spurred a nationwide wave of social protests by Latina/os and immigrants (protests asserting citizenship and rebuffing restrictive bordering practices), demonstrations and boycotts again spread throughout the country in 2010 involving Latina/os, immigrants, and other stakeholders. Mobilization was once more ignited in the most immediate sense by the passage of restrictive, nativist immigration legislation—Arizona's SB 1070.

This now-infamous legislation was signed by Arizona governor Jan Brewer on April 23, 2010, after heightened scrutiny and national media attention. Capitalizing on several federal programs encouraging state and local border enforcement, the Arizona law created a state crime of illegal immigration with stricter penalties than equivalent federal crimes, and it escalated the surveillance and persecution of suspected immigrants by state and local police. In the broadest sense, SB 1070 made undocumented immigrants doubly illegal and twice prosecuted: not only under federal law and by federal immigration officers but also at the state and local level.

The most controversial elements of SB 1070 concerned the further criminalization of work, hiring, and transporting of undocumented immigrants; police power of surveillance and detention of suspected immigrants; and the power of civil suit to force strict immigration enforcement. In the area of work, hiring, and transportation, for example, SB 1070 criminalized the "unlawful transporting, moving, concealing, harboring, or shielding of unlawful aliens," even by humanitarian organizations or so-called Good Samaritans.[4] SB 1070 also proposed to expand police power to profile suspected immigrants and verify their legal status by mandating that "for any lawful stop, detention or arrest . . . where reasonable suspicion exists that the person is an alien and is unlawfully present in the United States, a reasonable attempt shall be made, when practicable, to determine the immigration status of the person, except if the determination may hinder or obstruct an investigation."[5] Thus SB 1070 not only expanded powers of surveillance and prosecution, but it also targeted "illegal" immigrants in a roundabout way by criminalizing their livelihood.

In the opinion of many legal scholars, such as Kevin R. Johnson, SB 1070 strengthened already unspoken and "crude racial profiles" in immigration enforcement.[6] Its most controversial element, the provision concerning police surveillance, sanctioned state and local police to judge a subject's (il)legality ("immigration status") based on a "reasonable suspicion" drawn from factors such as the person's language, dress, demeanor, or presence in an area "where unlawfully present aliens are known to congregate."[7] These measures, I have argued elsewhere, meant that, under SB 1070, citizenship became a "performative affect defined only by difference," an affect (of difference) read and judged by state and local police on the bodies and in the performances of suspected immigrant "others."[8] In other words, police became critics of behaviors and demeanors, judging who performed citizenship (who seemed like they belonged) and whose performance communicated an affect of "alienness." According to the law, those suspects who gave police a "reasonable suspicion" they did not belong were presumed to be undocumented.

In addition to heightened surveillance of suspected undocumented immigrants,

SB 1070 also created controversy through a "citizen suit" provision. This measure authorized any "legal resident" of Arizona to bring a civil suit against a government agent who failed to enforce immigration laws to their strictest extent (See Senate Bill 1070, §2[G]). SB 1070, therefore, authorized residents themselves to become immigration agents implicated in the surveillance of suspected immigrants and the enforcement of the border. If Arizona residents believed that police or other state officials failed to adequately scrutinize and prosecute suspected immigrants, the legislation provided avenues for citizens to compel enforcement. In effect, citizens were encouraged to do their civic duty by helping to ferret out "illegal immigrants," or at the very least to surveil the government in its acts of surveillance. Because the legislation included measures for citizen enforcement of immigration laws, it implicated all residents in the practice of securing the border, converting border vigilantism into a mode of civic engagement, of doing one's citizenly duty.

The justification for the legislation went something like this. In the persistent absence of federal attention to the "problem" of immigration, state governments such as Arizona were forced to take action to secure their own borders. Governor Brewer emphasized this point during the signing ceremony for the legislation, stating, "We in Arizona have been more than patient waiting for Washington to act. But decades of federal inaction and misguided policy have created a dangerous and unacceptable situation." Brewer's stated desperation in the face of danger represented a broader sentiment of border anxiety. SB 1070 quickly became a rallying point for proponents of nativist immigration policy as well as a lightning rod for pro-immigrant activists. As a result, SB 1070 became one of the first and certainly the most publicized piece of a whole patchwork of state and local anti-immigrant measures to pass in 2010 that aimed to address immigration and border security in the absence of federal involvement. These anti-immigrant measures have since spread throughout the country and now include unprecedented levels of deportations and detentions, provisions preventing the aiding of undocumented immigrants, and efforts to block access to work, housing, or public schools.[9]

SB 1070 itself faced legal challenges by pro-immigrant and civil liberties groups, challenges that ultimately reached the U.S. Supreme Court in June of 2012. In its controversial and much-publicized decision, the Supreme Court ruled that several provisions of SB 1070 were unconstitutional because they usurped the federal government's presumed powers over immigration, naturalization, and border enforcement. Strikingly, however, the Supreme Court did not rule on the most controversial provisions of the Arizona law—those mentioned above regarding police surveillance and citizen suit. The Court reasoned that, since these provisions had not gone into effect (because of a previous court injunction blocking the law during its legal challenge) there was not sufficient evidence to judge whether these provisions would result in abuse and racial profiling, as the law's critics contended. (This decision was reached in spite of the opinions of many legal scholars and law enforcement officials that substantiated fears over profiling.)[10]

In September 2012, these controversial provisions of SB 1070 went into effect, resulting in continued public criticism and opposition. Activists have set up hotlines and educational campaigns for migrants to detect, prevent, and combat what they expect will be heightened levels of racial profiling and police abuse. The opponents of SB 1070 have also vowed to challenge these "show me your papers" provisions in future lawsuits. Perhaps most important, SB 1070 has spurred consideration and even adoption of copycat legislation (in many cases sponsored by the same anti-immigrant, Republican activists who backed SB 1070) in over twenty states. In spite of substantiated criticisms of the legislation and the Supreme Court's recent ruling, similar measures have been successfully passed in Mississippi, Alabama, Georgia, and Utah. Several states may still pass these strict anti-immigrant provisions. Thus what is important to emphasize, given the ever-shifting legal terrain around these laws, is the broader significance of these laws as heralds of a new approach to border enforcement.[11]

SB 1070 is the flagship of a broader patchwork approach to border and immigration policy that has come to be known as "attrition through enforcement." As guiding principle of immigration reform, attrition through enforcement aims to "choke out" undocumented immigrants by denying social services and economic opportunities, and through heightened persecution / prosecution. In other words, pursuing the attrition of immigrant communities has become the preferred means of immigration enforcement, thus making life almost unbearable for undocumented (and even some documented) immigrants. The proponents of attrition through enforcement aim to drive away undocumented immigrants (or what they call "self-deportation") and deter future immigration by creating a system of forced hardship. As I noted above, this approach is evident in many state and local policies; it was even endorsed by Republican presidential candidate Mitt Romney during the 2012 Republican primary. Arguably, this approach is even evident in the Obama administration's crackdown on unauthorized immigrants throughout 2011, in the form of increased deportations (more on this below).[12]

That bordering has taken on this militaristic and aggressive tone exemplified in attrition through enforcement is not surprising considering the persistent logics of citizenship and Latina / o identity discussed throughout this book. That is, when national belonging is wedded to an exclusionary gendered and racialized identity, and as long as some Latina / os can still be positioned as "others" by virtue of their difference(s), material and rhetorical bordering of U.S. citizenship remains the norm. Recent anti-immigrant provisions, of which SB 1070 is just an early example, demonstrate a persistent conflation of Latinidad with Mexican illegality, the representation of Latina / os as threats, and persistent fears of a racialized and gendered citizenship. However, it is also worth emphasizing that a color-blind double bind is evident in the increasingly militant and nativist immigration policies at the state and local level, including SB 1070. In the contemporary neoliberal moment, ideas of individualism, federal deregulation, and global free trade have come to structure immigration and border policy. Monica Varsanyi argues that "neoliberalizing economic policies . . . act as powerful push and pull factors promoting cross-border labor migration," and yet heightened bordering practices, workplace raids, and de-unionization efforts demonstrate that "the neoliberal ideology of the global free market has not . . . extended to the labor market." The push toward state and local immigration policy, the localization of border enforcement, and increasing focus on the individual immigrant as the locus of immigration policy—all elements of contemporary immigration policy—stem from the broader neoliberal ideology of federal deregulation and the focus on individualism.[13] In this vein, the nation formally celebrates its respect for diversity and multiculturalism, its status as a "nation of immigrants," and purports to enforce immigration and border policy in a "color-blind" way, all the while escalating the racialized and gendered policing and denial of full citizenship. The persistent celebration of a color-blind, post-race culture of individual responsibility masks the enduring significance of race, racialization, class, and gender in sociopolitical identity struggles including immigration policy. Thus our culture embraces "*race neutrality* even as it licenses 'limited' racial profiling for purposes of security maintenance, targeted policing," and immigration/border enforcement. Meanwhile, attempts to address racial disparities or achieve diversity, such as affirmative action or bilingual education, are criticized as "monocultural," anti-American, or even as reverse discrimination because they violate the supposedly color-blind and thus multicultural contours of contemporary society (by injecting race into the public sphere).[14]

As evidence of this neoliberal rhetoric, Arizona governor Brewer steadfastly denied traces of racial profiling or discrimination in SB 1070, despite criticisms to the contrary, asserting the law's racial neutrality and respect for diversity. During her signing statement, Brewer repeatedly rejected the assertion of critics that SB 1070 encouraged police profiling of Latina/os as "suspected" immigrants (because of language, race, and culture). Instead, Brewer assured that the law would be administered in a color-blind fashion: "While protecting our citizens is paramount, it cannot come at the expense of the diversity that has made Arizona so great. Nor can safety mean a compromise of freedom for some, while we, the many, turn a blind eye." Brewer's statement explained SB 1070 as an immigration policy fully in concert with the vaunted precepts of (neo)liberalism and cultural diversity. Brewer promised that in spite of provisions about the surveillance and "suspicion" of certain populations, SB 1070 would respect the color-blind ideology of contemporary racial neoliberalism. The law, after all, stated that officials could "not solely consider race, color or national origin" in determining someone's legal status (later, the word "solely" was dropped after sustained public criticism). Also, in response to concerns over racial profiling, Governor Brewer directed the Arizona Peace Officer Standards and Training Board (AZ POST) to clarify the standards for police surveillance and questioning of suspected immigrants. The promulgated guidelines stated that a number of factors taken in the "totality of the circumstances" (including "dress, demeanor . . . [or] significant difficulty communicating in English," "flight," the "attempt to hide or avoid detection," "possession of foreign identification," and presence "in [the] company of other unlawfully present aliens") could provide law enforcement a "reasonable suspicion" that a suspect was undocumented and that further inquiry—from questioning to detention—was justified.[15]

For proponents, the efforts to clarify and hone the law's application provided evidence that SB 1070 was aimed at enforcing immigration laws in a color-blind way. The enforcement standards provided by AZ POST, however, undermined Berewer's claim that the legislation was racially neutral and respected "the diversity that has made Arizona so great." In fact, the details of SB 1070 belie the neoliberal and color-blind ideology that surrounds it. The enforcement provisions by AZ POST link or "stick" together a number of behaviors or performances, such as language use, dress, co-presence with other suspected "illegals," and "flight" or nefarious intent, into an overall affect of alienness or Mexican illegality. The result is that police judge the *performances* of citizenship of those whom they suspect of not belonging. SB 1070 in one sense codified a performative dimension of citizenship by making one's performative affect (a "feeling" of belonging that one communicated) the warrant for a judgment of one's legal status. What Sara McKinnon terms "proper performances of citizenship" became avenues for "credibility" and markers of the suspected immigrants' "potential as a citizen-subject," just as performances of "alienness " or non-belonging (equated by AZ POST with foreignness, Mexicanness, or criminality) became evidence that one was an undocumented immigrant. The assumption that a government official could arrive at a "reasonable suspicion" of the legal status of a person by observing these various performances and behaviors demonstrates that lying at the heart of immigration enforcement were evaluations of racialized and gendered belonging. In the end, the officer would judge the potential of a surveilled subject to "come off" or pass as someone who "belongs." The fact that this same approach was emulated by other states and localities and embraced as color-blind, at least provisionally, by the U.S. Supreme Court, demonstrates its purchase in contemporary discourses of borders and citizenship.[16]

Thus the "affective economies" of SB 1070 undermined the neoliberal notion of respect for diversity that proponents of "attrition through enforcement" tried to attach to these measures. The ideology of racial neoliberalism, which holds that laws can be applied in a color-blind way and that discrimination has been all but eliminated, stands in stark contrast to the very real presence of discrimination and persecution of threatening "others," such as Latin American or Arab immigrants. Despite claims of respect and tolerance for difference within an inclusive American identity, and despite Brewer's claim that the law would be applied neutrally, SB 1070 demonstrates that it is still ethnic, cultural, religious, and linguistic differences of immigrants that are the basis for judgments of their nonbelonging. In fact, the idea of a color-blind or neoliberal SB 1070 (one focused on criminal individuals rather than race or ethnicity) fit in nicely with practices of racial profiling and suspicion (such as those promulgated by AZ POST). The law explicitly prohibited a focus on race while the practices of police and citizens circumvented those prohibitions. An increasingly militarized and nativist approach to immigration and border enforcement was rhetorically framed through a language of multiculturalism and color-blindness that helped it authorize the continued exclusion of those perceived as not belonging.[17]

In this respect, and as one piece in a nationwide retrenchment of immigration policy, SB 1070 represents a broader backlash against the vernacular, hybrid "coming out" of Latina/os and immigrants in 2006. For proponents of restrictive immigration and border policy, the "anti-American," or so they argued, protesters who took to the streets in 2006 constituted "evidence of an enemy in our midst whose force, like that of a virulent disease or inexorable flood, must be contained." The supposed (re) awakening of the Latina/o-immigrant "sleeping giant" in 2006 contributed to heightened anxiety about border integrity and demographic changes that threatened U.S. identity. SB 1070 cracked down on this "enemy" in our midst and aimed to secure the porous border, while similar efforts sought to secure the border and foreclose access to citizenship by immigrant communities. Perhaps the most extreme example of these efforts at attrition, of choking out undocumented immigrants by increasing hardships and removing supposed incentives to migration, was the effort at the state and national level to challenge the birthright citizenship provisions of the Fourteenth Amendment. These attempts were framed by proponents as a way to both punish undocumented immigrants and remove the inducement for future immigration.[18]

Moreover, I argued in the last chapter that performances of citizenship can create provisional belonging for otherwise alienized subjects, yet under SB 1070 the undocumented immigrant was tasked with the burden of always performing a credible affect of U.S. citizenship. Thus attrition through enforcement and its increasing focus on the performative dimensions of citizenship evinced a backlash against the protests of 2006. In essence, SB 1070 and other recent anti-immigrant legislation distinguish between right and wrong performances of citizenship. Police surveillance of suspected immigrants resulted from the performative affects of those suspects and whether or not they conformed to U.S. American "national affect." Not only immigrants but all subjects bore the burden of performing the affect of an American citizen (through dress, demeanor, language, behavior, and even race/ethnicity), or they risked being suspected of being an "undocumented alien" and subjected to police surveillance and possible detention. Rather than (or perhaps in response to) a performative strategy of challenging U.S. citizenship, performance now became a primary marker of a subject's citizenship.

To be sure, performativity has always been an integral component of a citizen-subject's assimilation into the national imaginary, as the previous chapters demonstrate. However, recent anti-immigrant measures are significant because they legalize and codify the surveillance and judgment of these performances of citizenship. In a sense, the undocumented immigrant has become responsible for her own alienization not only because of her "illegal act" of border crossing but also because she fails to adequately give the impression that she belongs. Under constant scrutiny and surveillance, forced to live in the shadows and in fear, and already suspicious because of her racial/ethnic and gender difference, it is likely that law enforcement can always infer "reasonable suspicion" that a suspected immigrant does not quite belong.[19]

These represent some of the political, cultural, and even emotional investments behind recent anti-immigrant legislation and the policy of attrition through enforcement, the most publicized example of which has been Arizona's SB 1070. Importantly, I have emphasized that these anti-immigrant laws can be seen as reactions to the very vernacular rhetorics of hybridity identified in the previous chapter. True to the contentious approach to immigration policy encapsulated in SB 1070, nationwide controversy over the law escalated even before its passage, thanks to round-the-clock cable news coverage. When it was signed into law on April 23, 2010, public debate had already calcified to the degree that the *Arizona Republic* reported on "clashes" taking place outside of the state capitol building.[20] Almost immediately after the bill's passage, activists, church leaders, and Brewer's political opponents mounted public challenges. And after the legislation went into effect in September 2012, activists once again organized demonstrations against it. In this respect, SB 1070 merely escalated an already-growing mobilization against anti-immigrant measures from a variety of immigrant and Latina/o organizations. Efforts against SB 1070, including protests, boycotts, public criticism, and a number of legal challenges, continued long into the summer of 2010. Because of the still-unfolding nature of these mobilizations and protests, I begin an analysis of the movement by briefly narrating the evolution of activism surrounding SB 1070 and other anti-immigrant legislation.

The Immigrant Movement(s) of 2010: Mobilization and Solidarity

On the day that SB 1070 was signed into law, over a thousand people demonstrated in Phoenix outside the state capitol.[21] Just a few days later, under the banner "We Are All Arizona," marches took shape in other cities throughout the Southwest. On April 27 in Dallas, for example, tens of thousands marched (following the same route as the protests of 2006) to show their opposition to Arizona's anti-immigrant law.[22] Students and Latina/os joined with immigrant organizers and labor unions not only to show solidarity with Arizona's immigrant communities, who would be subject to the restrictive legislation, but also to express concern about the prospects of similar legislation being emulated in other states and locales.

As in 2006, nationwide demonstrations occurred in over eighty cities and forty states on May Day, May 1, 2010. Los Angeles, for example, saw around sixty thousand people protest SB 1070—a demonstration second only in size to the 2006 marches.[23] The overarching theme that seemed to arise from these movements was not just political solidarity with Arizonans but, more important, a shared sense of persecution or criminalization of immigrant and Latina/o communities. In other words, the slogan "We Are Arizona" was deployed not only as a point of solidarity against SB 1070 but also, according to activists, as a warning that similar legislation could be on the horizon in other states.[24] Similarly, a little over a month after the law's passage, on May 29, 2010, tens of thousands of protestors engaged in a five-mile march through downtown Phoenix.[25] Though the march was heavily policed, demonstrators came to Arizona from across the nation, and clad in white T-shirts, they waved Mexican and American flags, chanted and sang, and listened to speeches in both Spanish and English from protest organizers and politicians (including the mayor of Phoenix, Phil Gordon).[26] One sign displayed during the protest of late May read, "We Can't Wait, We Won't be Criminalized," thereby directly refuting the presumption of criminality underlying anti-immigrant laws such as SB 1070. Tellingly, the May 29 march in Phoenix was the second-largest demonstration in Arizona history, second only to the protest organized in 2006 against the Sensenbrenner bill.

Protests such as these continued sporadically throughout the spring and summer of 2010, first in response to SB 1070 and then in opposition to copycat bills and anti-immigrant measures across the country.[27] In July, for example, while Utah considered legislation modeled after SB 1070, a group calling itself Concerned Citizens of the United States circulated a list to media and law enforcement sources in Utah accusing thirteen hundred residents of being "illegal" immigrants. The document listed individuals by name (all had Spanish surnames) and included birth dates, addresses, telephone numbers, and in some cases the due dates of pregnant women.[28]

Ultimately, the Latina/o individuals on the list were all proved to be legal residents, yet the list's circulation created significant public controversy and spurred investigations by state officials into privacy violations. The actions of these "concerned citizens" represented the affective investments behind anti-immigrant measures including SB 1070—of Latina/o immigrants (and particularly Latinas) as dangerous and threatening "others" and the trope of "dangerous" Mexicana/Latina fertility.[29] As state and local anti-immigrant measures proliferated, activists explicitly spoke of engaging in a nationwide, state-by-state mobilization for immigrant rights.

As I noted above, the hybrid performativity of the 2006 protests such as La Gran Marcha fueled greater border anxiety and, in many ways, energized the anti-immigrant and nativist movement, among other factors (such as the economic recession of 2007–8) contributing to a string of anti-immigrant measures at the state and local level. For many, the mobilizations of 2006 became evidence of the threat posed by the hidden masses of "illegal aliens" and validated the need to heighten border security and immigration enforcement. However, the 2010 demonstrations that took shape in response to recent bordering practices are significant in and of themselves because they represent a rearticulation of hybrid performativity, a modified vernacular of citizenship that responded to and challenged bordering measures and their underlying logics. Though the success of these contemporary vernaculars of citizenship and American identity may be difficult to evaluate, a point to which I will return in this chapter's conclusion, the performative discourses of hybridity and citizenship of ongoing immigrant rights movements portend significant changes and possibilities for belonging and civic identity in the United States.

In the next section I turn from this broad outline of the immigration activism of 2010 and analyze more closely the vernacular discourses of these nationwide mobilizations by focusing on my experiences during the Boston protest held on July 10, 2010. The NGA meeting that Arizona governor Brewer was attending in Boston served as an impetus for the organization of the demonstration, which drew its inspiration from earlier protests in Arizona, Texas, California, Utah, New York, and dozens of other states. My critical ethnographic analysis of this protest provides an entry into the larger vernacular rhetorics of citizenship and the Latina/o and U.S. identity of the contemporary immigrant movement.

Vernaculars of Citizenship and Borders

I came to the Boston protest at Copley Square on July 10 as both participant and observer. Before the designated start of the demonstration, I circled the square to survey the scene and to talk to the organizations and constituents of the protest. Copley Square, a grassy, tree-lined urban park, sits in one of the busiest parts of Boston, connecting an upscale shopping district with high rises and historic buildings. On the west and south sides, the square is bordered by busy streets and historic buildings—the impressive granite face of the Boston Public Library and the early twentieth-century Copley Plaza Hotel, respectively. On the northern side, Copley Square is lined with trees, monuments, and a fountain. The main part of the square where the protest was to take place is a flat lawn, at the eastern end of which is a pavilion and the nineteenth-century Romanesque and polychromatic stone face of Trinity Church.

Along the cement paths bordering the grassy square sat tables incrementally spaced a few feet from each other, most of which overflowed with buttons, signs, placards, or pamphlets from the representative organizations. The various groups that stood at tables or held signs marking their participation in the demonstration included the Service Employees International Union, the Brazilian Women's Movement, the People's Labor Party, the International Socialist Organization, Proyecto Hondureño (the Honduran Project), the Somerville Community Corporation, Direct Action for Rights and Equality (from Providence, Rhode Island), Unidad Latina en Acción (from New Haven, Connecticut), and several other groups from New York, Massachusetts, and other New England states. At the most crowded table, to the left of the grassy center of Copley Square, stood five members of the ANSWER Coalition wearing neon reflecting vests and handing out signs. I talked with several of these organizers and collected their materials for later analysis before I integrated into the swelling body of protestors. My questions involved the protestors' and organizers' motivations for participating in the protests, the political objectives of their organizations, their attitudes about SB 1070, and their involvement in struggles for immigrant rights.

As the demonstration's start time neared, people streamed into the square steadily, settling onto the lawn in front of the makeshift covered stage, under which a banner hung that read, "Say No to Anti-Immigrant Racism. Full Rights for All!" The crowd varied almost as much as the groups that had organized the protest, from white college-aged people and young couples to Latina/o families with their kids and groups of male laborers. When organizers ascended the stage, just as the sun broke through a patch of clouds, a series of thirteen activists from various organizations spoke to the crowd. Intermittent drizzle punctured the speeches, along with chants and drumming. As I will discuss below, each speaker addressed both the specific concerns of the protest and broader themes relevant to his or her organization. After about thirty minutes of speeches, the first speaker directed us to organize for the half-mile march to the Sheraton Hotel, where the NGA was holding its meeting. Police accompanied the demonstration as it moved. The stage built onto the back of a pickup truck led the march; on it musicians and speakers motivated the crowd with music and chants. At one point, two Latino rappers from New York rapped about SB 1070 and what they claimed was anti-Latina/o racism. Rain began to fall just as we started to march to the Sheraton Hotel, where we congregated and protested for approximately another twenty minutes. As I will discuss below, many protestors criticized or called on Brewer directly, while others had a broader message about immigrant rights.

After the demonstration I collected reports from national and local media outlets and compared their coverage to that given to similar demonstrations throughout the nation. According to media coverage, the Boston demonstration represented one in a wave of nationwide demonstrations. As in 2006, while some saw these demonstrations as delivering a radical message, others read them into a broader narrative of "amnesty" and immigrant rights. The *New York Times*, for example, called the Boston protest "raucous" in its stringent opposition to Brewer and Arizona and in its demand for immigrant rights. Meanwhile, the Associated Press commented on the "militant" tone of the Boston protest and its continual refrain that Brewer was a "bigot" and SB 1070 and other anti-immigrant laws were "racist."[30]

In the most immediate sense, of course, the protest functioned as an oppositional rhetoric against SB 1070 and as a demand for more progressive immigration reform. Because the protest mobilized in response to Governor Brewer's presence in Boston, Brewer and SB 1070 became stand-ins for the anti-immigrant legislation and nativism taking shape across the country. A promotional flyer for the protest produced by the Boston chapter of the ANSWER Coalition stated in English and Spanish, "Say 'No' to Anti-Immigrant Racism! . . . It's time for Brewer and the rest of the state governors to be met with the outrage felt by millions of immigrants and their supporters." One of the speakers from ANSWER built on this theme, praising people of all nationalities and backgrounds for uniting against SB 1070 and "standing up for what is right, fighting for the rights of all workers and undocumented people, fighting for the true freedom that we all deserve." Prominent signs read, "Defeat SB 1070 in the Streets" and "Jan Brewer is a Bigot." Chants included "What do we want? Amnesty! When do we want it? Now!" and "Arizona–Fight back!" Analogies between anti-immigrant legislation and Jim Crow segregation, apartheid, Japanese internment, or Nazism were prevalent in the organizers' speeches. Thus in its resistance to anti-immigrant legislation, the protest served to construct what Michelle Holling has called "oppositional social concord," the attempt to construct a united vernacular voice against a hegemonic order. Though the messages of the activists were diverse (as I will discuss below), their discourse was continually brought back under the same umbrella of opposition to anti-immigrant racism.[31]

In tandem with the protest's message of opposition, the vernacular discourses of the demonstration also featured appeals to citizenship and rights for immigrants. As one popular sign read, "A nation of immigrants is no place for xenophobia." Protestors echoed themes noted in the previous chapter, demanding that the nation embrace its immigrant past and provide rights and protections for the newest generation of immigrants. As we saw in the last chapter regarding earlier protests, the immigration demonstrations of 2010 represented a rhetorical enactment of citizenship. For those in the crowd who lacked formal citizenship, the protest provided an opportunity to assert their place in the nation. Another speaker supported this interpretation by stating that we were all exercising our citizenship in the act of protest. Even those who might be formally excluded from the nation and considered "aliens" were enacting their citizenship through this political act, and those protestors who possessed legal status expressed solidarity with immigrants, who were making a powerful argument for belonging.

In these ways the protest shared many affinities with the 2006 demonstrations. The Boston protest on July 10, and the nationwide movement it represented, folded the very different struggles of Latina/o and non-Latina/o citizens, residents, documented immigrants, and undocumented immigrants, progressives, and student activists (and all the possible permutations of these groups) into a collective demand for national belonging. While I as a Latino citizen marched out of solidarity with immigrants, documented migrants marched to secure avenues to their legal inclusion, undocumented immigrants marched to enact their citizenship, and the protest as a whole was organized to express opposition to the alienizing discourses of SB 1070. Latina/o immigrants' struggles became intertwined with the struggles of various other groups against nativist bordering practices, creating a hybrid, collective enactment of U.S. citizenship.[32]

However, I want to emphasize not only what connected the protests of 2010 with those of 2006 but also what changed about vernaculars of citizenship and Latina/o identity. In the remainder of this section I discuss the unique vernacular rhetorics of the 2010 movement and the ways in which they responded to and challenged the reenergized bordering practices of dominant society. The Boston protest and the larger immigrant movement it represents challenged dominant bordering logics in at least three ways. First, through hybrid performativity (exemplified in the slogan "Do I look illegal?"), the immigrant protest(s) staged the impossibility of judging the affect of the citizen and the performance of (il)legality and reclaimed hybridity as a positive and productive performative identity. Second, the protest(s) demonstrated broader organizational constituencies and coalitional politics (exemplified in the slogan "We Are All Arizona") that expanded the struggle beyond immigration reform to economic policy, labor rights, and neoliberal ideologies of citizenship. Third, through their slogan that "No human being is illegal," contemporary movements performed a cosmopolitan identity that transcended the nation-state and rooted belonging in an ethic of hospitality and shared humanity.

"Do I Look Illegal?" Hybrid Performativity

SB 1070 and attrition through enforcement, a developing regime of anti-immigrant legislation, locate illegality in the performative affect of suspected immigrants. Anyone who looks or acts "illegal" or like they do not quite belong is subject to police questioning, detention, prosecution, and possible deportation. Anyone suspected of being "illegal," again because of their failed performances of belonging (or their performances of alienness), can be denied basic opportunities to work, travel, or seek social services. One significant element of the protests of 2010 was that they challenged these affective economies of SB 1070. They subverted an easy distinction between legal and illegal and problematized the reliance on performative affect to judge someone's belonging. The question by protestors, "Do I look illegal?" enacted the impossibility of determining citizenship based on race, look, or behavior. In this way, the Boston protest and many of the larger demonstrations it emulated aimed to return to a more radically hybrid performativity of citizenship by demonstrating that there was, in fact, no "right" way of performing citizenship, no way to judge someone's belongingness or alienness based on their performative affect.

The hybrid performativity of the protest suffused many of its elements, from the slogans, signs, and chants to the words of protest organizers and the embodied rhetoric of the protestors themselves. Many of its slogans (deployed across a variety of media, from buttons to posters) sought to reappropriate the discourses surrounding SB 1070—of reasonable suspicion, of the performative affect of foreignness as marker of illegal status—to challenge its very logics. "Reasonably Suspicious," "I could be illegal," and "Immigrant" read some of the prominent signs/buttons/placards. These slogans, some worn or carried by those who might be racialized as Latina/o and others as whites, deployed markers of illegality and "suspicious" immigrant status to demonstrate the arbitrariness of these judgments. What did it mean to look illegal or to be reasonably suspicious, they asked? Several speakers who addressed the protest echoed the common refrain that "we are all immigrants!" Though these statements in one sense drew on the mythos of a nation of immigrants to argue that we all came from immigrants, in another sense the claim that "we are all immigrants" also worked alongside slogans such as "Reasonably Suspicious," "Immigrant," and "I could be illegal" to perform the undecidability of reading legal status on people's bodies or performative affects. Similarly, we could see the refrains that "We Are All Arizona" and "Somos Uno" (We are all One) not only as expressions of political solidarity but also as statements of equivalence between those with and without legal status.

Other protests in the spring and summer of 2010 provide similar themes. Though SB 1070 conflated illegality with a certain performative affect of not belonging, the popular slogan of many of these protests—"Do I look illegal?"[33]—highlighted the arbitrariness of determinants of legality/illegality and refuted the presumption that judgments of belonging could or should be based on performative affect. If language use, dress, demeanor, or even presence in an area "where unlawfully present aliens are known to congregate" could provide justification for a "reasonable suspicion" of someone's illegal status (as per SB 1070), then perhaps even those protestors (like myself) who were legal citizens but were "congregating" with undocumented immigrants were also reasonably suspicious. Would marching for immigrant rights and recognition constitute justification for suspicion? Perhaps all Latina/os, because of their language or affects of "foreignness," should be presumed to be "illegal," despite Governor Brewer's assurances to the contrary. Following the affective economy of SB 1070, all of these performances would imply a potentially foreign and suspicious identity. To borrow from Muñoz, the logics of performativity, affect, and citizenship exemplified in SB 1070 illuminated "a phobic majoritarian public sphere that continuously elides or punishes the existence of subjects who do not conform to the phantasm of normative citizenship." Thus the discourses of "I could be illegal," "Do I look illegal?" and "Reasonably Suspicious" represented a process of "disidentification" with and from SB 1070, a working "on, with, and against [this] cultural form" to "transform" affects of citizenship and enact "structural change" in immigration policy.[34] Put simply, these slogans (such as "Do I Look Illegal?") implicitly asked what it meant to *look* legal and/or illegal. By asking whether or not they too looked suspicious, it seemed that these discourses ultimately questioned what it truly meant to look (il)legal. Rather than presuming performances of the national affect (of legality) to be the norm and criminalizing any deviations from it, we all could be immigrants; we all could be "reasonably suspicious." This rhetoric made clear that performances of citizenship were only marked by their relationship to difference and could never be defined in a universal way so as to include all citizens. Presumptions of legality and illegality were arbitrary and politicized judgments, and there was, in fact, no pure affect of the U.S. American. If citizenship was performative, if what police and citizens judge is an individuals' performative affect of (non)belonging, then anyone could perform "reasonable suspicion." Determinations of citizenship and belonging were ultimately demonstrated to be undecidable.

Another example of this hybrid performativity can be found in the intersections of the Boston protest's embodied and verbal rhetoric. On one side, there were the Mexican and Central American immigrants wearing shirts from the Service Employees International Union (SEIU) stating "Brown & Proud." On the other side were the white college students who carried Mexican flags, bells and drums to pound out "ethnic" beats, and some of whom even wore comical sombreros. In the former case, individuals who might be presumed "reasonably suspicious" because of their skin color, but most of whom were legal residents, affirmed their "affective excess" as part of their performances of political subjectivity. In the latter case, cultural stereotypes were appropriated with the effect of extending the status of "reasonable suspicion" to those who were otherwise within the bounds of the political community. In both cases, the rhetoric of racial and cultural identity was potentially problematic, in the former case because of the deployment of racially essentialist elements of "brownness"; in the latter case, strategic reappropriations of Mexican stereotypes also subtly reaffirmed some sort of essential "Mexican" identity. Nonetheless, both performances seemed to aim in the same direction, challenging the logic that one's performative affect—including the feelings drawn from one's language, culture, demeanor, and dress—could be the basis for judgments of one's legal status.

Using the hybrid positionality of migrants and minorities, protests subverted the conflation of citizenship with certain affects and performances. To be "brown and proud" and also enacting one's citizenship illuminated the racialization of anti-immigrant policy and embraced the possibility of performing a hybrid citizenship that held in tension multiple nationalities and racial/cultural difference. Unlike the neoliberal and multicultural logics of a "color-blind" U.S. identity, the protests affirmed the necessity of identity and difference within the parameters of national belonging. If legal citizens, documented immigrants, and those who would normally be considered "good citizens" could perform reasonable suspicion and affects of illegality, then it undermined the very premise that belonging could be restricted based on factors such as race, language, and performative affect. It meant citizenship and illegality could be performed, thus undercutting the naturalization of civic identity.

"We Are All Arizona": Coalitional Politics

Apart from (or in tandem with) its hybrid performativity of citizenship, the constituents and goals of the Boston protest broadened to include connections with struggles against neocolonialism, globalization, and transnational capitalism as well as struggles for legalization. The Boston protest, then, demonstrated the degree to which contemporary immigrant movements engage in what Karma Chávez called "social movement coalition-building." Chávez's analysis of coalitions between immigrant rights and queer rights movements emphasizes the coalition building that takes shape "behind the scenes" in social movement enclaves. This coalitional dimension of the Boston demonstration was evident most directly in the range of organizations serving as co-organizers—from the ANSWER Coalition (involved in the 2006 demonstrations) to the International Socialist Organization and Proyecto Hondureño. However, the coalitional politics of the immigrant rights movement were also enacted in its public discourse. Though, as Chávez demonstrates, coalition building takes shape behind the scenes before the movement reaches out into the public sphere, it is also true that links between struggles are rhetorically reiterated and re-enacted through the public discourses of the movement(s) themselves. To respond to alienation and build solidarity between movement constituents, the protests of 2010 highlighted struggles for wages, labor rights, economic reform, and against colonialism, connecting these to the immigrant struggle for citizenship rights.[35]

In light of contemporary neoliberal immigration policy, immigrant activists in the Boston protests—and the larger demonstrations of 2010—expanded the movement beyond the politics of belonging to re-create linkages between struggles and broaden the immigrant movement. One of the clearest connections struck during the protest was between the immigrant rights struggle and movements against transnational capitalism, globalization, and neoliberal economic policy. The very same promotional flyer from ANSWER mentioned above, which featured Brewer, SB 1070 and other anti-immigrant legislation as exigencies of the protest, also included "the wave of budget cuts and mass unemployment," racial profiling, and border enforcement as mobilizing causes. In a list of demands, the flyer included repeal of Arizona's SB 1070 and Arizona HB 2281 (a bill banning ethnic studies programs in public K-12 schools) as well as a number of other goals relating to budget cuts and unemployment. Furthermore, speakers challenged neoliberal economic policies by connecting anti-immigrant sentiment to a broader regime of labor exploitation. Reconstituting this coalition between immigrant rights and the workers' struggle, one speaker stated that immigrant activists had "ignited a movement on our [that is, Socialists'] side," had "ignited a conversation" about economic exploitation. This statement stressed the importance of a broader movement, a movement against economic exploitation and against borders on laborers. Other speakers similarly connected exploitation of undocumented immigrants to transnational capitalism and the stripping of workers' rights in neoliberal economic policies. A member of the ANSWER Coalition perhaps put it most bluntly: "They steal our country, steal our resources, force us to migrate, then criminalize us."

According to these statements, the immigrant movement(s) could not just aim to secure rights to live and work but had to challenge a whole economic system that made immigration into at best a necessary and exploitable resource. Some speakers commented on the need to address and move beyond anti-Communism and anti-Socialism in the immigrant movement, while a flyer from the People's Labor Party (PLP) stridently demanded coalitions and solidarity between immigrant and labor struggles: "U.S. capitalists need the 12 million undocumented workers in America as a source of low-wage labor to maximize profits. . . . Obama and his ruling-class bosses are not trying to help immigrants at all. . . . They need workers especially black and Latin workers to accept low-wage working conditions. . . . The U.S. bosses are pushing patriotism and the idea that we can all unite under a multicultural banner within the U.S. . . . We say: *Smash all Borders!* Workers have no nation. The real enemy is . . . capitalists of all nations." Not all advocates subsumed the immigrant movement under the banner of anticapitalist struggle. For example, representatives from UNITE HERE (a union primarily of workers in hotel and food service industries) and the SEIU emphasized connections between immigrant rights and labor rights but, unsurprisingly, stopped short of embracing a revolutionary strategy. Rather than paint anti-immigrant laws as symptomatic of capitalism, they framed them as antiunion and antiworker laws that restricted the rights of all people to earn a living and organize for their well-being. The coalitions struck between movements were not of one voice. While some emphasized the immigrant struggle, others framed the immigrant struggle as part of the fight for workers' empowerment, and still others subsumed immigration under a broader worldwide struggle against capitalism. These examples demonstrate how various vernacular discourses of the protest created and reconstituted coalitional politics and different linkages between movements that could broaden the struggle.

Not only the speakers but also the protestors themselves reinforced this message through verbal and visual rhetoric. For example, some of the signs prevalent in the protest read, "¡No Hay un problema de inmigración! ¡Si hay un problema de capitalismo!" (There is not an immigration problem! There is a capitalism problem!), "Resist U.S. EMPIRE," and "Arizona was $tolen from Mexico!" These rhetorical fragments broadened the immigrant mobilization to target the neocolonialism of U.S. economic policy as well as demands for legalization. Slogans such as "Arizona was $tolen from Mexico" connected past colonial legacies to present-day trade and labor policy, which (according to this slogan) was colonialism by other means.

The connection between the immigrant movement and the labor and anti-capitalist/Socialist movement, as Alicia Schmidt Camacho writes, has broad historical roots, including Luisa Moreno's Congress of Spanish-Speaking People and Huerta and Chavez's United Farm Workers.[36] However, we could also argue that immigrant rights discourses—with their focus on the right to work, to support the nuclear family, and on narratives of the exemplary immigrant—sometimes draw on neoliberal ideology just as much as they challenge it.[37] The immigration protests of 2010 employed a fair amount of neoliberal rhetoric themselves. Protestors and organizers demanded the right to work and make a living and highlighted immigrants' status as laborers as justification for their inclusion. Yet the protest also reworked these rhetorical linkages between neoliberalism and borders/immigration, evincing a more complex relationship between movements and goals. In other words, these protests were enactments of citizenship that in some ways were consonant with neoliberalism and in other ways problematized neoliberal logics and addressed larger causes of migration and labor disparities.

The slogan "We Are All Arizona," which was deployed throughout the demonstrations of 2010, can be seen as not just a statement of solidarity with Arizona's immigrants but as representing a broader politics of coalition building that took shape both before and during the larger demonstrations of 2010. The connections and divergences between these different frames demonstrate coalitional subjectivities.[38] That is, the very identities of the movement organizers and protestors seemed contingent, intersectional, and, to some degree, in flux as the coalitions and connections between diverse constituents were (re)constituted. The struggle of and by Arizona became a synecdoche for a number of radical, even revolutionary movements against neoliberal economics, racism/racial profiling, and even against capitalism. The goal became not just reform of immigration laws or even a claiming of cultural citizenship (though these goals certainly suffused the protest); rather, the protest featured a simultaneous working toward and on behalf of multiple intersecting positionalities. In this sense, any effort to define the protests' goals or the identity of the protestors beyond the statement that "We Are All Arizona" has to account for the coalitional subjectivities and complex coalition building of the movement.

"No One Is Illegal": Performing Cosmopolitanism

One of the most prevalent and defining slogans of the demonstrations and movements throughout 2010 was the refrain "No human being is illegal" or, alternately, "No one is illegal." The insistence that "no one is illegal" took shape in a variety of discursive fragments in the Boston protest in which I participated. It appeared on signs, placards, and buttons: "¡Alto Arizona! Ningun Ser Humano es Illegal" (Stop Arizona! No Human Being is Illegal), "We Don't Need No Stinking Papers," "Deporten a la Migra!" (Deport Immigration and Customs Enforcement, or ICE), *"Smash all Borders!,"* or "Fight For a World *Without* Borders." The slogan was also used in protestors' chants ("Why you checking papers? No one is illegal!") and in speeches by a variety of activists addressing the demonstration. It was widespread in the Boston protest as well as in the larger nationwide movements. Analyzing this slogan can illuminate one final dimension of the demonstrations. Mainly, though on the one hand the protests served as demand for and enactment of citizenship, on the other hand, the protests claimed that "no human being is illegal" and challenged the very binary logic of belonging through a project of vernacular cosmopolitanism.[39]

"No one is illegal" or "No human being is illegal" is attributed to Elie Wiesel who, it is said, coined the phrase during a speech he gave in 1985 in Tucson, Arizona (a striking coincidence!) during a conference on U.S. sanctuary policy for refugees. Drawing on his own experiences as a refugee, Wiesel argued for an ethical/religious obligation to welcome all the persecuted and marginalized who seek refuge into the national community regardless of legal status or immigration laws. As he later wrote, "[A] human being is never illegal."[40] In 1997 "No one is illegal" was appropriated as both a rallying cry and as the name for a network of activists and groups protesting deportation policy and challenging immigration and border policy in several western European countries. The organization that now calls itself No One Is Illegal connects antiborder and antideportation groups in Canada, the United Kingdom, Germany, Poland, and Australia, among other countries—organizations that not only mobilize against immigration policy but also contest deportations and defend refugees and immigrants targeted by the state. "According to No One Is Illegal," writes Jakub Burkowicz, "immigration controls and international borders must be completely opposed and dismantled because they perpetuate human suffering by constructing a system of global apartheid."[41] No One Is Illegal is both an organization of activists and a broader struggle against borders and immigration restrictions. Of course, the slogan itself has also been appropriated by a number of nonaffiliated movements and activists to challenge the notion of the "illegal" person and to resist deportations and restrictive immigration policy. For example, Peter Nyers identifies "No One Is Illegal" as a guiding principle of the movement for Canadian sanctuary cities.[42] Though in the United States the organization No One Is Illegal has yet to establish a foothold, the immigrant demonstrations of 2010 demonstrate that the slogan has been appropriated by immigrant activists at the national and local level.

At the risk of oversimplification, we can compare the slogan "No human being is illegal" or "No one is illegal" to the slogan "Hoy marchamos, mañana votamos" (Today we march, tomorrow we vote), which Alfonso Gonzales claims is one of the predominant themes of the 2006 demonstrations. Recall the words of one of the speakers at La Gran Marcha in Los Angeles in March 2006 that I quoted in the last chapter: "Today we march for amnesty, tomorrow for citizenship, and after that, to gain the right to govern civilly along with the rest of the honest workers of this country." This slogan, despite its hybrid performativity in the context of La Gran Marcha, clearly spoke to an integrationist strategy of many of the promoters of the 2006 protest, who, as I noted in the last chapter, objected to the introduction of "foreign" political traditions or practices and demanded instead allegiance to U.S. American identity. As we know, the emphasis on civil rights and citizenship faces limitations since it works within the system and demands recognition from those who can confer it, thus subtly entrenching dominant logics. In spite of this, for many activists, the performance of citizenship served as a crucial demand for inclusion into the nation.[43]

However, anti-immigrant legislation such as SB 1070 bespeaks anxiety about and resistance to immigrant inclusion at a fundamental level. Measures that heighten border security and enforcement and that escalate the surveillance and persecution of all those suspected to be undocumented immigrants represent a broader effort to restrict the right to have rights. No example is more telling than the growing effort to remove birthright citizenship from the Fourteenth Amendment. The logic of (il)legality marks certain people as (un)desirable, (un)worthy of inclusion, and (therefore) worthy of surveillance, prosecution, and ultimately exclusion. Contemporary immigration policy and border enforcement at some level problematize the possibility of an integrationist, civil rights discourse because they refuse to acknowledge that most immigrants are worthy of rights. Thus while "Today we march, tomorrow we vote" represents a demand for inclusion into a political and social community, "No one is illegal" makes an ontological claim about the very definition of human community. This reminds us of José David Saldívar's statement "The paradigm of the border"—and we could also say the paradigm of legality and citizenship—"involves us in an ontological question: What kinds of world or worlds are we in?" In this case, "No one is illegal" seems to problematize the world we inhabit, which is based on territorial sovereignty, nation-state citizenship, and borders.[44]

This is why, on its face, the statement "No one is illegal"—and its persistence in contemporary immigrant movements—is vexing because it seems to miss the way that citizenship and immigration law criminalizes people by criminalizing their *acts*. After all, "illegal" status means the nation-state is deeming individuals in violation of the law because of their illegal actions (border crossing, illegal residence), not making a definitive statement on the immigrant's humanity. At the same time, these status claims are often imputed to be pronouncements about immigrants' character, when undocumented status is conflated with all kinds of markers of "worthiness" for inclusion. Yet this is precisely one way in which the phrase "No human being is illegal" works to challenge the logics of citizenship and nationalism by shifting the emphasis from an individual's legal actions and/or status to a more fundamental shared level of humanity. In other words, "No one is illegal" passes over and refutes the legal judgment of an individual's actions and/or status and the moral judgment of an individual's worthiness, justifying compassion and identification based on the immigrant's humanity. By focusing on shared humanity rather than legal status, the slogan "No one is illegal" implicitly argues that "illegality" itself is a political and thus partisan judgment of an individual's belongingness. As Nyers explains, these slogans are "more than moral pleas for better, more humanitarian treatment" but instead are "declarations that are generative of a political subjectivity" and "subjectification" that "allow non-status groups to extract themselves from the hegemonic categories by which political identity is normally understood."[45] Nyers is echoing here the relationship between citizenship and subjectivity/subjectification, namely, that citizenship is a form of political identity and agency but also a mode by which the nation-state maintains its sovereignty through the creation of citizen-subjects. In this way, "illegality" is a mode of subjectification (or subjection) of individuals who cross and have been crossed by the border and are thus deemed as unworthy of subjectivity (citizenship). Undocumented immigrants and refugees are nonsubjects for whom subjectivity is impossible but who remain an integral part of the economy of citizenship and civic belonging nonetheless (as the "aliens" against whom citizenship remains exclusive). "No one is illegal" is an expression of *il*legal belonging, of demanding recognition from a constitutive exclusion. The slogan has a dual function of both subverting understandings of nation-state citizenship and foregrounding an alternative form of identification. Let me further illustrate this claim through examples from the 2010 demonstrations and the Boston protest specifically.

Protestors with whom I participated chanted regularly, "Why you checking papers? No one is illegal!" Signs and placards read, "We Don't Need No Stinking Papers" and demanded, "Deport la Migra (ICE)" rather than immigrants. There is no need to check papers and, more than that, belonging does not require papers! These slogans and statements, as well as many others from the speeches illustrate how "No one is illegal," as a broader vernacular rhetoric of the 2010 demonstrations, broke with binaries of belonging and citizenship. This rhetoric extended "No one is illegal" into a reversal of the discourse of citizenship and belonging: immigrants didn't need papers and defied the logic of legality underpinning ICE. The rhetoric fundamentally challenged the paradigm of legality underlying citizenship. Taking the hybrid enactments of 2006 one step further, the premise that "No one is illegal" not only transcended the binary between citizen and alien but subverted that binary head-on, decriminalizing the act of border crossing and denaturalizing the frame of (il)legality and nation-state citizenship. "No one is illegal" not only contested the subjectification of immigrants as illegal but also constituted an alternative, critical, and vernacular cosmopolitan subjectivity *outside* the nation-state.

The term *cosmopolitan* has a long and complex history every bit as contentious as the term *hybridity*. Broadly speaking, cosmopolitanism represents a contrasting form of identification, one that foregrounds the similarity and unity of all humankind rather than the particular communal identities of nationalism.[46] However, rather than engage these broader theoretical questions about the status and validity of cosmopolitanism as a universalist identity paradigm, I want to focus here on cosmopolitanism as a particular vernacular discourse that is situated, contingent, and performative, much like hybridity. In other words, I understand cosmopolitanism, like hybridity, as particularized and localized discourse rather than universal identity paradigm. Put another way, I am thinking of cosmopolitanism not as a universal project or model for community but rather as what Walter Mignolo terms a "critical" or "decolonial" project that shifts "from imperial cosmopolitanism (or cosmopolitanism without modifiers and without parenthesis) to cosmopolitan localisms (co-existence of cosmopolitanism with modifiers and with parenthesis)." This way of thinking about cosmopolitanism as vernacular, plural, localized, and performative would strive not for a universality (or universal community) but for pluriversality. Thus I argue that the immigrant protests of 2006 were enacting an "actually existing" cosmopolitanism or a "cosmopolitanism from below" that sought to challenge dominant logics of borders and citizenship and to situate an alternative and pluriversal standard of belonging.[47]

Important to recognize, in terms of understanding the cosmopolitan rhetorics of contemporary immigrant movements, is that, as Sheldon Pollock et al. argue, "Cosmopolitans today are often the victims of modernity, failed by capitalism's upward mobility, and bereft of those comforts and customs of national belonging," including "refugees, peoples of the diaspora, and migrants." Similar to hybridity, cosmopolitanism often functions in the mode of an "abject cosmopolitanism," a subjectification that positions immigrants as outside the bounds of the nation-state, as free-floating aliens, lacking an identity or "home," thus resulting in exclusion and marginalization. U.S. citizenship or Western identity often becomes representative of true, universal cosmopolitan multiculturalism, and immigrants and minorities represent an abject cosmopolitanism because they are in between places, they are cosmopolitan in a negative sense, as those who belong neither here nor there, everywhere, and thus nowhere, representative of inassimilable cultures.[48]

Yet this abject cosmopolitanism, like the abjectness that accompanies the supposed hybridity of immigrants, paradoxically can become the grounds for subjectivity and for challenging the binary logics of the nation-state. Vernacular cosmopolitanism can take shape in discourses through which individuals performatively enact and position themselves at the interstices of local, national, and global borders and imagine an alternative standard for community. In the context of immigration, vernaculars of cosmopolitanisms function similarly to hybridity as a sort of both/and condition of the migrant. In the case of "No human being is illegal," we see a performance of vernacular cosmopolitanism that undermines the logic of the nation-state and displaces identification from citizenship onto a different register.[49]

Recall that affects and logics of citizenship and migration naturalize the framework of legality and illegality, belonging and alienness; borders not only demarcate the nation but also serve to "border" the terrain of "the political" (in the sense of who counts and who can speak as a subject). Because they are abject cosmopolitans—because they lack national status—immigrants are excluded from the nation and the realm of politics. This is quite obvious in contemporary anti-immigrant laws, which attempt to choke immigrants out of the political, social, and cultural community. However, the claim that "No one/human being is illegal," the call to "smash all borders," and the defiant *rejection* of the logics of citizenship, as in "We don't need no stinking papers!" and "Deport la Migra," all performatively place the political into question. The contestation and refusal of these logics repoliticize the question of legality and illegality (resituate it in the realm of the political). Though some argued that these slogans and protest(s) served as demands for legalization, I believe the vernaculars of citizenship and identity also served as a critique of logics of belonging. Papers, legalization, and borders were rejected for a political identification as resident, worker, member of the human community deserving of hospitality and respect.[50] One of the organizers noted at the beginning of the march that the protest was not only "fighting" for rights for the undocumented but, more broadly, "fighting for the true freedom that we all deserve," while another speaker stressed that the chants of "We don't need no stinking papers" and "No one is illegal" were attempts at "fighting for a world with no borders." These slogans and speeches highlighted how the rhetoric of "No one is illegal" worked not as a universal or global design but as a performative strategy to contest logics of (il)legality and highlight a link between local and global communities. In its enactment of a vernacular cosmopolitanism, the protest emphasized that legality / illegality did not have to be the sole paradigm of political community, that belonging should be based on hospitality toward migrants, and that citizenship was a process of political action rather than a static legal category.

Again, it is important to emphasize that the immigrant protests of 2010 featured multiple vernacular cosmopolitanisms. The constituents and agendas of the protestors was complex, and for some cosmopolitan identity was articulated as the workers' revolutionary struggle ("a world where people work and struggle together for the common good"),[51] while for others cosmopolitan claims that "No human is illegal" privileged a mode of belonging based on work and residence, on hospitality for all of humanity. By foregrounding a politics based on residency and freedom of movement and work, activists performed a form of citizenship that was both "unbounded" in its (trans)national access and "grounded" in residency, presence, and the local realities and needs of immigrant communities.[52] In contrast, the movement in support of the federal DREAM (Development, Relief and Education for Alien Minors) Act featured young undocumented immigrant activists, or "Dreamers" (as student-immigrant activists called themselves), painting themselves as U.S. Americans who wanted to become integrated members of the American community and live out the American Dream. The DREAM activists aimed not to challenge the parameters of belonging or to constitute an alternative, cosmopolitan mode of belonging but rather worked to demonstrate their cultural citizenship and fittingness for formal inclusion.[53]

Nevertheless, though it was not ubiquitous in the immigrant movement, the rhetoric of "No one is illegal" is significant because it was pregnant with the possibilities of multiple dimensions of identity and agency for the movement. The diverse ways in which the slogan "No one is illegal" was deployed throughout the nationwide protests, boycotts, and mobilizations demonstrate its hybrid performativity since it could at times serve as a warrant for inclusion (as in the sign "No one is illegal. Amnesty

Now!") and at other times could challenge that very logic (as in the chant "Why you checking papers? No one is illegal!"). In the latter sense, the slogan "No one is illegal" enacted a critical cosmopolitanism that subverted binaries of legality / illegality and displaced identification from the nation-state. Mignolo notes how in contemporary society "the problems of rights, justice, equality, and so on are thought out by way of inclusion." "But," he writes, "[t]oday, silenced and marginalized voices are bringing themselves into the conversation of cosmopolitan projects, rather than waiting to be included. Inclusion is always a reformative project. Bringing themselves into the conversation is a transformative project that takes the form of . . . the recognition and transformation of the hegemonic imaginary from the perspectives of [subaltern] people."[54] For nonimmigrant protestors, "No one is illegal" became both a challenge to conventional logics of nation-state citizenship and an affirmation of a more fundamental form of belonging. For migrants, the slogan appropriated the supposedly "abject" cosmopolitanism of migrants—in between worlds and nations—into a form of cosmopolitan subjectivity outside the bounds of the nation-state from which to speak and act.

Ours is a world that celebrates the free flow of capital and goods and that valorizes the entrepreneurial individual and yet criminalizes the movement of people and exploits the hard work of a whole class based on the circumstance of their movement. Citizenship privileges those who become part of the national community in theory, but in practice it violently polices the boundaries of belonging. It is in this light that protestors throughout the country contested the logic of nation-state belonging. Through a constellation of discourses represented in the slogan "No one is illegal" protestors performed cosmopolitan belongings in opposition to the nation-state, a notion of citizen without citizenship, or perhaps a return to the root of citizen as the inhabitant of a city rather than a legal member of a nation.[55] "Our received traditions of the political require that some human beings be illegal," writes Nyers; thus "to say that no human is illegal is to call into question the entire architecture of sovereignty, all its borders, locks and doors, internal hierarchies, etc."[56] Some might argue that any such appeals to a cosmopolitan community risk entrenching the marginalization of migrants because human rights always codify nation-state sovereignty and citizenship—frameworks that ultimately underpin the exclusivity of belonging.[57] This critique may indicate one of the shortcomings of the vernacular rhetorical strategy identified above. At the same time, the vernacular cosmopolitanism of contemporary movements helps to expose and undermine the very logics of nation-state sovereignty that contribute to immigrants' marginalization, even if only partially and tenuously. If borders pose an ontological question about the world in which we live, this vernacular cosmopolitanism seemed to imagine a world without borders, at least in the conventional way in which we see them. The different strands of discourse, verbal, visual, and embodied, in these contemporary immigrant rights protests represented a type of "reworlding" that constructed multiple alternative imaginaries of citizenship outside of the paradigm of borders, that constituted alternative worlds in which unauthorized immigrants could be recognized as belonging without formal or legal recognition.[58]

My analysis has unpacked three significant elements of the Boston protest that I argue distinguish the discourses of citizenship in the 2010 immigrant movements. First, in response to SB 1070 and other anti-immigrant measures, which sought to survey and prosecute immigrants for their purported performative affects of "alienness," the demonstrations of 2010 can be read as subverting those affective economies and embracing hybrid performativity and the impossibility of determining (il)legality. Second, the confluence of diverse goals, constituents, and themes analyzed above represents the coalitional politics of the protests. While pro-immigrant organizations were organizing in opposition to anti-immigrant legislation and in support of immigration reform, other issues—unemployment, labor rights, and racial discrimination—were also represented in the movement's agenda and constituent list. Third, the broadening of the protests' messages, from enactments of citizenship to the assertion "No one is illegal," demonstrated a vernacular cosmopolitanism that challenged logics of nation-state citizenship and enacted belonging as localized and rooted in an ethic of hospitality and shared humanity.

Conclusion

This chapter has traced the development of contemporary movements against SB 1070 and the gathering of organizations making up those movements. By focusing on a critical ethnographic analysis of one particular protest in the nationwide wave of 2010, I have attempted to elucidate the contours of contemporary vernacular rhetorics of citizenship and their relationship to bordering practices. I have also situated and contextualized this event within the broader movements that took place throughout the country against SB 1070 and other anti-immigrant state and local laws. Collectively, the rhetorical fragments of the protest I have analyzed provide a richer understanding of the discourses of citizenship in the 2010 protests and their relationship to the 2006 demonstrations. In the remainder of this chapter I trace the rhetorical effectivity of this evolving movement, as best we can, and the limitations it faces.

Much of this chapter has focused on direct demonstrations and protests against SB 1070, but to begin to trace these movements' circulation we can look to the variegated forms of activism against anti-immigrant legislation that worked in tandem with and drew inspiration from anti-SB1070 protests. Protests broadened into legal challenges to anti-immigrant laws as well as other forms of activism, including boycotts of Arizona and corporate supporters of the Arizona Republicans who crafted SB 1070. For example, inspired by the demonstrations against the law, several groups mounted public protests of Arizona's Major League Baseball (MLB) team the Arizona Diamondbacks because the team's ownership had contributed to the campaigns of Republican senators responsible for spearheading the legislation. Several protests outside of Diamondback games and facilities attracted public attention, and organizers also pushed a boycott of the team and lobbied the leadership of MLB to relocate the 2011 Major League All-Star Game, which was scheduled to take place in Phoenix. They argued that the large number of Latino professional baseball players demanded that the MLB resist Arizona's racist and nativist law. Though the commissioner of the MLB refused to move the All-Star Game for purportedly economic reasons, several Latino players publicly stated their opposition to SB 1070 and joined in the calls for a boycott, which drew even more public attention to the struggle.[59]

Efforts to exert economic pressure on Arizona's government through boycotts grew. For example, over thirty performers and musical acts pledged to boycott the state, refusing to perform and/or canceling previously scheduled performances there. Over twenty city governments also voted to boycott Arizona, including Los Angeles, Bloomington, Indiana, and Hartford, Connecticut; dozens of other city and local governments passed measures objecting to the law. Other public bodies, from the Denver Public Schools to Milwaukee Area Technical College, imposed various levels of boycotts or travel bans, and many organizations canceled or relocated conferences or other events previously scheduled in Arizona. Although the success of these individual boycotts varied, they drew attention to the national boycott. By June 2010 figures suggested that Arizona had already lost nearly $10 million in revenue, and a report issued in November 2010 estimated the loss at $140 million from canceled conferences alone, not including the economic impact of canceled contracts for services and reduced tourism. Activists and unions were buoyed by these boycotts as well as by expressions of solidarity by public figures such as musicians, performers, athletes, and even by Arizona's National Basketball Association team the Phoenix Suns, who wore Spanish-language jerseys reading "Los Suns," usually reserved for special "Latino"-themed promotions, in direct protest of SB 1070. The political statement by the professional basketball team drew criticism from many of the Phoenix Suns' fans who opposed the team's political stance or objected to the mixing of sports and politics.[60]

These events raise the question of rhetorical impact for the still-unfolding immigrant movement. In the most immediate sense, the persistence of mobilizations against SB 1070 and other anti-immigrant legislation throughout the country demonstrates that the oppositional social concord hardened into a concerted movement.

The convergence of multiple constituents in opposition to SB 1070, from laborers and service workers to immigrants, white citizens, and Latina/os, demonstrates that the movement has been able to capture the attention and support of a broad coalition through its opposition to racist and nativist immigration restriction. The anti–SB 1070 protests and movements contributed to opposition to the law and its challenge by the U.S. Supreme Court, but the efforts to build public opposition to SB 1070 and lobby for legal challenges have failed to overturn some of SB1070's most controversial provisions. As I noted above, while the Supreme Court overturned many of the law's provisions, those concerning "reasonable suspicion" and police surveillance have gone into full effect. Also, the efforts listed above, such as boycotts and the support of public figures, waned once court injunctions were issued and increased once again in the wake of the law's implementation. Similar anti-immigrant provisions at the state and local level remain in place, but arguably, the complex and intersecting appeals of citizenship, antiracism, labor, and cosmopolitanism provide a wide berth for the mobilization of activists against anti-immigrant legislation.

However, we could just as well argue that the reach and success of these demonstrations is limited, in spite of the successful court challenge, when considering the persistence of border anxiety and restrictive immigration policies. In spite of protests, boycotts, public relations campaigns, and lawsuits, efforts to reverse anti-immigrant laws have been met with stiff opposition. Public polls indicate that the national mobilizations against SB 1070 in 2010 served to polarize public opinion on immigration and harden anti-immigrant sentiment. Efforts to protest SB 1070 fueled a proliferation of similar state and local anti-immigrant measures. To date, copycat provisions have passed in several states and have been debated in over twenty. Even where the local version of SB 1070 has failed, other measures have passed, such as those preventing immigrants from working or acquiring housing. Governor Brewer herself issued an executive order in August 2012 barring undocumented immigrant students who receive deferred action from deportation from receiving state benefits or drivers' licenses.[61]

Despite its public opposition to state initiatives like SB 1070, the Obama administration itself has presented a mixed message on immigration policy. On one hand, the federal government escalated anti-immigrant measures, including deportation efforts and information sharing between ICE and local law enforcement to facilitate state-level enforcement.[62] In particular, the administration's intensification and formalization of the Secure Communities deportation program, which purports to target "dangerous" and "criminal" immigrants, has resulted in the deportation of over one million immigrants just during Obama's presidency (and the arrest and temporary detention of many times that). The result is that the president stressed his bona fides as a border enforcer by publicly proclaiming he had deported more undocumented immigrants than his predecessor. On the other hand, the administration released a number of clarifying memos in 2012 announcing the intent of federal immigration officials to exercise "prosecutorial discretion" when initiating or reviewing deportation cases (meaning discretion to exempt those who are not "bad" immigrants on a case-by-case basis). Later in the year, the administration also enacted a "soft" version of the DREAM Act known as "deferred action," in which some youth eligible for the DREAM Act could apply for a two-year stay from deportation, subject to renewal. These efforts were praised by some as proof of the immigrant movement's success in spurring action on immigration policy despite congressional gridlock. At the same time, others pointed to the administration's ongoing deportation efforts and to statistics that demonstrate that these promises have gone unrealized, which supposedly belie a pro-immigrant image for the administration.[63] At the time, immigration activists noted the proximity of Obama's discretionary programs to the 2012 presidential election, arguing that his decisions were politically motivated since Obama's reelection depended at least in part on Latina/o turnout. However, emboldened by his reelection (or at least so said his administration), and to the surprise of some activists, the president initiated a push for his own "comprehensive" immigration reform legislation in 2013—a proposal that bore a significant resemblance to that of Obama's Republican predecessor. At the time of this writing, congressional gridlock has prevented any substantial consideration of immigration reform. Nevertheless, all of this is to say that events at the federal level as well as the state and local level problematize easy estimations of the immigration movements' successes. Some point to the administration's softening as evidence of shifting sentiments while others argue that whatever momentum was gained in 2010 has been lost.

It has always been difficult to evaluate an ongoing movement through instrumental markers of success because movements are complex coalitions of different constituents and goals and because they operate by fits and starts. Vernacular rhetorics are always at a disadvantage against dominant power brokers. It is undeniable that anti-immigrant measures and a general climate of border anxiety and "Latino threat" persist, if only because of the institutional sanction of these dominant logics. The border has crossed and continues to cross Latina/o, immigrant, and non-immigrant communities, demarcating the exclusive and exclusionary boundaries of civic belonging. Nonetheless, it is also important to acknowledge some significant rhetorical impacts that we can trace in these vernacular rhetorics. In an era of "impure politics," an era in which "no tactical choice is pure," the question should be how coalitional and provisional activism can enact change. Contemporary Latina/o-immigrant activist vernacular discourses represent both the coalitional possibilities of social movement(s) and the continuing efforts to bring forth alternative forms of belonging.[64]

Not only unauthorized immigrants but also citizens, labor unions, and other progressives identified dominant logics of citizenship as restricting the possibilities of belonging for all. For Latina/o citizens and other documented immigrants, the fear seemed that stricter immigration laws would result in more racial profiling and persecution. In a climate of anti-immigrant and anti-Latina/o nativism, the mobilizations were able to reclaim at least provisionally the performative affect of hybridity and affirm a more expansive, hybrid citizenship. For other activists, the nativism and racism of SB 1070 represented broader forces of neoliberalism that foreclosed the possibility of full belonging—social, economic, and cultural—for all. Thus the contemporary activism against SB 1070 and other anti-immigrant legislation bespeaks the potential of a complex movement that can involve political economy, national belonging, and cultural/identity politics.

Even in the world of globalization of culture, capital flow, and neoliberal political economy, the civic imaginary can expand or evolve to take into account new challenges and experiences. If the border involves us in an ontological question, then contemporary immigrant and Latina/o movements, by expanding the very meanings of citizenship and borders, forge new visions of the type of world we can inhabit. They move beyond what kind of world we are in to imagine what kind of world we can create. In this vein, it is to questions of citizenship and identity, borders and belonging that I return in the conclusion. What are the consequences and challenges, the lessons and possibilities that Latina/o vernaculars of citizenship and civic identity provide for the politics of belonging, for conceptions of U.S. American identity, and for the growing Latina/o community in the United States?

Conclusion

Denaturalizing Borders and Citizenship

The analysis, elaboration, and bringing into question of power relations and the "agonism" between power relations and the intransitivity of freedom is an increasingly political task—even, the political task that is inherent in all social existence.

—Michel Foucault

Yo no cruce la frontera, la frontera me cruzo
América nació libre, el hombre la dividió.

—Los Tigres del Norte, "Somos Mas Americanos"

It has become quite commonplace for scholars and social commentators to begin their work on Latina/os in the United States by remarking on the growth of the Latina/o population, on the relative youth of the Latina/o community, and on its increasing political mobilization. These studies regularly point out that Latina/os (or "Latins," "Hispanics," "Latinos," "Spanish," or whichever moniker by which they are referenced) have become the largest minority group in the United States. According to this demographic research, Latina/os account for over half of the population growth of the last decade, and the bulk of this increase comes not from immigration (though that is still a significant factor) but from "natural" population growth (births).[1] In light of these observations, there is a relentless heralding of the cultural and political rousing of Latina/os. At different moments over the last three decades we have supposedly witnessed the rise of "Spanglish," the "Decade of Hispanics," the "Hispanic nation," and the "Latin explosion."[2] No such refrain is more persistent and thus more clichéd than that of Latina/os as a "sleeping giant" beginning to awaken (whether for good or ill, depending on who is heralding the coming "awakening").[3] For some, Latina/os are the "new Americans," while for others, they are overrunning U.S. borders and communities. Underlying both of these views is the persistent representation of U.S. Latina/os as a growing demographic community poised to overtake or at least transform U.S. society.

In the face of such pronouncements, this book has sought to explore the contours of borders, U.S. citizenship, and Latina/o identity across history. I have focused on the rhetorical and material bordering and rebordering of U.S. citizenship and identity in the context of and by Latina/os. The four case study chapters have analyzed important moments of anxiety about citizenship and the nation, anxieties that propelled rhetorical and material bordering and that spurred attempts by Latina/o groups to rhetorically reborder, reshape, and challenge those boundaries of belonging and the terms of citizenship. The preceding case studies have recontextualized persistent claims of a Latina/o "awakening" by examining both historical and contemporary Latina/o vernaculars that helped to redefine U.S. citizenship and identity. Tracing Latina/os' struggles with U.S. citizenship through situated moments, I have sketched a partial picture of how borders are rhetorically constructed and contested and how citizenship is enacted. As should be evident by now, the popular belief that Latina/os' presence in the United States and the political activities of Latina/o citizens is a modern phenomenon, or one that is just on the horizon of possibility, is not only historically inaccurate but, more important, occludes the real struggle by Latina/o communities over the meanings and material conditions of citizenship and U.S. identity throughout U.S. history.

A host of other struggles surrounding U.S. citizenship and national identity are prevalent in contemporary politics. Latina/o vernacular rhetorics of borders and U.S. citizenship are evidenced in the proliferation of political groups mobilizing for Latina/o rights, controversies over bilingual education and ethnic identification, and mobilization for political power, visibility, and cultural representation. In light of these and other continuing struggles for belonging, this conclusion offers lessons for our understandings of Latina/o identity, for the politics of borders and U.S. citizenship, and for scholars interested in these enduring issues. After exploring some of the themes of the preceding chapters, I outline several theoretical and programmatic insights about rhetorics of borders and citizenship for future scholarship. I also use the conceptual and methodological frameworks I have deployed in this book to meditate on broader questions, including the pitfalls and possibilities of a Latina/o identity politics (a politicized Latinidad) as well as the future trajectories of citizenship and national identity.

"The Border Crossed Us"

The "problem" of the border defines contemporary concerns about immigration, citizenship, and U.S. identity. This border problem is most regularly reiterated in the public imaginary through images of the porousness of the U.S.-Mexico frontier, its violation by illegal aliens, and the supposedly evaporating borders between U.S. American and foreigner. Anxiety over the (U.S.-Mexico) border fuels efforts to police the physical borders of the nation and the legal and cultural borders of citizenship. More broadly, the borders of belonging—racial, cultural, economic, and gendered—continue to manifest in contemporary controversies over citizenship and civic identity in the United States.

As I have shown, the crossing of the border—both physical and figurative—historically defined the reality of colonized Mexicans in the middle of the nineteenth century. After this initial crossing (over) of the border and the imposition of citizenship, the relationships of citizenship and Mexican "alienness" gradually hardened, creating racialized categories such as "illegal immigrant" that worked to secure the boundaries of U.S. American identity. Even now, borders and citizenship are strictly policed in the most literal sense (in the form of border patrolling and border militarization) as well as through restrictions on legal and cultural belonging. These multiple crossings of and by the border demonstrate how rhetorical and material bordering is intricately tied to the definition of citizenship and civic identity. A crisis of the border(s) and of citizenship results in efforts to distinguish legitimate from illegitimate border crossings and worthy from unworthy subjects. Bordering practices take shape in contemporary concerns over immigration, civil rights, and culture as well as in increasingly organized and aggressive efforts to police the boundaries of the civic imaginary through immigration enforcement and anti-immigrant measures. Even in popular culture, a number of stereotypes and discourses about Latina/o and immigrant identity still circulate, often contributing to the marginalization of communities and the stratification of citizenship status. Thus the border has continually crossed and recrosses communities, and it is through border rhetoric that the boundaries of the nation and citizenship are drawn. When contemporary immigrant rights movements state, "We didn't cross the border, the border crossed us," they seem to reference this enduring legacy of the crossing of and by U.S. borders.

Also, this popular slogan suggests that borders and citizenship are rhetorical practices—that they can be contested or challenged by those very groups who are defined on the margins (or borders) of belonging. The "border" is a physical place at which nations meet and a cultural space at which national identity and community are demarcated. But the border not only demarcates and divides, it also provides the possibility for contact and crossing. It takes shape through the reiteration and performance of those borders in public discourse. The border is pliable and, more than that, rhetorical, such that rhetorical and performative practices materialize the border and demarcate belonging. Obviously, this does not mean that borders and bordering practices are wholly rhetorical or symbolic. However, recognizing borders and citizenship as rhetorical practices situates them as sites for negotiation, contestation, and affirmation of identity and agency. In other words, the "dominant civic" border rhetorics—those that come from "mainstream" society and represent tradition and empowered positions—exist in relationship with "vernacular" attempts to (re)define U.S. citizenship and (re)draw the borders of belonging.

Through this framework, *The Border Crossed Us* has examined both historical and contemporary border rhetorics and the ways that Latina/o vernaculars worked in tandem with and sometimes in opposition to mainstream attempts to define the parameters of the civic imaginary. The preceding chapters provided several interventions into the popular narrative of Latina/o "awakening" by focusing on historical moments of negotiation over citizenship and borders. The California Constitutional Convention of 1849, which I analyzed in chapter 1, represented a proving ground for Californio elites to negotiate and contest the racial and cultural borders of U.S. citizenship, a political identity forced upon them through colonization and conquest. Chapter 2 focused on the rhetoric and activism of Reies Tijerina and the Alianza Federal de Mercedes, which demonstrated a vernacular discourse of citizenship that contended with the segregation, exclusion, and second-class citizenship of Mexican Americans (and other Latina/os) through a differential border discourse. As explicit counterpoints to the presentist bias in contemporary discussions of borders and citizenship, these two historical interventions demonstrate how Latina/o citizenship vernaculars formed fundamental constituents of the U.S. national imaginary and shaped the racial, cultural, and political boundaries of the nation. These chapters are meant to show that those interested in addressing contemporary challenges of Latina/o citizenship must attend to how tensions of U.S. national belonging have been negotiated successfully or unsuccessfully throughout history. Latina/os are not "sleeping giants" but rather have been (forcibly and willingly) part of the U.S. civic imaginary for centuries. Latina/os and Latina/o immigrants have been integral to the making and remaking of U.S. citizenship and identity.[4]

Chapters 3 and 4 engaged with contemporary manifestations of border and citizenship struggles, showing how public anxiety has manifested in new ways as well as how Latina/o and particularly Latina/o immigrant movements have reorganized to negotiate and contest exclusionary border politics. Several highly publicized and controversial anti-immigrant initiatives, such as HR 4437 and SB 1070, represent a broader escalation of the legal, cultural, and physical bordering of U.S. citizenship in the last thirty years. These decades have witnessed escalating militarization of the U.S.-Mexico border and heightened criminalization of immigrants. Yet this rhetorical and material bordering has been met with a number of movements concerning citizenship and civic identity. Nationwide protests, boycotts, and mobilizations against anti-immigrant legislation and for immigrant and labor rights over the last ten years demonstrate just one contemporary vernacular discourse that crosses social positions and broadens the struggle for belonging.

Apart from contributing to our situated understanding of Latina/o vernacular rhetorics, these case studies have also advanced a broader theoretical argument about the relationships between rhetoric, borders, and citizenship. One of the goals of this book has been to advance the view that borders and citizenship are not just the situations that give rise to rhetoric but rather that rhetoric itself creates and defines the border and the identity of the citizen. I have argued that, as rhetorical practices, borders and citizenship go hand in hand. Border rhetorics define the parameters of U.S. citizenship and civic identity—who belongs and who should be excluded. Discourses of citizenship, national identity, and national culture represent the reiterative rhetorical materials out of which bordering takes place and often operate at the level of common sense and become sedimented in particular configurations and institutional practices. Citizenship and nationalism, in fact, are wedded to this very process of bordering the civic imaginary.

Up to now I have developed this argument through analysis of discourses surrounding the U.S.-Mexico border and Mexican Americans, Chicana/os, and Latina/o immigrants. However, I believe that the critical focus on border rhetorics and rhetorics of citizenship has purchase beyond these particular historical and political contexts. Here another example—the nomination debate over Supreme Court justice Sonia Sotomayor—can help us to understand the significance of border rhetorics in defining citizenship and Latina/o identity beyond the U.S.-Mexico border as well as the importance of a critical rhetorical project of denaturalizing borders and citizenship.

During her 2010 confirmation debate, controversy arose about Sotomayor's proud Latina and Puerto Rican identity. In particular, Sotomayor received criticism for her repeated public statement that "a wise Latina woman with the richness of her experiences would more often than not reach a better conclusion than a white male who hasn't lived that life." This statement, delivered in a number of public lectures, was largely either decried as racist or dismissed as an unfortunate and misguided misstatement. For some, the comment was interpreted as racist because it forwarded her Latina identity as a source of difference and pride. Many of the senators in the confirmation hearings as well as reporters and political commentators noted that this was not an appropriate sentiment for a potential Supreme Court justice to express and that it potentially indicated a source of bias in Sotomayor's past decisions, a prejudice for Latina/os and against whites. Others merely argued that Sotomayor inelegantly expressed pride in her cultural identity but did not advocate any racial or cultural bias in her judicial decision making. In fact, Sotomayor herself eventually made this point in the Senate confirmation hearings when questioned about her statement, describing it as "a rhetorical flourish that fell flat."[5]

Notwithstanding the irony of these criticisms of Sotomayor's statement, especially when compared to the strong evidence that discrimination actually exists in the legal system against blacks and Latina/os, the protestations of media pundits and politicians represented a public moment of reckoning with the proper amount of Latina/o cultural, racial, and gender "difference" that could be tolerated in "mainstream" America. Concerns over Sotomayor's "passion" and the rumors that she was a "terror on the bench" surfaced stereotypes and dominant discourses about Latina race, gender, and sexuality that worked to define the proper performance of citizenship and reasonability. The very same purported "spiciness" and "emotionality" that often make Latina pop culture icons so desired and hyper-sexualized in U.S. society was immediately equated with Sotomayor's identification as a Latina woman and, even more, was understood as a liability during the nomination debate, as Sotomayor was accused of being too emotional, too fiery, too much of a "wise Latina" for the job of Supreme Court justice. For some, Sotomayor's Latina identity, often celebrated and even fetishized in other Latinas, was an unacceptable form of difference supposedly at odds with more appropriate (white, male) qualities of reasonableness and objectivity.

Though Sotomayor was eventually confirmed, she ultimately had to denounce the statement and publicly apologize under scrutiny. Sotomayor's previous identification as a "wise Latina woman" was a threat to her confirmation, and thus she had to explicitly and publicly affirm her "objectivity" (presumably associated with white, masculine, Americanness) for Republicans during the course of her nomination. During the Senate confirmation hearings, Sotomayor worked to perform a national affect of a reasonable and objective citizen-subject. In fact, one journalist described Sotomayor's behavior during the confirmation hearings as "deliberate" and "well-controlled" and praised her for successfully "color[ing] her words beige." Other journalists commented after the confirmation hearings that Sotomayor had successfully demonstrated "restraint" and left her "passion" behind, thus proving that she possessed the temperament and judgment necessary for the position of Supreme Court justice.[6]

This example illustrates the rhetorical and material bordering faced by many Latina/os and immigrants in contemporary U.S. public culture through discourses including race, gender, sexuality, colonialism, and class. Sotomayor's confirmation debate illuminates how border rhetorics deploy dominant logics of Latina/o and immigrant identity to concretize and police the boundaries of acceptable U.S. identity. In cases such as this, something is "off" or different about certain individuals that often marks them as "other" even when they do "belong" in a strictly legal or limited sense. In order to achieve full recognition they are often expected to put aside this difference and assimilate as much as possible to the dominant expectations of U.S. citizenship. This was true for Sotomayor, a U.S. citizen, born in New York, educated at the nation's best schools, and respected as a prominent federal judge, yet who was immediately understood through the trope of Latina "exoticness" as a source of uncertainty and trepidation. In response, one of Sotomayor's biggest hurdles in the confirmation process was displaying the proper performance of U.S. citizenship for the critical eyes of certain senators and the public. This demonstrates how the parameters of U.S. identity and belonging are continually constituted through rhetorical bordering in relation to (Latina/o) others. It demonstrates how performances of citizenship help to draw people into or outside of the civic imaginary.

That border rhetorics and particular civic imaginaries are naturalized through rhetoric masks the fact that the border moves and materializes differently across space and time, that the borders of citizenship as they are conceived in any one space and time are unnatural. By thinking about border rhetorics as rhetorical and performative practices we can recognize that any particular configuration of borders and citizenship is situated and contingent no matter how sedimented, natural, or normal it may seem. The borders and/of U.S. citizenship are aberrant in the sense that they are exceptional and abnormal. According to the popular Mexican band Los Tigres del Norte, "Yo no cruce la frontera, la frontera me cruzo / America nació libre, el hombre la dividió" (I didn't cross the border, the border crossed me / America was born free, it was man who divided it). This lyric obviously resonates with and draws upon the popular saying, "We didn't cross the border, the border crossed us" that forms the title of this book. In this case, the lyric echoes my broader argument that borders are rhetorical and ideological constructions (though, of course, I would differ with this lyric in that I do not recognize any such "free" time period that existed before borders). Border rhetorics define the norm by situating an aberrant or abject other. However, my focus on borders and citizenship as rhetorical and ideological processes demonstrates that it is borders themselves that are particular and situated and thus are aberrant. The borders of U.S. citizenship—territorial, legal, racial, cultural, and linguistic—are rhetorically produced, imposed, and maintained. Borders cross people just as people cross borders. Border rhetorics demand attention precisely because they make the physical and figurative borders of belonging seem natural.[7]

In this light, one programmatic theoretical and critical lesson we can draw from these case studies is to problematize border rhetorics as well as particular understandings of citizenship. This relates to the critical rhetorical approach I discussed in the introduction, which seeks to understand how truths are imbricated in power and language and how rhetorical and material conditions are ideologically grounded. Border rhetorics naturalize citizenship and civic identity and influence institutions, laws, and practices of exclusion and inclusion. But since borders and citizenship are situated, historical, and contingent, this means, crucially, that they are not natural. Our understandings of the boundaries of belonging, ideas about U.S. citizens and "illegal" immigrants, entrenched as they may be, are grounded in particular moments and serve ideological purposes: to remove border anxiety, to protect the exclusivity of U.S. identity, and/or to secure the interests of citizens from the supposed threat of new arrivals. Thus the critical task is to understand the ideological and historical groundings of border rhetorics and the ways that they make certain political and material conditions seem natural. Historicizing particular configurations of borders and citizenship is important in light of repeated efforts to rigidify those borders. In particular, tracing the rhetorical and historical constitution of borders and citizenship denaturalizes the physical and figurative boundaries that define and demarcate citizens and aliens. This entails exploring the interests these logics serve(d) in restricting citizenship to certain groups as well as the alternatives to accepted notions of borders and citizenship. In sum, because the border is rhetorical—in the sense that it is situated, pragmatic, and contingent—borders and/of citizenship are produced through rhetorical practices, in particular moments, and to serve practical, political, and ideological purposes.

As follows, a second insight I want to suggest is the importance of studying vernacular discourses, and Latina/o vernacular rhetorics in particular, as part of this critical project of denaturalizing and reimagining borders and citizenship. As I noted throughout the preceding chapters, border rhetorics draw the parameters and terms of belonging, but performing citizenship can redefine those borders and redraw the boundaries of the civic imaginary. Citizenship can represent a rhetorical practice of claiming belonging and recognition for those who are considered nonsubjects. It is often concluded that border rhetoric "all but *guarantees* an irredeemable non-place for the racialized, alienized, border-crossing migrant in the United States today."[8] Yet logics of citizenship can be productive in creating and redefining identities and social positions. Privileging questions concerning how Latina/os and migrants (as well as other minoritarian groups) are represented in dominant society and ignoring their vernacular discourses may contribute to the flawed perception that these groups are apolitical and/or "awakening."

Therefore, *The Border Crossed Us* has sought to attend to the efforts of migrant groups and Latina/os to challenge borders and redraw the nation in more inclusive ways. Latina/o vernacular discourses point to the role of border rhetoric and citizenship as both modes of subjectification (the making of national subjects) and as constitutive of subjectivity, or affirmative identity and agency within (or outside of) the nation-state. As part of the rhetorical project of denaturalizing borders and citizenship, scholars need to consider the interplay between dominant and vernacular appeals. This task represents the dimension of critical rhetoric that foregrounds and "voices" alternative logics as counterpoints to sedimented understandings of social imaginaries. To this end, the rhetorical moments demonstrate that conventions of U.S. citizenship and identity can be enacted as well as problematized through rhetorical performance. Another example from a different Latina/o context, as above, can illustrate the power of attention to vernacular discourse and to the role of Latina/o vernacular discourses in particular.

On January 3, 2012, the American Broadcasting Company (ABC) aired the pilot of its new television show *Work It*, a comedy in which two unemployed men dress as women to attain jobs at a pharmaceutical company. The show was universally panned by critics and canceled after a few episodes, but it also created significant controversy among lesbian, gay, bisexual, transgender, and queer (LGBTQ) communities as well as among Puerto Rican and Latina/o communities for its content. While LGBTQ groups objected to the concept of the show, which trivialized transgender issues and whitewashed workplace discrimination, Puerto Rican groups mounted opposition to the show based on a single joke from the pilot episode, in which the unemployed character Angel (played by Puerto Rican actor Amaury Nolasco), discussing his future employment prospects, stated, "I'm Puerto Rican. I'll be great at selling drugs." The comment caused a firestorm on social media and among bloggers, who criticized the show and ABC for such a disparaging joke. Many of those who objected to the joke on *Work It* argued that ABC had drawn on stereotypes of Puerto Ricans as racially, culturally, and economically aberrant in spite of their status as legal citizens within the United States.[9]

To combat such discourses, Puerto Ricans in New York organized the group Boricuas for a Positive Image and mounted protests and an organized social media campaign against ABC, demanding that the network apologize for its stereotyping of Puerto Ricans as drug dealers. These activists engaged in a vernacular discourse of citizenship, positioning themselves as full members of the nation while also engaging in strategic identification with Puerto Rican identity and nationalism. For example, one of the main slogans of the group, displayed in protests, on blogs, and distributed through social media, was "I'm Puerto Rican, and I do not sell drugs," which was accompanied by a display of the Puerto Rican flag. Through this simple rhetorical refutation, the group sought to denaturalize the images that contribute to Puerto Ricans' marginalization within the national community, to reaffirm their U.S. citizenship status, and to strategically deploy symbols of national identity as affirmations of political and cultural agency for Puerto Ricans. Its goal was both to refute the otherization of Puerto Ricans and (re)claim their status as U.S. citizens through identification. Meanwhile, through the use of the Puerto Rican flag these activists also engaged in strategic discourses of Puerto Rican nationalism that subtly affirmed a space of difference and cultural pride in the face of Puerto Rico's enduring colonial relationship to the United States. According to scholars such as Ana Yolanda Ramos-Zayas, this type of layered national performance has been used as a vernacular rhetorical strategy of Puerto Rican groups in similar contexts. The group's weekly protests in front of ABC offices and its public media campaign led ABC officials to issue a public apology and meet with members of the activist group to discuss the representation of Puerto Ricans and Latina/os on network television and in the television industry. The success of the Boricuas for a Positive Image in moving ABC to respond to the group's concerns also mobilized support from other Puerto Rican political organizations and Latina/o public figures and drew national media attention from the major news networks and online news sources.[10]

This brief example demonstrates the broader point that Latina/o vernacular discourses contest and constitute physical and figurative borders, rebordering the U.S. civic imaginary. Citizenship and civic identity are accessible to rhetorical struggle. This is not to deny, of course, that citizenship remains tied to legal categories and political status but only to recognize that these institutional dimensions of citizenship take shape only in relation to its reiteration and performance as a mode of identity. Vernacular discourses are not necessarily liberatory, for they can contribute to and sometimes work within those selfsame dominant logics they seek to challenge. In the case of the Boricuas for a Positive Image, this group did not necessarily challenge or expand the boundaries of the U.S. national imaginary in fundamental ways as much as it tried to foster an understanding of Puerto Ricans as both "normal" members of the national community and as inheritors of their own nationalist imaginary. As we have seen, this type of identificatory strategy can often reinforce exclusionary dimensions of belonging in other contexts.

Nevertheless, attention to vernacular discourse can highlight the constitution and contestation of belonging and citizenship. Accessing, voicing, and analyzing vernacular discourses of citizenship—the ways in which belonging is contested in the "everyday" rhetoric of counterpublics—is an important part of the critical rhetoric project. To borrow from Roderick A. Ferguson, if we view border rhetorics as aberrant rhetorical constructs, as I suggested above, this also means recognizing these discourses "as the sites of ruptures, critiques, and alternatives." Vernacular discourses can illuminate the evolution of borders, citizenship, and civic identity as well as the negotiation of identity and agency for minoritarian groups. As Ono and Sloop write, "[U]nless critical attention is given to vernacular discourse, no new concepts of how community relations are interwoven and how communities are contingent is possible."[11] Past vernacular discourses of citizenship such as those discussed in the preceding chapters can perhaps serve as rhetorical resources in contemporary struggles regarding border and immigration policy, citizenship rights, and national and cultural belonging. By foregrounding vernacular voices as part of a broader project of critically investigating borders and U.S. citizenship, we can contribute to recasting forms of belonging and explore alternatives to dominant ideologies.

With these insights in mind, the next section reflects on how the particular Latina/o vernacular discourses considered in this book enact agency and identity, or "voice," for Latina/os and Latina/o immigrants. According to Calafell and Holling, the concept of voice "calls attention to marginalized speaking subjects who rely upon distinct cultural forms as a means of self-assertion to reject and/or challenge oppressive social and political conditions."[12] The metaphor of voice presumes a verbalization that is grounded in embodiment and personal experience and that serves as a grounding for identity, expression, and agency. I will begin by discussing the lessons we can draw from this book about Latina/o voice, its potential, pitfalls, and possibilities. Latina/o discourse is not of one voice, but thinking about Latina/o voice and identity (Latinidad) through the insights of the preceding chapters provides a provisional perspective on political and rhetorical agency, or "voice," for Latina/o communities. Later, I expand the discussion beyond Latina/os to consider the applicability of these forms of voice, identity, and agency for other marginalized groups on the borders of belonging.

Latina/o Voice and Identity

The topic of Latina/o identity or Latina/o voice has long been vexing for scholars and political activists. The issue is expressed, among many ways, in an ongoing debate about terminology. Should these groups be referred to as Latina/os, Hispanics, or through their particular nationalities, such as Mexican, Cuban, or Guatemalan? What about more politically charged terms like Chicanos, La Raza, or Boricua? Is it even worth speaking of some sort of common term, let alone a pan-ethnic unity, among Latina/o groups? Several scholars have attempted to outline unifying elements that tie together diverse groups into some sort of Latina/o collective, elements that include a common language, common cultural traits, a similar history, and so forth. These shared experiences and characteristics are understood as providing a common denominator of Latina/o identity. However, other scholars argue that there is a danger in searching for such a universal or all-encompassing Latinidad, which risks overessentializing and abstracting Latina/o identity so much that it loses any significance.[13]

Despite these admonitions, in this section I engage the question of Latina/o voices and identities and the prospects for Latinidad, well aware of the possibilities for homogenization, essentialism, or overgeneralization but also aware of the productive possibility of such a form of political and cultural identity. Though in the next section I broaden this discussion beyond Latina/os to consider the possibilities of political and rhetorical agency for other marginalized groups, it is first important to address the specific question of Latina/o voice or identity, both because it is a vexing and persistent question for Latina/o scholars and also because questions of Latina/o identity implicate the broader possibility of identity politics in contemporary neoliberal society. That is, if Latina/o can be a strategic identification performatively employed for political and rhetorical purpose in spite of its challenges and in the face of the pressures to move beyond identity politics that characterize our supposedly "post-race" society, then perhaps a similar defense can be made of other forms of minoritarian identification in the public sphere.

The debates over Latina/o terminology and Latinidad mentioned above encapsulate the larger difficulties of identity politics and self-identification in contemporary neoliberal culture.[14] In this light, the debate over Latina/o identity represents the broader reaction against identity politics as a supposed "ideological fiction." A backlash against identity and identity politics (on the right and the left) contributes to the difficulty of speaking of identity in concrete political terms and occludes the fact that identity is a reality of social location and part of a potential program for liberation and social change. There is a disconnect between, on one hand, the supposed fragmentation and incoherence of the category "Latina/o" (or any identity category, for that matter) and, on the other hand, the "persistent meaningfulness" of "Latina/o" (and other such identifications) in contemporary society. Thus, despite claims to the contrary, racial, cultural, sexual, and gender identities—in this case "Latina/o"—continue to matter in the way society is organized and in the workings of institutional politics.[15]

The Latina/o vernacular rhetorics I have explored throughout this book point to both the productive potentials and the pitfalls of Latina/o identity and Latina/o voice. In particular, these case studies demonstrate that a focus on rhetorical and performative practice can also provide perspective on Latinidad as an inherently limited, protean, but also important identity category. Though the groups examined in previous chapters differed in their self-identifications (Californios, Mexican Americans, Chicana/os and Hispanos, and modern-day transnational migrants), they were all constructed, in the specific historical moment, as (non)subjects on the borders, that is, as displaced in relation to a racialized, gendered, and predetermined "center" of citizenship. These groups were defined through border rhetorics and in opposition to U.S. national identity as outside the bounds of the U.S. civic imaginary, unifying them in a struggle for citizenship in the face of racialization, nationalism, and colonialism. In the same way, Mexican Americans, Chicana/os, and Latina/os are regularly faced with the crossing of, over, under, and/or through borders, culturally, linguistically, figuratively, and physically; they often "find themselves," as Lisa Flores puts it, "with a foot in both worlds."[16] The historical and contemporary Latina/o discourses discussed in this book point to this fundamental struggle with and against border and citizenship rhetorics. Latina/os have been crossed by borders, defined by borders (of colonialism, racialization, gender, and so forth), and have sought *both* belonging in *and* distinctness from the borders of the U.S. civic imaginary.

Some might say that this notion of Latina/os as displaced by and contending with borders of race and gender, colonialism, culture, and migration has the tendency to universalize a Chicana/o experience onto all Latina/os. I should emphasize, though, that I am thinking here of border rhetorics in the broadest sense, as ways in which citizenship is demarcated through difference. The physical and figurative borders of territory, nation, and cultural community produce displacement and dislocation. As Edna Acosta-Belén and Carlos Santiago note, it is from the struggle of and living within this "displacement" and "dislocation" that "emerge the tensions, contradictions, and reconfigurations that influence and mold the construction of our contemporary Latina/o identities."[17] By trying to negotiate the tension of exclusion and inclusion endemic to U.S. citizenship, the vernacular discourses I have considered worked from and have illuminated the powerful but problematic position of "displacement" at the borders of belonging and the possibilities of vernacular discourses to create discursive and political space for Latina/os. In other words, border rhetorics displace Latina/os in U.S. society when they are positioned as a racialized, displaced group. This physical and cultural space (of displacement) also represents a potential rhetorical strategy for agency within and resistance of bordering logics. Latina/o vernacular discourses can represent efforts to displace the conventions and borders of citizenship.

In addition to the preceding chapters we could also look to the two examples I provided above, which demonstrate how dominant rhetorics displaced Puerto Ricans, who were otherwise full citizens, through gendered racialization and sexualization. Puerto Ricans were bordered outside of the U.S. civic imaginary, displaced from the space of citizen to that of other, and framed as less than full participants in the national imaginary. In both cases, rhetorical and performative practice provided avenues for reasserting these individuals' subjectivity and citizenship. Latina/os can be subjectified, or made into certain kinds of subjects (or, more likely, nonsubjects—what Ngai calls "impossible subjects," or those outside of the bounds of belonging) through discourses of citizenship, race, identity, and alienness.[18] These border rhetorics can constitute physical displacement, as is the case of the many elements of Latina/o diasporas, as well as cultural, social, and political displacement. At the same time,

Latina/o vernacular discourses provide opportunities to displace the borders of the civic imaginary and emplace particular Latina/o groups within the bounds of belonging. This is why, as a form of subjectification as well as a form of provisional subjectivity, Latinidad seems to remain a central component of our political and social organization despite the pitfalls it entails as an identity category.

The contrast or contradiction between the backlash against identity politics and the persistence of dominant logics of identity in public debates about citizenship and political rights points to the necessity of rearticulating identity through a logic that can provide for its flexibility and political significance. It is the persistence of these identity categories that demands their rearticulation as modes of solidarity, community, and agency for Latina/os (and other minoritarian groups). I see it as most productive to think of Latina/o identity in terms of performance and in relation to the state, community, and self. Viewing Latinidad as performative and strategic provides the possibility of political unity while maintaining the many differences within Latina/o voices; it affords the opportunity to reclaim a situated and contingent identity politics. As Calafell summarizes, "[P]erformance matters and identities matter, especially in the space of the everyday as people . . . negotiate power-laden terrains." Despite the dangers involved in identity politics, there is value in maintaining a performative or positional sense of "Latina/o." This view recognizes what Juan Poblete calls the "plurality of identification processes" of Latina/o groups, the rhetorical and performative practices that materialize provisional and contingent Latina/o identities but also tack between local and national forms of identification.[19] We saw in the preceding case studies that Latina/o groups moved between registers of racial, national, and cultural identification in a struggle with the realities of bordering and exclusion. In this way, the performance of a collective identity of solidarity can work in tandem with (or sometimes in opposition to) the exclusive discourses of nationalism and racial/cultural identity that seem to displace particular Latina/o communities.

As activists continue to mobilize for more humane immigration policy or more expansive rights for Latina/o communities, it is important to balance the particularities of Latina/o voices with the strategic essentialism of a larger Latina/o voice. This book suggests that a performative framework provides the best way to conceptualize this political and rhetorical process. The important thing that this approach would keep in mind is that articulations of "Latina/o" identity or community are as much an active process of invention as they are an attempt to draw out essential characteristics of Latina/os living in the United States. Rather than attempting to condense characteristics or conditions that unify Latina/o experience and provide a grounding for identity, this rhetorical and performative approach would see multiple and provisional Latina/o identities arising out of the moments in which they are crafted for political and cultural agency. Rather than eschewing the possibility of a Latinidad because of the dangers of essentialism or homogeneity, this rhetorical/performative approach would recognize all identity categories, including Latinidad, as contingent inventions and as sites of "necessary trouble" that can also be productively troubling.[20] Therefore, rhetorically constructing Latina/o identity or "voice" would demand a situational approach that took into account the possibilities and the problems of a unifying voice in the specific contexts that gave it rise. We would recognize how performative enactments of Latinidad could materialize certain affective and political connections between particular Latina/o groups and de-emphasize others. We would appreciate that these performative practices too would be subject to self-reflexive critical analysis.[21]

Rather than attempt to distill a list of certain characteristics that could compose Latinidad, I have emphasized provisional and strategic points of identification for Latina/o communities. In light of a persistent struggle with and against bordering practices and the exclusivity of U.S. citizenship, I have suggested a way of thinking about Latinidad as a strategic and provisional emplacement in response to the displacements wrought by logics of borders, citizenship, race, colonialism, and gender. Latina/o identities are performative, positional, and relational but, for those very reasons, hold the possibility of creating agency and challenging dominant modes of relating with publics and the state. Most important, affirming the possibility of Latina/o voice and voices (and those of other marginalized groups) could help to problematize the exclusive and exclusionary dimensions of our modern social imaginaries. To elaborate this point, the next section will illuminate several particular rhetorical and performative practices found within the preceding case studies that may materialize agency and identity for Latina/os and other minoritized groups that find themselves displaced within or outside the bounds of political, social, and cultural belonging.

Crossing and Contending with Borders

Throughout the book we have identified a number of common axes around which citizenship and belonging are drawn, including race, ethnicity, sex, gender, sexuality, and social class. Though in principle the United States may welcome those who are tired or poor or hungry or yearning to breathe free, in practice U.S. national belonging is a more contentious and oftentimes exclusionary process. The case studies I analyzed provide a window into how Latina/o groups enact and contend with national belonging in the absence of full symbolic and legal recognition. As presumptive racialized and gendered "foreigners" (or, at the very least, as not full citizens), many of these Latina/o groups I examined in the preceding chapters struggled to access the recognition and political agency that attend U.S. national belonging. Sometimes this struggle for belonging took shape through explicitly racialized dimensions, as in the Californios' attempts to move into whiteness and thus citizenship, while at other times the borders of belonging involved negotiation with intersecting coalitions and identity formations, as has been evident in contemporary Latina/o immigrant movements. By comparing these different vernacular discourses, we can outline their applicability as strategies for enacting and rebordering citizenship for other marginalized groups. In particular, I will suggest an overarching strategy by which marginalized groups simultaneously access and problematize conventions of borders and citizenship through performative enactments.

After the Mexican-American war, Mexican citizens were forcibly made U.S. Americans when the border literally crossed over them. Now "Americans," at least in purely legal terms, Californios found themselves living within and forced to assimilate into a foreign logic of civic belonging. Californios crafted a vernacular border rhetoric that performed citizenship but also sought to create slippage in the colonial and racial logics of U.S citizenship. Embracing but also subtly challenging dominant traditions of white, patriarchal U.S. citizenship, Californio delegates performed U.S. identity and negotiated entry into citizenship but also contested the racialized and colonial terms of belonging. However, as a form of agency this border rhetoric did not express enough disobedience to the colonial and racial logics that it was redeploying. The result was that, by struggling for inclusion within conventional categories of race, identity, and colonialism, Californios entrenched these selfsame borders and exclusions. It should not have been necessary for Californios to embrace these racial and colonial logics within their rhetorical enactments of citizenship; that they reified the exclusion of indios, mestizos, Afro-Mexicanos, and women was a testament to the Californios' willing or perhaps unwilling ignorance of the darker side of their own rhetorics of identity and agency. In this respect, though we might affirm their overall project—that of challenging border rhetorics while also seeking pragmatic political and social inclusion—we would be forced to reject the Californios' particular vernacular rhetorics of Latina/o identity and citizenship because they were blind to their own coloniality.

The Alianza Federal de Mercedes also performed a border rhetoric, enacting citizenship in tandem with its rejection. In contrast to that of the Californios, the Alianza's rhetoric oscillated between appeals to citizenship and foreignness, identification and ethnic separatism, civil rights and radical revolution. In response to the racial and cultural bordering of U.S. citizenship, the Alianza constructed a border rhetoric of its own that crossed borders and was betwixt and between the recognized traditions of U.S. citizenship. The aliancistas did not merely try to achieve a degree of recognition or acceptance within the boundaries of the civic imaginary, though that was certainly an element of their integrationist rhetoric. Rather, the Alianza enacted citizenship in tandem with its critique and eschewal, highlighting the exclusionary dimensions of the civic imaginary and gesturing toward a pan-ethnic and nationalist form of identification for Chicana/os and Latina/os (the new breed). In this sense, the Alianza's rhetoric was a direct response to the bordering that Mexican Americans had faced for over a century, and it demonstrates the possibilities but also the pitfalls of a vernacular discourse of citizenship and Latina/o identity. The Alianza's border rhetoric provided agency for Chicana/os and opened up avenues to an alternative paradigm of political and cultural belonging. However, the group also embraced a masculinized ethnic nationalism that marginalized Chicanas and reinforced some of the very essentializing and exclusionary elements of the national imaginary.

La Gran Marcha in Los Angeles on March 25, 2006, the largest of the year's nationwide protests, demonstrated a hybrid citizenship that fused multiple identities, nationalities, and traditions. Its vernacular discourse enacted citizenship but also transcended the binary between exclusion and inclusion by refuting the preeminence of single-nation-state identification. To borrow from Molina-Guzmán and Valdivia, the 2006 protests "render Eurocentric discourses of racial and national purity untenable, and challenge us to acknowledge the uneasy harnessing of transnational, hybrid, and gendered bodies."[22] As we saw, the reappropriation of hybridity within La Gran Marcha demonstrated how these Latina/o immigrant groups could redeploy the "hybrid" conditions that often lead to abjection as an opportunity to (re)border U.S. citizenship and national identity. La Gran Marcha integrated and created something new through its rhetorical and performative practices, but it also had its own limitations as a vernacular strategy of citizenship and Latina/o identity. For one, the reliance on discourses of hybridity entrenched problematic associations of Latina/os as racial and cultural hybrids despite efforts to redeploy these stereotypes. More important, La Gran Marcha's hybrid rhetoric was difficult to replicate and limited in its applicability as a political program for a broader community of marginalized people.

Likewise, the immigration movements I analyzed in chapter 4 are emblematic of hybrid rhetoric in form, content, and constituents. The body of protestors created an overall rhetoric of citizenship that embraced affective excess, cultural difference, and transnational political traditions under the banner of "No human being is illegal." As a vernacular rhetoric of borders, citizenship, and Latina/o identity, these protests demonstrated the possibility of belonging outside of the nation-state and of citizenship without assimilation. These movements provided subjectivity not just for migrants but for all the different constituents of the movement. "We are all immigrants," was a coalitional subjectivity that drew together immigrants and citizens and that centered migrant identity rather than making migration peripheral to citizenship. Instead of immigrants exclusively performing a demand for inclusion (drawing themselves into the bounds of the national imaginary), these contemporary protests featured nonimmigrants performing the role of the immigrant—claiming that they too were reasonably suspicious or "illegal." This succeeded in moving migrant identity from the periphery to the center of the public sphere and blurring the territorial, legal, and cultural boundaries of nation-state citizenship. These protests created a form of subjectivity through which migrants could not just claim belonging but through which all participants could claim migrant or "cosmopolitan" identity as a challenge to citizenship and as a form of identification with a shared common humanity. This rhetorical strategy also holds potential for a broader form of belonging that is "neither derivative of, nor separable from, the political dominance of U.S. nationalism."[23] Yet even in this case, the vernacular discourses discussed in the chapter had their own pitfalls that demand recognition, namely, the danger of migrant identity and illegality as a rhetorical and performative strategy in light of increasing border militarization as well as the limited applicability of these forms of identity to certain groups of Latina/os.

Though each moment was fraught with limitations, each chapter also illuminates distinct discursive strategies of contesting bordering logics. Though they range from political oratory and deliberation to social movement rhetoric and public protest, these chapters demonstrate the changing rhetorical form and content of Latina/o discourses of citizenship, performances of identity and agency that seek to negotiate the borders of belonging and citizenship. All remain legitimate modes of performing (and thus accessing) citizenship and inclusion into the national imaginary while also expanding these boundaries. Vernacular border rhetoric, for example, may provide the flexibility to migrate between and across modes of belonging and thus enact a differential mode of social movement. Performing hybridity can materialize a "homeland" or community that recognizes cultural fusion and the intersectionality of identity, and cosmopolitanism may hold within it the potential to expand understandings and practices of belonging. Each of these modes of agency authorizes a way to negotiate tensions of assimilation and exclusion and to affirm a space of identity. Whether these vernacular rhetorical strategies are specific to certain Latina/o groups, to the Latina/o context writ large, or even more broadly to other minoritarian groups struggling for political and cultural belonging is a question that I cannot hope to answer definitively here. However, there are certainly reasons to believe these particular vernacular rhetorical strategies may provide lessons that can apply to broader contexts.

One form of vernacular rhetoric that might have broader purchase is the performance of citizenship as a means of claiming belonging as well as challenging or expanding its exclusionary dimensions. Each of these case studies featured the rhetorical enactment of citizenship (particular to the time period and context) that constituted particular groups as citizens and contested the exclusionary borders of U.S. citizenship. Rhetorical theorists have long argued that public discourse is constitutive of self and other, and, in this vein, we see how constituting oneself as citizen through the public enactment of citizenship identity provides an avenue for agency and "voice" within the civic imaginary, even in the absence of formal recognition as a political and legal subject. While some scholars claim that citizenship increasingly loses its relevance as a political identity in a globalized, transnational world, this book argues for the persistent relevance of citizenship and borders when thought of, at least partly, as rhetorical and performative practices. Citizenship is a civic imaginary and thus is actively imagined, performed, and contested in concrete discourses. Whether found in grand civic rituals or the quotidian actions of citizen-subjects, citizenship is articulated through civic performances that constantly rearticulate the contours of U.S. civic identity. Both dominant and marginal visions of what it means to be a citizen are forwarded, staged, and negotiated through these rhetorical enactments. While citizenship can often take shape through its performative positioning against those whose difference excludes them from belonging, efforts by those who purportedly do not belong to access citizenship, at least in part, through rhetorical enactment bespeak its nonessentialized and performative dimension.

However, it should be clear from the preceding chapters that Latina/o groups did not just enact U.S. citizenship as a form of social inclusion; they also critiqued exclusionary dynamics of U.S. citizenship and rebordered the civic imaginary. In other words, though they lacked the power to change the parameters of U.S. citizenship outright, their performances of citizenship exposed the limits in the logics of national belonging, reshaping the boundaries of civic identity along the way. This process of contestation points to the fact that rhetorics of borders and citizenship can be undermined through disidentification, overdetermination, or appropriation. Since borders and citizenship are performative, the "stock characters" and roles of the U.S. civic imaginary can be adapted and appropriated to challenge the conventions of belonging. This process of performative reappropriation, incomplete and contingent as it is, and always taking shape within the logics laid out by dominant society, represents a process of subject making through which individuals can constitute provisional identity, agency, and community.[24]

Precisely because rhetorics of race, gender, sexuality, and other forms of social identity continue to define the landscape of contemporary citizenship for many minoritarian groups, not just Latina/os and immigrants, the case studies I analyzed here speak to the possibility of performatively reappropriating border and citizenship rhetorics as means of rebordering the civic imaginary. These citizenship enactments are more than just avenues toward cultural inclusion; they politically remake the parameters of citizenship and materialize new possibilities of belonging. They speak to the possibility of performative rhetorics of borders and citizenship to function as "outlaw discourse," negotiating material relations of power, placing into question particular ways of being, and remaking the boundaries of the civic imaginary.[25] Just as institutions use rhetoric as a tool of control and as a means for materializing the boundaries of the political and cultural community, so too can vernacular rhetorics break apart and rebuild material relationships of power.

Perhaps, in a similar way, other vernacular discourses may hold within them possibilities for challenging and reorienting societal practices, borders, and belonging. Perhaps this "writing" and rewriting of borders, citizenship, and belonging through performative enactments can "refuse" its colonization and marginalization "even as," to summon a quotation from Judith Butler in the preface of the book, it is "colonizing discourse [that] enables or produces this stumbling block, this resistance." In particular, could other instances of border, hybrid, or cosmopolitan rhetoric portend new relationships of belonging that elide the exclusionary politics of citizenship? Can citizenship be reimagined or rewritten by using, at least in part, the very terms that enable its bordering to begin with? Could it be that performative rhetorics of borders and citizenship, which materialize inclusion within but also problematize the boundaries of the national imaginary, represent a broader strategy of vernacular discourse beyond the particular Latina/o contexts I have discussed here? The discourses studied in this book perhaps may provide an entrée to contest the exclusionary logics behind national belonging in other contexts as well, keeping in mind that, as the above quotation suggests, the disruptive potential of these very performative rhetorics emanates from within the colonizing logics of borders and citizenship they seek to disrupt.

Critical Rhetoric and Political Futures

Throughout this book I have sought to follow Foucault's (and critical rhetoric's) call to analyze, elaborate, and bring into question power relations, in this case, surrounding borders and citizenship. As the quotation in the epigraph indicates, this scholarly project has also been a "political task" aiming to denaturalize particular and exclusionary borders and point to alternative possibilities for imagining belonging. Foucault states that this scholarly and political project would seek to identify the "agonism" (that is, the contestation) between power and "the intransitivity of freedom." In this vein, this book has analyzed and questioned the workings of power relationships surrounding citizenship, borders, and Latina/o identity in our society. Focusing on performances of citizenship enacted in both historical and contemporary discourses, I have elaborated the possibilities, however intransitive, for conditions of freedom within those vernacular rhetorics of borders, citizenship, and Latina/o identity.

I have argued for a critical rhetorical approach to rhetorics of borders and citizenship, one that can explore the rhetorical constitution of the civic imaginary and that can study the relationships between borders (both physical and figurative) and citizenship. An intertwining of Latina/o studies, citizenship studies, rhetorical/performance studies, and Latina/o communication studies has helped me to trace the practices of democratic citizenship and borders in Latina/o contexts. On the one hand, this interdisciplinary collaboration should demonstrate the importance of rhetoric and performance for those interested in borders, citizenship, and Latina/o identity, and on the other, it should illuminate the significance of Latina/o communication and Latina/o identity within the discipline of communication and rhetorical studies. Greater conversation between these subject areas can help to foster avenues of critical theory and praxis. A critical rhetoric project can be indispensable in the goal of understanding how borders and citizenship are constituted and sedimented into our political and cultural realities—not just as they persist but also as they are negotiated, contested, and reimagined. In sum, I hope this project provides impetus for continued struggles to denaturalize borders and reimagine the civic imaginary in more inclusive ways.

Here I have also ventured some conclusions about agency and identity politics not only for Latina/o communities but for marginalized groups struggling for political and social inclusion in the neoliberal moment. Certainly, within these historical and contemporary case studies we see strands or fragments from which social movements and activists perhaps can draw as they weave new tapestries of belonging and community. In this sense, perhaps this book could provide inspiration and a rhetorical toolbox for those struggling for belonging both in the "everyday" and in the political realm. Apart from the rhetorical strategies I have examined, general attention to how vernacular rhetoric both uses the colonial and challenges it simultaneously, doing so in part through activist performance, can help us think about how minoritarian groups claim belonging and construct new imaginaries of community belonging. At the very least, this book denaturalizes the exclusionary logics of borders and citizenship that structure the U.S. civic imaginary and foregrounds the voices of those subalternized subjects who are struggling for recognition. It provides a counterpoint to incessant heralding of a Latina/o "awakening" and proves that Latina/o communities have long been active subjects helping to craft U.S. identity, society, and culture.

The Border Crossed Us also demonstrates the importance of a rhetorical perspective on borders and U.S. citizenship. Certainly, the legal, political, social, and symbolic dimensions of U.S. citizenship prove enduringly important throughout history. Borders are undoubtedly material and legal constructs that divide communities and do real violence to people. But this project illustrates that borders and citizenship are about more than that. Borders are physical and figural; they divide and demarcate but also are emblematic of contact, crossing, and (thus) provide the possibility of crafting alternative cultural and political space. Citizenship, likewise, is more than just legal status or social contract; it is about enacting belonging, having voice, and being seen. Furthermore, borders and citizenship go hand in hand such that rhetorically invoking one constitutes the other. Bordering practices strengthen not only the physical boundaries of the nation but also the borders of belonging (citizenship). Expanding or contracting citizenship implicates the parameters of the national imaginary and represents a (re)bordering practice. These dimensions of borders and citizenship (as well as, in many cases, their material and institutional dimensions) are accessed and remade through discourse. Attention to rhetorics of borders and citizenship is central to understanding how the national imaginary is materialized and contested. This attention can inform prevalent debates about public participation and the future of U.S. democracy, recognizing that enactments of citizenship materialize new possibilities of legal or civic belonging.

It may seem that, in this book, my task has been to provide cause for optimism about borders and citizenship, partly because of my focus on liberal, vernacular discourses. This might lead the reader to believe that I am heralding the pluralization of the civic imaginary. Yet as one door opens, others close. With increased recognition have also come stereotyped and marginalized representations of Latina/os in media, public debate, and political rhetoric. Along with more power and prestige has come an increase in hate crimes, extremism, and anti-Latina/o, anti-immigrant initiatives at the state and local level.[26] These events are merely manifestations of enduring contradictions and conflicts in U.S. citizenship. This interplay between bordering practices and challenges to those practices represents the engine that drives the evolution of the U.S. national imaginary.

The persistence of this contestation between competing ideas of borders and citizenship reminds us of Foucault's statement about the "'agonism' between power relations and the intransitivity of freedom." The focus of this book has been the analysis and critique of this contestation between borders and citizenship, between restriction and freedom. The process of critically interrogating rhetorics of borders and citizenship is daunting and never complete, yet this is a "political task." This is true not only for activists who are engaged with the ever-shifting dimensions of power but also for scholars seeking to understand the construction of national, racial, and cultural identities and the possibilities of new political futures. This political task is relevant not only for those interested in questions of borders and citizenship in Latina/o contexts and communities but also for all of those interested in listening to alternative voices and entertaining new imaginaries. Exploring the rhetorics of borders and citizenship, denaturalizing borders, and voicing vernacular rhetorics—these form a necessary project that is worth undertaking not only by and for those groups on the borders but for all those who long for more expansive and enduring dimensions of belonging.

Notes

Preface

1. Calafell and Holling, introduction, xvi.

2. On the history of these terms, see Oboler, *Ethnic Labels, Latino Lives*. My original preference was to use the term "Latin@" throughout the book because the "@" is meant to achieve gender subversion by breaking down the strict dichotomy between masculine and feminine that is implicated in the "a/o" of "Latina/o." However, I have been persuaded by the editorial staff at The University of Alabama Press to use "Latina/o" instead, to prevent problems with the listing and searching of the book in online databases that could be posed by using the "@" sign. This terminological choice elicited much deliberation and discussion, and it has demonstrated to me the need for continued scholarship on Latina/o identities so as to influence the broader academic community to consider the theoretical, conceptual, and terminological issues involved in this research.

3. The obvious exception will be when quoted material renders Spanish words or phrases in italics. For further discussion of this issue, see Holling and Calafell, "Tracing the Emergence of Latin@ Vernaculars in the Studies of Latin@ Communication."

Introduction

1. Chavez, *The Latino Threat*; Cisneros, "Contaminated Communities"; Cisneros, "(Re)Bordering the Civic Imaginary"; DeChaine, "Bordering the Civic Imaginary"; Lyall, "Vigilante State"; Pantoja, Menjívar, and Magaña, "The Spring Marches of 2006."

2. Anguiano and Chávez, "Dreamers' Discourse"; Shahani and Greene, "Local Democracy on ICE"; Varsanyi, "Rescaling the 'Alien.'"

3. I could cite examples of anxiety surrounding borders and immigration in news and entertainment media, in political debates about health care and the economy, and even in concerns about race, ethnicity, and "national culture." See Chavez, *The Latino Threat*; Goldberg, *The Threat of Race*.

4. DeChaine, "Introduction," 1.

5. See Brady, "Border"; Balibar, "At the Borders of Citizenship." This distinction between the border as a place (as a physically real location) and a space (as a figurative and discursive locus) is drawn from Michel de Certeau's distinction between space and place in *The Practice of Everyday Life*, 117–18. For a discussion of borders and citizenship as both spaces and places, see Córdova, "*Nuestro Himno* as Heterotopic Mimicry."

6. Anzaldúa, *Borderlands/La Frontera*, 3, vii. Perhaps more important, Anzaldúa advances a notion of borderlands as productive spaces of identity and agency that has heavily influenced a number of related theories discussed and deployed in this book, including the idea of "border thinking," differential consciousness, and hybridity theory. I will return to this aspect of Anzaldúa's theory in chapter 1.

7. Saldívar, *Border Matters*, xii. Saldívar's book offers one of the definitive explorations of the physical and figurative border from a Chicana/o perspective. His analysis traces the border in a variety of discourses, including literature, film, music, and politics—as a contact zone where culture and power clash and where identity and agency are forged. See also Saldívar, "On the Bad Edge of *La Frontera*"; Saldívar, "Unsettling Race, Coloniality, and Caste"; Saldívar, *Trans-Americanity*.

8. Ono, "Borders That Travel," 21. See also Aldama, "Millennial Anxieties."

9. For a review of some of the many different trajectories of citizenship studies, see Bloemraad, Korteweg, and Yurdakul, "Citizenship and Immigration"; Klusmeyer, introduction; Shafir, "Introduction."

10. Social imaginaries, as Dilip Gaonkar summarizes, "are ways of understanding the social that become social entities themselves, mediating collective life." Gaonkar, "Toward New Imaginaries," 4. On social imaginaries see also Enck-Wanzer, "Decolonizing Imaginaries"; and Taylor, *Modern Social Imaginaries*. The now-classic formulation of this argument regarding citizenship and national identity as imaginaries is Anderson's *Imagined Communities*, in which he traces the development of nationalism as the dominant way that we imagine political and cultural community.

11. Bloemraad, Korteweg, and Yurdakul, "Citizenship and Immigration," 156. For an explanation of these overlapping and conflicting dimensions of citizenship, see Miller, *Cultural Citizenship*, chapter 2.

12. For two elaborations of this view, see Kymlicka, "Multicultural Citizenship"; and Rosaldo, "Cultural Citizenship."

13. Castles and Davidson, *Citizenship and Migration*; Del Castillo, "Illegal Status and Social Citizenship"; William V. Flores and Benmayor, *Latino Cultural Citizenship*; Johnston, "The Emergence of Transnational Citizenship"; Aihwa Ong, *Flexible Citizenship*.

14. Bennett, *Banning Queer Blood*, 7.

15. Bosniak, *The Citizen and the Alien*, 1–2, 31.

16. On "alienization," see DeChaine, "Bordering the Civic Imaginary."

17. Beasley, *You, the People*, 5.

18. DeChaine, "Introduction," 3.

19. Though I am referring here to rhetoric as a specific mode of discourse that is situated, public, and persuasive, I also view rhetoric as a perspective taken toward all discourse insofar as all reality is representational and contains constitutive force. See McGee, "Text, Context, and the Fragmentation of Contemporary Culture." For a useful primer on rhetoric, see Bizzell and Herzberg, *The Rhetorical Tradition*.

20. Examples of the broadening of the rhetorical perspective include Biesecker and Lucaites, *Rhetoric, Materiality, and Politics*; Goodale, *Sonic Persuasion*; Olson, Finnegan, and Hope,

Visual Rhetoric; Selzer and Crowley, *Rhetorical Bodies*. For an elaboration of the roots of rhetoric in public address, see Murphy, "Theory and Public Address."

21. Conquergood, "Rethinking Elocution"; Gunn, "On Speech and Public Release." Notwithstanding the important differences between a rhetorical act and a performance, in this book I draw on both performance studies and rhetorical studies to continue to develop the affinities between those two allied disciplines. In the chapters to follow, rhetoric and performance help to define the parameters and operations of borders and citizenship as they are enacted in and through discourses. For more on the connections between rhetoric and performance, see Calafell, *Latina/o Communication Studies*; Holling and Calafell, "Identities on Stage and Staging Identities"; Gencarella and Pezzullo, *Readings on Rhetoric and Performance*; Pezzullo, "Resisting 'National Breast Cancer Awareness Month.'"

22. Burke, *A Rhetoric of Motives*.

23. Asen, "A Discourse Theory of Citizenship," 203–4. Other examples of this approach include Bennett, *Banning Queer Blood*; Cisneros, "(Re)Bordering the Civic Imaginary"; Dickinson, "Selling Democracy"; Isin and Nielsen, *Acts of Citizenship*; Miller, "Culture, Dislocation, and Citizenship"; Ray, "The Permeable Public"; Ray and Richards, "Inventing Citizens, Imagining Gender Justice."

24. Berlant, "Citizenship," 38; emphasis added. See also Berlant, *The Queen of America Goes to Washington City*, 20.

25. DeChaine, "Introduction," 3. See also Enck-Wanzer, "Tropicalizing East Harlem"; Julia R. Johnson, "Bordering as Social Practice"; Ono, "Borders That Travel."

26. Ono and Sloop, *Shifting Borders*, 5. Ono and Sloop's important book examines the public debate surrounding California Proposition 187, a 1994 ballot initiative that banned social services for undocumented immigrants. Analyzing news media rhetoric, political discourse, and the anti–Proposition 187 rhetoric on listservs and alternative media, they map the contesting "logics," or understandings, of the border and citizenship and how these discourses imagine the border between U.S. citizens and "aliens" in more or less restrictive ways. These logics, argue Ono and Sloop, entail more or less humane identifications for U.S. citizens and immigrants and more or less expansive boundaries on U.S. civic identity.

27. Julia R. Johnson, "Bordering as Social Practice," 35. My understanding of borders and citizenship as performative draws heavily on Judith Butler's theory of performativity, which entails that identity is nonessentialized and constituted through its performance in a stylized repetition of acts. The performance of identity, whether gender, race, or, in this case, citizenship, operates within constraints of sedimented roles and norms, bodies, and materiality. Performativity entails citationality, the ability to rewrite and stylize these norms into more expansive options of identity and agency. Butler, *Gender Trouble*; Madison and Hamera, "Performance Studies at the Intersections." On borders, citizenship, and performance, see also Calafell, "Love, Loss, and Immigration"; Cisneros, "Looking 'Illegal'"; Goltz and Pérez, "Borders without Bodies"; Joseph, *Nomadic Identities*; McKinnon, "Citizenship and the Performance of Credibility," On the connection between rhetoric and performance, see note 21 above.

28. As this sentence should make clear, my approach to borders and citizenship works from the broad, meta-theoretical perspective within rhetorical studies known as "critical rhetoric."

Influenced by post-structural theory and cultural studies, critical rhetoric focuses on the analysis and critique of public discourse as it implicates power relationships. Michael G. Lacy and Kent A. Ono explain that critical rhetoric "seeks to understand discourse and its effectivity, especially the way that power operates to constitute subjects through discourse." Lacy and Ono, introduction, 4. The goal of critical rhetoric is first to examine how rhetoric constructs dominant ideologies, subjectivities, and material realities; and second to explore alternative voices that can problematize and/or pluralize these common ways of knowing and being. On critical rhetoric, see Ono and Sloop, *Shifting Borders*; Lacy and Ono, *Critical Rhetorics of Race*; McKerrow, "Critical Rhetoric"; Sloop, *Disciplining Gender*. For critical rhetorical studies of borders and citizenship, see Cisneros, "Contaminated Communities"; Cisneros, "(Re)Bordering the Civic Imaginary"; DeChaine, "Bordering the Civic Imaginary"; Chávez, "Border (In)Securities"; Hasian and Delgado, "Trials and Tribulations of Racialized Critical Rhetorical Theory."

29. On this broader point, see especially the essays in DeChaine's edited collection *Border Rhetorics*.

30. As critical rhetorician John M. Sloop puts it, "[T]he discourse of power itself [is] material." Sloop, *Disciplining Gender*, 18. For more on this point, see Ono and Sloop, *Shifting Borders*.

31. Beasley, *Who Belongs in America?*; Chávez, "Border Interventions"; Demo, "Sovereignty Discourse and Contemporary Immigration Politics"; Hasian and McHendry, "The Attempted Legitimation of the Vigilante Civil Border Patrols"; Inda, *Targeting Immigrants*. For historical studies of borders, citizenship, and subjectivity, see Ngai, *Impossible Subjects*; Smith, *Civic Ideals*; Schudson, *The Good Citizen*. On the racialized, gendered, and classed dimensions of U.S. citizenship, see Berlant, *The Queen of America Goes to Washington City*; Haney-López, *White by Law*. While the category of the citizen is a central focus in this book, I do not intend to endorse a normative ideal of citizenship as universality. This is because, as Roderick A. Ferguson notes, "The universality of the citizen exists in opposition to the intersecting particularities that account for material existence, particularities of race, gender, class, and sexuality." Ferguson, *Aberrations in Black*, 12. Normative discourses of citizenship themselves can function as modes of bordering who belongs and who does not. Thus my goal is to explore different formations of the citizen-subject, who is defined as citizen, and how those subjectivities are both enabling and constraining.

32. Aihwa Ong, "Cultural Citizenship as Subject-Making," 737–38. This argument is evocative of Michel Foucault's statement about the fluidity and contestation of power. He writes, "Where there is power, there is resistance, and yet, or rather consequently, this resistance is never in a position of exteriority in relation to power" but rather "can only exist in the strategic field of power relations." Foucault, *The History of Sexuality*, 1:95–96.

33. Inda, *Targeting Immigrants*, 8. On subjectivation as both empowering and constraining, see Foucault, "The Subject and Power." On governmentality, see Foucault, "Governmentality."

34. Isin, "Theorizing Acts of Citizenship," 18.

35. Condit and Lucaites, *Crafting Equality*; Brouwer, "ACT-ing UP in Congressional Hearings"; Terrill, *Malcolm X*; Ray, "The Rhetorical Ritual of Citizenship"; Ray and Richards, "In-

venting Citizens, Imagining Gender Justice"; Wilson, "The Racial Politics of Imitation in the Nineteenth Century."

36. According to Gerard A. Hauser, vernacular discourse describes "the vast and complicated terrain across which social actors converse with assertions, challenges, and invitations to create social meaning." Hauser contrasts vernacular expressions to institutional discourses and focuses on how publics, public opinion, and democracy work through "everyday dialogue of symbolic interactions" through which people "share and contest attitudes, beliefs, values, and opinions." Hauser, *Vernacular Voices*, 7, 36, 99. Following Hauser, I am suggesting that counterpublic groups constitute, reify, and/or challenge ideas and material realities of borders and citizenship through their "everyday" rhetoric, just as institutional, legal, or cultural discourses materialize borders and citizenship.

37. This is what critical rhetoric scholars Ono and Sloop refer to as a "commitment to telos," or an attempt "to imagine new ways of constructing the world, and to replace the logic of dichotomies [such as citizen vs. alien] with alternatives." Ono and Sloop, "Commitment to Telos," 50.

38. As Raymond Rocco explains this point, "[T]he current pattern of politics of contestation over citizenship in Latino/a communities has been framed and shaped by the modes of exclusion [and incorporation] that were established during [this] period." Rocco, "Transforming Citizenship," 305.

39. Amaya, "Dying American; or, The Violence of Citizenship," 12. On Mexican Americans and U.S. citizenship, see Acuña, *Occupied America*; De Genova, "Introduction"; Gómez, *Manifest Destinies*. On Puerto Ricans and the imposition of citizenship, see Córdova, "The Incomplete Subject of Colonial Memory"; Ramos-Zayas, *National Performances*; Thomas, "'How They Ignore Our Rights as American Citizens.'"

40. Schmidt Camacho, *Migrant Imaginaries*, 24. See also De Genova, *Racial Transformations*; Lisa A. Flores, "Constructing Rhetorical Borders."

41. Juan González, *Harvest of Empire*, 129. See also Daniels, *Coming to America*, chapter 15.

42. Hasian and Delgado, "Trials and Tribulations of Racialized Critical Rhetorical Theory," 257.

43. To say that Latina/os and U.S. citizenship have been "racialized" means that these identities took shape through a socio-historical and rhetorical process of subject formation (the creation of subjects) involving dimensions of racial meaning and hierarchy mapped onto social relations. In this case, Mexican Americans and Latina/os were racialized and thus defined outside the bounds of the (white) U.S. civic imaginary. On racialization, see Omi and Winant, *Racial Formation*. On Latina/o racialization, see De Genova and Ramos-Zayas, *Latino Crossings*; Haney-López, *White by Law*; Oboler, *Ethnic Labels, Latino Lives*.

44. Chavez, *Covering Immigration*; DeChaine, "Bordering the Civic Imaginary"; Lisa A. Flores, "Constructing Rhetorical Borders"; Lisa A. Flores, "Constructing National Bodies"; De Genova, "Migrant 'Illegality' and Deportability in Everyday Life"; Santa Ana, *Brown Tide Rising*; Ono and Sloop, *Shifting Borders*; Mehan, "The Discourse of the Illegal Immigration Debate."

45. According to Leo Chavez, a "Latino threat narrative" is prevalent in mass media and political rhetoric and takes shape through concerns about Latina/o population growth and

fertility, the supposed decline of the English language and U.S. culture, and the continual concerns about the Latina/o "sleeping giant." Chavez, *Latino Threat*. Perhaps the clearest example here is Samuel P. Huntington's infamous article "The Hispanic Challenge," in which he argues that "Hispanics" represent "the single most immediate and most serious challenge to America's traditional identity" because of immigration and demographic pressures but also because of their un-American and unassimilable language and culture. Samuel P. Huntington, "The Hispanic Challenge," *Foreign Policy*, March 1, 2004, http://www.foreignpolicy.com/articles/2004/03/01/the_hispanic_challenge (accessed February 28, 2012).

46. On representations of Latina identity, see Calafell, "In Our Own Image?"; Molina-Guzmán, *Dangerous Curves*; Molina-Guzmán and Valdivia, "Brain, Brow, and Booty."

47. Aparicio and Chávez-Silverman, introduction; Calafell, *Latina/o Communication Studies*; Dávila, *Latino Spin*; Valdivia, *Latina/o Communication Studies Today*. For further discussion of this "sleeping giant" trope, see Allatson, *Latino Dreams*, 50–51.

48. Butler, "Imitation and Gender Insubordination," 312.

49. Stan Steiner argues that it was adapted from "We didn't come to America, America came to us," an earlier slogan popular among Chicano and Native American movements of the 1960s and 1970 (a slogan that has obvious parallels to Malcolm X's famous statement, "We didn't land on Plymouth Rock, my brothers and sisters—Plymouth Rock landed on us"). Others trace the saying to the protests and demonstrations in 1994 against California's anti-immigrant state ballot initiative, Proposition 187. See Martinez, "Fighting 187," 29; Steiner, *La Raza*, 14. In addition to protest movements, "We didn't cross the border, the border crossed us" appears in a variety of other cultural contexts, from songs to films: for example, as lyrics in the 2001 song "Somos Más Americanos" (We Are More American) by Grammy-award winning Mexican band Los Tigres del Norte and as a battle cry by the character Sartana Rivera (played by Jessica Alba), an immigration enforcement officer turned revolutionary, in the 2010 action film *Machete* by Mexican American filmmaker Robert Rodriguez. It should be obvious that I do not intend to conflate my voice and experience with those that I analyze in this book by drawing myself into this "us."

50. According to Jeanne Fahnestock, a "'corrective' *antimetabole*" describes a phrase in which "one half has a negative term (*not*), so the form says in effect, 'It's not A . . . B, but B . . . A.'" The most famous example of this type of antimetabole may be President John F. Kennedy's phrase delivered during his presidential inaugural address, "Ask not what your country can do for you; ask what you can do for your country." In this example we can see the way that antimetabole argues through rhetorical reversal. "The form itself," writes Fahnestock, "epitomizes, or expresses iconically, the connection between the two key terms" and enacts the argumentative reversal, refuting one viewpoint and advancing another. See Fahnestock, *Rhetorical Style*, 234–35.

51. Ono and Sloop, "The Critique of Vernacular Discourse," 20. See also Holling, "Forming Oppositional Social Concord"; Sloop and Ono, "Out-law Discourse"; Ono and Sloop, *Shifting Borders*.

52. Foucault, *"Society Must Be Defended,"* 7.

53. See Hauser, *Vernacular Voices*, especially chapters 1 and 4.

54. Fahamisha Patricia Brown, *Performing the Word*, 2. See Baker, *Blues, Ideology, and Afro-American Literature*, introduction.

55. Ono and Sloop, *Shifting Borders*, 14. See also Holling, "Forming Oppositional Social Concord."

56. Holling and Calafell, "Tracing the Emergence of Latin@ Vernaculars in the Studies of Latin@ Communication," 21.

57. Communication scholars have identified and explored Puerto Rican, Chicana/o, Mexican American, and Latina/o vernacular discourses in a variety of contexts. For example, a number of studies of political rhetoric or Latina/o social movements outline vernacular rhetorical strategies that define Latina/o identity and challenge social exclusion. Anguiano and Chávez, "DREAMers' Discourse"; Cisneros, "(Re)Bordering the Civic Imaginary"; Córdova, "*Nuestro Himno* as Heterotopic Mimicry"; Enck-Wanzer, "Trashing the System"; Enck-Wanzer, "Gender Politics, Democratic Demand and Anti-essentialism in the New York Young Lords"; Enck-Wanzer, "Decolonizing Imaginaries"; Scholz, "Hablando por (Nos)Otros, Speaking for Ourselves"; Sowards, "Rhetorical Agency as *Haciendo caras*"; Sowards, "Rhetorical Functions of Letter Writing." Others explore Latina/o vernaculars in media discourses or in the performances of Latina/o artists and writers, arguing that through decolonial performance practices, these rhetorics engage and challenge dominant discourses of Latina/o racialization and illegality. Avant-Mier, "Of Rocks and Nations"; Calafell, *Latina/o Communication Studies*; Calafell and Delgado, "Reading Latina/o Images"; Delgado, "When the Silenced Speak"; Garza, "The Rhetorical Legacy of *Coyolxauhqui*"; Alberto González, "Listening to Our Voices"; Holling and Calafell, "Identities on Stage and Staging Identities"; Moreman and Calafell, "Buscando Para Nuestra Latinidad"; Rivera-Servera, "Exhibiting Voice/Narrating Migration"; Sowards and Pineda, "*Latinidad* in *Ugly Betty*"; Westgate, "When Sexual Becomes Spiritual." For an extensive review and bibliography of the scholarship on Latina/o vernacular discourse and Latina/o communication, see Holling and Calafell, "Tracing the Emergence of Latin@ Vernaculars in the Studies of Latin@ Communication."

58. I draw this idea of performative reappropriation generally from the work of Butler and specifically (in the Latina/o context) from that of José Esteban Muñoz and Bernadette Marie Calafell. Calafell, *Latina/o Communication Studies*; Muñoz, *Disidentifications*. For further discussion of Butler's notion of appropriation, see Shugart, "Counterhegemonic Acts."

59. Calafell and Holling, introduction, viii.

60. For further discussion of rhetorical criticism as performance, see Dow, "Criticism and Authority in the Artistic Mode"; McKerrow, "Critical Rhetoric"; Ono and Sloop, "The Critique of Vernacular Discourse."

61. Holling and Calafell, "Tracing the Emergence of Latin@ Vernaculars in the Studies of Latin@ Communication," 25.

62. Solnit, *Storming the Gates of Paradise*, 76.

Chapter 1

1. Griswold del Castillo, *The Treaty of Guadalupe Hidalgo*, xii; Anzaldúa, *Borderlands/La Frontera*, 3.

2. The relevant portion of the treaty dealing with citizenship is article 8, which provided Mexican citizens the choice of whether to take on American citizenship or retain their Mexican citizenship, but if the choice was not made within a year all Mexican citizens would thenceforth be considered American citizens. Article 9 called on the federal government to grant citizenship to all those Mexicans who chose to accept it, and extended rights and protections to those newly assimilated Mexicans.

3. Anzaldúa, *Borderlands/La Frontera*, vii, 79. Anzaldúa calls the in-between space of the borderlands "nepantla" and the new identity to which it gives rise the "new mestiza." See Alarcón, "Traddutora, Traditora"; Anzaldúa and Keating, *This Bridge We Call Home*; Quiñonez, "Re(Riting) the Chicana Postcolonial." Following Anzaldúa's path-breaking work, one vein of scholarship on which I will draw in this chapter conceives of the border as a material and cultural space with(in) which Mexican Americans as well as other Latina/os have lived and struggled in the context of U.S. citizenship and identity. Aldama and Quiñonez, *Decolonial Voices*; Amoore and Hall, "Border Theatre"; Schmidt Camacho, *Migrant Imaginaries*; Ramirez, "Toward a Borderlands Ethics." A second and broader yet related view, which I also draw upon in this chapter, builds upon Anzaldúa's notion of borderlands as productive spaces of identity and agency to theorize decoloniality and decolonial thinking beyond Latina/o contexts. Mignolo, *Local Histories/Global Designs*; Saldívar, *Trans-Americanity*; Sandoval, *Methodology of the Oppressed*.

4. Throughout this chapter, I use the term "Californios" to refer to native Mexican Californians because that was the term that they generally used and preferred at the time. When I refer more specifically to "indigenous" (precolonial) societies of California I use that term, or I use the term "indio" (the Spanish term at the time) or its translation "Indian." I refer to "U.S. American" immigrants to California by that term or as "Anglo-Americans" or "Anglos" rather than "Euro-American" or "white" (even though many U.S. Americans were not of Anglo-Saxon descent, such as Irish Americans) to distinguish them from the Californios, many of whom also traced their lineage to Europe and identified as white. Readers should not confuse my use of these terms for an unproblematic endorsement of them. For a more in-depth discussion of the complexities of this terminology, see, Heidenreich, *"This Land Was Mexican Once,"* 7–8.

5. Murphy, "The Language of the Liberal Consensus," 136. My analysis in this chapter draws upon the perspective of rhetorical history. For more on this approach, see Zarefsky, "Four Senses of Rhetorical History."

6. Mignolo, "Philosophy and the Colonial Difference," 82; Mignolo, *Local Histories/Global Designs*, 25.

7. Maldonado-Torres, "On the Coloniality of Being," 243.

8. Grosfoguel, "The Epistemic Decolonial Turn," 219. See also Grosfoguel, "Transmodernity, Border Thinking, and Global Coloniality." In fact, Anibal Quijano argues that modernity itself is tied to and constituted by coloniality so that they are two sides of the same coin. In other words, our modern ideas about identity (race, gender, sexuality, and class), citizenship, humanity, civilization, knowledge, and progress were/are defined through (epistemic and ontological) coloniality. Quijano, "Coloniality and Modernity/Rationality."

9. Stuart Hall, "When Was the 'Post-colonial'?" 248. The relationship between postcolo-

nial theory and coloniality theory is complex and controversial. While some coloniality theorists see themselves as enacting a radical break with postcolonialism, others try to dialogue with postcolonial theory. On this question, I generally agree with Walter Mignolo, who sees postcolonial theory and coloniality theory as "complementary trajectories with similar goals of transformation" that emerge from "different geneolog[ies] of thought." Throughout the chapter I will draw on both theories when relevant, in the spirit of embracing multiple "decolonial options." Mignolo, *The Darker Side of Western Modernity*, xxvi–xxvii. For a different take on this theoretical debate, see Enck-Wanzer, "Decolonizing Imaginaries."

10. Gómez, *Manifest Destinies*, 51. As Douglas Monroy argues, colonial Mexico saw the coexistence of an obsession about racial purity and classification with the officially sanctioned practice of "racial mixing." Monroy, "Guilty Pleasures." For a discussion of the links between coloniality, racialization, and gender, see Schiwy, "Decolonization and the Question of Subjectivity."

11. Fisher and O'Hara, "Introduction," 5.

12. Tavárez, "Legally Indian," 81. See also Almaguer, *Racial Fault Lines*.

13. Mignolo, "Delinking," 479. See Maldonado-Torres, *Against War*. Though it is out of the specific purview of this chapter, coloniality and racialization stemming from Spanish colonial society bear a brief mention here, especially because many elements of Spanish coloniality persisted after Mexican independence. Tomás Almaguer argues that the distinctions between "heathen" or "savage" and "Christian" or "civilized" "provided [the Spanish] ideological basis for a social order that stigmatized the Indian population." Almaguer, *Racial Fault Lines*, 21. This ideology of coloniality was reflected in and helped shape political/economic conditions of colonialism in the Spanish colonies. For example, the Franciscan missions, some of the earliest Spanish settlements in California, served as the primary tool of Christianizing, Hispanicizing, and thus subjugating the indigenous population. Similarly, the "hacienda-peon" system of Spanish colonial society, which relied on the indentured servitude or even slavery of indigenous people tied to large and wealthy landowners, was justified using the coloniality of knowledge about indigenous people as supposedly heathen, inferior, or uncivilized. Heizer and Almquist, *The Other Californians*, 5–18.

14. Quijano, "Coloniality," 169.

15. Morelli, "Entre el Antiguo y el Nuevo Régimen." For further discussion of post-independence Mexican citizenship reforms, see Guerra, "Mexico from Independence to Revolution"; Herzog, *Defining Nations*; Reina, Servín, and Tutino, "Introduction."

16. Menchaca, *Recovering History, Constructing Race*, 163. See also Almaguer, *Racial Fault Lines*; Heizer and Almquist, *The Other Californians*; Fisher and O'Hara, "Introduction"; Monroy, "Guilty Pleasures"; Pitt, *Decline of the Californios*; Tavárez, "Legally Indian."

17. Menchaca, *Recovering History, Constructing Race*, 156; Monroy, "Guilty Pleasures," 38–39. This process of whitening, or blanqueamiento, was true throughout Latin America, where race served as a crucial issue in the negotiation of national identity in the wake of independence from Spanish colonialism. Spickard, *Race and Nation*.

18. Quijano, "Coloniality," 169. The concept of gente de razón in particular entrenched ideas of Western knowledge as universal, Western subjects as the only rational beings capable

of subjectivity, and all other societies/civilizations as uncivilized. Mexican citizenship still relied on intersecting and exclusionary elements of race, gender, and social class, through the norm of the white, reasonable, masculine, and upper-class criollo person of reason.

19. Gabriel Gutiérrez, "Affirmative Action of the First Kind," 17.

20. Grosfoguel, "The Epistemic Decolonial Turn," 215. Heizer and Almquist's *The Other Californians*, for example, provides ample documentation and historical evidence of the oppression and abuse faced by freed Indians and mestizos despite citizenship pronouncements. Freedom and economic mobility were still difficult to attain, and "by 1846," a select group of families "of substance, influence, or political power ruled California." Pitt, *Decline of the Californios*, 10.

21. Robinson, *Land in California*, 59. For a historical survey, see Goodwin, *The Establishment of State Government in California, 1846–1850*, chapter 1.

22. Smith, *Civic Ideals*, 242, 198. Recent research on nineteenth-century U.S. identity illuminates these racialized and gendered dimensions. Altschuler and Blumin, "Limits of Political Engagement in Antebellum America"; Wander, Martin, and Nakayama, "Whiteness and Beyond."

23. Monroy, "Guilty Pleasures," 47; Almaguer, *Racial Fault Lines*, 54. Further discussion of the racialization of Californios and other Mexicans by U.S. settlers can be found in Gómez, *Manifest Destinies*; Heidenreich, *"This Land Was Mexican Once"*; Menchaca, *Recovering History, Constructing Race*.

24. Saldívar, *Trans-Americanity*, xiv. Saldívar uses the term "Americanity" here to describe the "invention" of the "Americas" as a geospatial place and the invention of "American" as an identity, arguing that U.S. American identity was constituted through the coloniality of power.

25. Greenberg, *Manifest Manhood*, 21. Apart from Greenberg's excellent historical analysis of the gendered racializations that animated feelings of Manifest Destiny, see also Russel y Rodríguez, "Mexicanas and Mongrels"; and Gabriel Gutiérrez, "Affirmative Action of the First Kind."

26. Royce, *California*, 2; Almaguer, *Racial Fault Lines*, 52.

27. De Genova, "Introduction"; Greenberg, *Manifest Manhood*, chapter 1; Heidenreich, *"This Land Was Mexican Once,"* chapter 3. For a broader history of filibustering in Latin America, see Juan González, *Harvest of Empire*.

28. Menchaca, *Naturalizing Mexican Immigrants*, 19.

29. Heidenreich, *"This Land Was Mexican Once,"* 92. See also Acuña, *Occupied America*; De Genova and Ramos-Zayas, *Latino Crossings*.

30. Manuel G. Gonzales, *Mexicanos*, 90.

31. Enck-Wanzer, "Decolonizing Imaginaries," 6; Almaguer, *Racial Fault Lines*, 20. For further discussion of the historical context summarized in this section, see Almaguer, *Racial Fault Lines*; Camarillo, *Chicanos in California*; Gómez, *Manifest Destinies*; Griswold del Castillo, *The Treaty of Guadalupe Hidalgo*; Haney-López, *White by Law*; Heidenreich, *"This Land Was Mexican Once"*; Heizer and Almquist, *The Other Californians*; Menchaca, *Recovering History, Constructing Race*; Pitt, *Decline of the Californios*.

32. Burns, "Taming the Elephant," 9; Heidenreich, *"This Land Was Mexican Once,"* 167;

Holling and Calafell, "Tracing the Emergence of Latin@ Vernaculars in the Studies of Latin@ Communication," 21. Two recent examples of "decolonial" history (though admittedly not identifying with the Latina/o vernacular discourse approach) are Heidenreich, *"This Land Was Mexican Once"* and Pérez, *The Decolonial Imaginary*.

33. Conmy, *The Constitutional Beginnings of California*. Historian Hubert Howe Bancroft provides a catalog of the delegates, their places of origin, and personal histories in his *History of California*, vol. 6.

34. Pitt, *Decline of the Californios*, 43–44.

35. Browne, *Report of the Debates in the Convention of California*, 22. The proceedings of the California Constitutional Convention of 1849 were written and compiled by J. Ross Browne, a printer elected by the delegates to serve as the convention reporter. In the tradition of eighteenth- and nineteenth-century constitutional conventions, Browne recorded the debates and proceedings at times in the delegates' first-person voice, but at other times he recorded speeches in the third person, referencing (and sometimes summarizing) what the delegates stated on the convention floor. This accounts for the peculiar narrative conventions of the proceedings, though we can suppose that Browne's report was regarded as trustworthy, since it was approved by the U.S. Congress. I will henceforth use parenthetical citations to reference quotations from the convention proceedings.

36. Mignolo, "Delinking," 453.

37. Mignolo, *Local Histories/Global Designs*, 66–67.

38. Saldívar, "Unsettling Race, Coloniality, and Caste," 339. See also Mignolo, *Local Histories/Global Designs*; Saldívar, *Trans-Americanity*. I am referring here to the work of Walter Mignolo, José David Saldívar, Ramón Grosfoguel, Nelson Maldonado-Torres, Freya Schiwy, and others. Though these scholars differ in the emphasis they give to different sources and regions (Chicana/o, South American, Caribbean, African, Middle Eastern), they collectively turn to subaltern, colonized literatures and voices from the borders of coloniality (rather than to the scholars of the first or Western world) to draw a decolonial theory that can challenge race, class, gender, sexuality, and nationality. In this respect, there are significant similarities and resonance between scholars of coloniality and the decolonial project of Latina/o vernacular discourse. For further elaboration of these connections, see Enck-Wanzer, "Decolonizing Imaginaries."

39. Alcoff, "Mignolo's Epistemology of Coloniality," 93.

40. Holling, "Retrospective on Latin@ Rhetorical and Performance Scholarship," 304.

41. I am drawing this term "darker side" from Mignolo, who claims that coloniality is the "darker side" of Western modernity. *The Darker Side of Western Modernity*.

42. Recall that, at the time, legal status was distinct from full consideration as a citizen, including rights of property ownership and suffrage, hence the disenfranchisement of women and freed slaves. Smith, *Civic Ideals*.

43. Bancroft, *California Pioneer Register and Index, 1542–1848*, 172.

44. The exception is Manuel Dominguez, whom I will discuss below. For further discussion of de la Guerra, see Bancroft, *History of California*, 284–89; Menchaca, *Recovering History, Constructing Race*, 221.

45. Mignolo, *Local Histories/Global Designs*, 67.

46. Nakayama and Krizek, "Whitenes." Almaguer makes a similar argument in, *Racial Fault Lines*, chapter 2.

47. Pitt, *Decline of the Californios*, 43. Pitt refers to Dominguez as "the Indian member" of the Californio delegation, suggesting that he was the one delegate who was unanimously considered nonwhite (though it is unclear whether the other delegates considered Dominguez mestizo or indio). In any case, Dominguez would later face racism in the new state, despite his role in drafting its constitution, when he was barred from testifying in a trial because he was presumed to be nonwhite and thus a noncitizen.

48. Bhabha, *The Location of Culture*, 201.

49. Mignolo, "Philosophy and the Colonial Difference," 82.

50. The racism and coloniality embedded within de la Guerra and the Californios' own system is even more evident considering that, in Mexico, blacks were explicitly excluded from citizenship. Annino, "The Two-Faced Janus."

51. Rhetoricians call this strategy the locus of essence, which accords higher value to those things that purportedly embody a true essence (e.g., whiteness) while disparaging those things that are supposedly diluted (e.g., nonwhites and mestizos). On the locus of essence, see Perelman and Olbrechts-Tyteca, *The New Rhetoric*, 83–85, 93–94. For further discussion of this rhetorical strategy in contemporary discourses of race and whiteness, consult Lisa A. Flores, Moon, and Nakayama, "Dynamic Rhetorics of Race." Quijano argues in his "Coloniality and Modernity/Rationality" that the question of racial essence is a central part of the rhetoric of modernity and coloniality.

52. Cloud, "Hegemony or Concordance?"

53. Dissociation describes the rhetorical strategy of breaking apart a conceptual unity into two separate parts, redefining and complicating the notion under contestation. As we have seen, the delegates dissociated indigenous people into "mixed-blood" descendants of Indians, who they claimed might potentially be acceptable (on an individual basis) and "real," or "full-blooded" Indians, whom they considered wholly unacceptable. On dissociation, see Perelman and Olbrechts-Tyteca, *The New Rhetoric*, 411–16.

54. This reading of de la Guerra's comments also could suggest conciliation to U.S. "Hispanophobia" and Manifest Destiny, which framed Spanish society as inferior to Anglo-Saxon civilization. It should be clarified that this speech took place during a later point in the convention, when the issue of suffrage was reintroduced for further debate. As I said, the debate over suffrage recurred several times throughout the convention before a suitable compromise was reached.

55. Mignolo, *Local Histories/Global Designs*, 26.

56. Mignolo, "Philosophy and the Colonial Difference," 82. On the topic of colonial mimicry, see especially Bhabha, "Of Mimicry and Man" in *The Location of Culture*. Wilson's "The Racial Politics of Imitation in the Nineteenth Century" discusses racial imitation as a performative logic.

57. Appadurai, *Fear of Small Numbers*. Further examples of this position were expressed

by Mr. Steuart, Mr. Sherwood, and others. Browne, *Report of the Debates in the Convention of California*, 305–6.

58. Bhabha, *The Location of Culture*, 87–88.

59. Constitution of the State of California, 1849, art. 2, sec. 1; emphasis added. The California Constitution of 1849 was replaced by a new constitution in 1879, under which the state of California still operates.

60. Pitt, *Decline of the Californios*, 43; Bancroft, *History of California*, 285; Menchaca, *Recovering History, Constructing Race*, 221.

61. Carrillo's plan to split California into two halves to address its vast regional, geographic, and cultural differences mirrored the regional structure of Mexican citizenship. Furthermore, Californios saw themselves as citizens of their towns, their regions, and their province (California) primarily, even though they also saw themselves as Mexican citizens. In fact, this was consistent with the hyper-regional tradition of vecindad I discussed above and should be evident in the Californios' insistence on being called "Californios" as well as or in place of "Mexicanos." Pitt, *Decline of the Californios*, 2–7.

62. Though lack of space prohibits its discussion here, another fascinating moment can be found in debates over language policy in the new state. Unlike the controversies over suffrage or borders, in the debate over language rights the Californios were able to achieve accommodation with the Anglo delegates. Ultimately, the delegates voted unanimously to "require publication" of all "laws, decrees, regulations, and provisions emanating" from the state into both English and Spanish. Browne, *Report of the Debates in the Convention of California*, 273.

63. Mignolo, *The Darker Side of Western Modernity*, 250.

64. Pitt, *Decline of the Californios*, 44. For a discussion of other important debates in the convention, see Almaguer, *Racial Fault Lines*; Heizer and Almquist, *The Other Californians*.

65. Mignolo, "Philosophy and the Colonial Difference," 82.

66. Mignolo, *The Darker Side of Western Modernity*, 222, 228.

67. Mignolo, *Local Histories/Global Designs*, 66–67. For an explanation of dominant vernacular discourses, see Ono and Sloop, *Shifting Borders*, 20–21.

68. Heidenreich, *"This Land Was Mexican Once,"* 144. For a further discussion of de la Guerra's case, see Menchaca, *Naturalizing Mexican Immigrants*, 67–70. Heizer and Almquist discuss the actions of the first California legislature in their *The Other Californians*.

69. Pitt, *Decline of the Californios*, 46, 86. On the 1879 Constitutional Convention, see Grodin, Massey, and Cunningham, *The California State Constitution*; Swisher, *Motivation and Political Technique in the California Constitutional Convention*.

70. Camarillo, *Chicanos in California*, 13–15. The quote from West is found in Willis and Stockton, *Debates and Proceedings of the Constitutional Convention of the State of California*, 802. Analysis of the 1879 California constitution in comparison to that of 1849, especially with regard to its institutionalized racism and exclusion of Californios and Mexican and Asian immigrants, can be found in Swisher, *Motivation and Political Technique in the California Constitutional Convention*, 86–92.

71. Despite the overall process of marginalization experienced by Mexican Americans in

the ensuing decades, there was vernacular resistance in California and throughout the Southwest during the late nineteenth and early twentieth centuries, including through cultural organizations, Spanish-language press, and informal community networks. For example, see Heidenreich, *"This Land Was Mexican Once."*

72. Bancroft, *History of California*, 284–85.

Chapter 2

1. Gardner, *Grito!* 156. See also Nabokov, *Tijerina and the Courthouse Raid*. I will elaborate on this event later in the chapter, but for a more detailed history of New Mexico's land grant struggle, see Maciel and Gonzales-Berry, *The Contested Homeland*.

2. I use the phrase Chicano movement(s) with parentheses because what we call a movement was in fact a multitude of different organizations and loosely coordinating activist networks throughout the Southwest—including in Denver the urban Crusade for Justice, in south Texas the Raza Unida Party, in Los Angeles the Brown Berets and the student walkouts of East LA, and in New Mexico the land grant movement led by the Alianza. Also, when I use the term Chicano I do so deliberately to denote the masculine and patriarchal dimensions of the movement. At other times, I reference self-identified Chicana/o people (rather than specific movements or Chicano ideology) through the gender-inclusive term.

3. Mignolo, *Local Histories/Global Designs*, 67.

4. Sandoval, *Methodology of the Oppressed*, 58–59.

5. Menchaca, *Recovering History, Constructing Race*, 278. The extent of this exclusion, of course, extended to African Americans as well, who continued to experience both de jure and de facto segregation despite the amendment's guarantees.

6. Gómez, *Manifest Destinies*; Haney-López, *White by Law*; Meier and Ribera, *The Chicanos*; Menchaca, *Naturalizing Mexican Immigrants*; Roediger, *Working toward Whiteness*; Rosales, *Chicano!*

7. Rodriguez, *Mongrels, Bastards, Orphans, and Vagabonds*, 127. See Acuña, *Occupied America*; Manuel G. Gonzales, *Mexicanos*; Menchaca, *Recovering History, Constructing Race*; Orozco, *No Mexicans, Women, or Dogs Allowed*.

8. LULAC was founded in 1929 and advocated for political inclusion and economic mobility. The American G.I. Forum, though founded after World War II as a veterans' organization, grew by the 1950s into one of the premier organizations demanding Mexican American civil rights. Hall Kells, *Héctor P. García*; Orozco, *No Mexicans, Women, or Dogs Allowed*; Rodriguez, *Mongrels, Bastards, Orphans, and Vagabonds*.

9. Acuña, *Occupied America*, chapter 6; Schmidt Camacho, *Migrant Imaginaries*.

10. Acuña, *Occupied America*, 158. See Orozco, *No Mexicans, Women, or Dogs Allowed*; Rodriguez, *Mongrels, Bastards, Orphans, and Vagabonds*.

11. Manuel G. Gonzales, *Mexicanos*, chapter 7.

12. Rosales, *Chicano!* 109. For an excellent primer, see Juan González, *Harvest of Empire*.

13. García, *Chicanismo*, 41.

14. Delgado, "Chicano Ideology Revisited," 98, 109. See also Alaniz and Cornish, *Viva La Raza*.

15. The influence of the Alianza on other Chicano movements is discussed in Bebout, "Hero Making in El Movimiento." For a thorough review of scholarship on Tijerina and the Alianza, see Busto, *King Tiger;* and Cisneros, "Reclaiming the Rhetoric of Reies López Tijerina."

16. Maciel and Peña, "La Reconquista."

17. In New Mexico, the term "Hispanos" was more common as a form of ethnic self-identification than Mexicano, Mexican American, or Chicano. In part, this was based on mythic identification with the original Spanish colonizers of the territory. It also stemmed from the sparsely settled nature of the territory, whose inhabitants were far removed from and thus never fully identified with the Mexican national government.

18. The slogan is taken from Tijerina, *They Called Me "King Tiger,"* 47. Histories of the Alianza movement include Blawis, *Tijerina and the Land Grants*; Nabokov, *Tijerina and the Courthouse Raid.*

19. It is well known that the late 1960s saw a growing convergence of "confrontation" in social movements. On confrontational rhetoric, see Stewart, "The Evolution of a Revolution"; Andrews, "Confrontation at Columbia"; Scott and Smith, "The Rhetoric of Confrontation."

20. For accounts see Blawis, *Tijerina and the Land Grants*, chapter 6; Gardner, *Grito!* chapter 9.

21. "Spanish March to Santa Fe over Lands," *Tucumcari Daily News*, July 4, 1966, Reies Tijerina Papers (MSS 654 BC, box 60, folder 5), Center for Southwest Research, University Libraries, University of New Mexico (hereafter abbreviated as CSWR).

22. Alianza Federal de Mercedes, Minutes of the Fourth Annual Convention, Albuquerque, September 3–4, 1966, Reies Tijerina Papers (MSS 654 BC, box 1, folder 21, CSWR.

23. "Families to Claim Land in Rio Arriba," *Raton Daily Range*, October 14, 1966, Reies Tijerina Papers (MSS 654 BC, box 60, folder 7), CSWR.

24. José Angel Gutiérrez, introduction, xvi.

25. For more information on these events, see Gardner, *Grito!* 286–89; Nabokov, *Tijerina and the Courthouse Raid*, 223; Tijerina, *They Called Me "King Tiger,"* 101.

26. Maciel and Peña, "La Reconquista," 274; Rosales, *Chicano!* 154; Blawis, *Tijerina and the Land Grants*, 36; Gardner, *Grito!* 70.

27. Hammerback, Jensen, and Gutierrez, *A War of Words*, 160–62. See also Bebout, "Hero Making in El Movimiento"; Busto, *King Tiger;* Hammerback and Jensen, "The Rhetorical Worlds of César Chávez and Reijes Tijerina"; Oropeza, "The Heart of Chicano History."

28. Manuel G. Gonzales, *Mexicanos*, 196.

29. Mignolo, *Local Histories/Global Designs*, 66.

30. Gardner, *Grito!* 44; Hammerback, Jensen, and Gutierrez, *A War of Words*, 25; Rosales, *Chicano!* 157. In a book chapter and a few academic essays, John C. Hammerback and Richard J. Jensen provide the most comprehensive discussion of Tijerina's rhetoric, in particular an understanding of his rhetorical background, his motivations to speak, and the basic themes of his early discourse. See Hammerback and Jensen, "The Rhetorical Worlds of César Chávez and Reijes Tijerina"; Hammerback and Jensen, "Reies López Tijerina: Founder of the Alianza, Minority Leader"; Hammerback, Jensen, and Gutierrez, *A War of Words*; Fernandez and Jensen, "Reies Lopez Tijerina's 'The Land Grant Question.'" Busto's *King Tiger* focuses on the religious vision animating Tijerina's career as an activist, including his rhetoric. For a more

thorough review of this literature, see Cisneros, "Reclaiming the Rhetoric of Reies López Tijerina."

31. The speech appears in Gottheimer, *Ripples of Hope*; and Tice, *The Rhetoric of La Raza*.

32. Tijerina, "The Land Grant Question," 7, 23, 2–3, 18–19, 4.

33. Ibid., 22.

34. Ibid., 4, 12.

35. Ibid., 12–14, 23, 15.

36. Other examples of this border rhetoric can be found in ibid., 12–14, 14–15, 22–24.

37. The hemispheric dimensions of Tijerina's rhetoric are discussed more fully below. In "The Land Grant Question," Tijerina argued that the "Indo-Hispano" or "new breed" included not only Mexican Americans but Latina/os and Latin Americans across the hemisphere. Throughout his rhetoric, he framed the "new breed" as a separate, hemispheric race/nation united by blood, a common experience of white imperialism, and a common struggle for land. As Tijerina stated, "As our land grants were taken away here in New Mexico, in Mexico were taken away from the Indians and the new breed by blue eyed Spaniards. . . . In Argentina the same, in Brazil, Chile, Peru—all throughout South America." Ibid., 18. In this sense, Tijerina's "new breed" or "Indo-Hispano" nationalism was more expansive and more evocative of the modern term "Latino" than conceptions of "Chicano" nationalism (which were limited to Mexican Americans). For more on this point, see Cisneros, "Reclaiming the Rhetoric of Reies López Tijerina." This hemispheric appeal is a rhetorical tactic similar to that other scholars identify in the rhetoric of black nationalism, including that of Malcolm X. Terrill, *Malcolm X*.

38. Tijerina, *They Called Me "King Tiger,"* 101.

39. Blawis, *Tijerina and the Land Grants*, chapter 14.

40. Busto, *King Tiger*, 154. Tijerina, "A Letter from Jail." For more on *El Grito del Norte*, see Longeaux y Vásquez et al., *Enriqueta Vasquez and the Chicano Movement*.

41. Tijerina, "A Letter from Jail," 88.

42. La Raza Cósmica was the theoretical concept of a cosmic race developed by twentieth-century Mexican philosopher and politician José Vasconcelos. It symbolized the coming birth of a supposed new race that would be a superior combination of all the previous races. Vasconcelos saw Latin America as the birthplace of this race because of its unique cultural and racial hybridity, and thus, for him, La Raza Cósmica became a strong marker of cultural and racial identity. A similar view is evident in the Chicano term La Raza, which I will discuss below. On the Raza Cósmica, see Schutte, *Cultural Identity and Social Liberation in Latin American Thought*, 13; Gracia, *Latin American Philosophy in the Twentieth Century*, 53; Vasconcelos, *La Raza Cósmica*. Obviously, the biological essentialism and patriarchal roots of this concept have received much criticism, to which I return later in the chapter.

43. Tijerina, "A Letter from Jail," 97.

44. On consubstantiality, see Burke, *A Rhetoric of Motives*, 21–22.

45. Tijerina, "A Letter from Jail," 88–89, 95–96.

46. Delgado, "Chicano Movement Rhetoric," 448. Though classifying Tijerina's rhetoric as "Chicano rhetoric" would be inaccurate, it does share several common elements with the evolving Chicano ideology of the time period, including the affirmation of an ethnic identity,

a critique of the dominant social order, and a call to action. Bebout, *Mythohistorical Interventions*, chapter 2.

47. Busto, *King Tiger*, 152–54.

48. Tijerina, "From Prison: Reies López Tijerina," 215.

49. Ibid., 216.

50. Busto, *King Tiger*, 151.

51. Condit and Lucaites, *Crafting Equality*, 192.

52. Tijerina, "From Prison: Reies López Tijerina," 219.

53. Leff and Utley, "Instrumental and Constitutive Rhetoric in Martin Luther King Jr.'s 'Letter from Birmingham Jail,'" 49.

54. Tijerina, "From Prison: Reies López Tijerina," 219.

55. Alianza Federal de Mercedes, Minutes of the Fourth Annual Convention, Albuquerque, September 3–4, 1966, Reies Tijerina Papers (MSS 654 BC, box 1, folder 21), CSWR.

56. "Alianza Will March, Claim Chama Grant," *Albuquerque Tribune*, October 14, 1966, 2.

57. "Against Alianza: Legal Loop Delays Federal Charge," *New Mexican*, October, 24, 1966, Reies Tijerina Papers (MSS 654 BC, box 60, folder 8), CSWR. "Spanish Americans Seeking Showdown," *Portales News-Tribune*, October 24, 1966, Reies Tijerina Papers (MSS 654 BC, box 60, folder 8), CSWR. *Albuquerque Tribune*, January 4, 1967, Reies Tijerina Papers (MSS 654 BC, box 60, folder 11), CSWR.

58. Peter Kelly, "Alliance Camps Out in Forest; Claiming Area," *Albuquerque Journal*, October 16, 1966, D-1; "New 'Republic' Is Staked Out in Forest Camp," *Albuquerque Journal*, October 17, 1966, B-14; "Forest Service Given Notice to 'Move Out,'" *Clovis News-Journal*, October 18, 1966, 14.

59. Clark Knowlton, "Guerillas of Rio Arriba: The New Mexican Land War," *Nation*, June 17, 1968, 794, Reies Tijerina Papers (MSS 654 BC, box 50, folder 47), CSWR.

60. "Squatters Court Tries 2," *Arizona Republic*, October 23, 1966, A-12.

61. Pictured in "Against Alianza: Legal Loop Delays Federal Charge," 1.

62. "U.S. Takes Steps to Bar Alliance in Claim of Land," *Albuquerque Journal*, October 26, 1966, A-2.

63. Bob Levey, "Alliance Can't Create Town in US Forest, Judge Rules," *Albuquerque Tribune*, October 26, 1966, A-2.

64. Oropeza, "The Heart of Chicano History."

65. Manuel G. Gonzales, *Mexicanos*, 203.

66. Gardner, *Grito!* 70; Rosales, *Chicano!* 154.

67. "Officials Mum on Motorcade," *Albuquerque Tribune*, October 15, 1966, A-9; "Land Grant Seizure Strategy Meets Held," *Albuquerque Tribune*, October 17, 1966, A-1.

68. "Land Alliance Chiefs Are Arrested by FBI," *Albuquerque Journal*, October 27, 1966, A-7.

69. "Against Alianza: Legal Loop Delays Federal Charge," 1; Martha Buddecke, "Alliance Members Abandon 'Republic,'" *New Mexican*, October 27, 1966, A1. When asked at the beginning of the takeover whether the armed guards were merely for show, Tijerina replied, "They're not keeping anyone out . . . yet." "Land Grant Seizure Strategy Meets Held," A-1.

70. Leslie Bottorff, "'Alianzistas' Standing Pat," *Taos News*, October 27, 1966, 1.

71. "Officials Mum on Motorcade," A-9.

72. "Against Alianza: Legal Loop Delays Federal Charge," 1.

73. "'Rebel' Flag Still Flies in Forest as Squatters Defy Uncle's Agents," *Arizona Republic*, October 24, 1966, 9; emphasis added.

74. Ruben D. Salaz, "Believes Treaty Broken," the People's Column, *Albuquerque Journal*, October 27, 1966, A-5.

75. Bottorff, "'Alianzistas' Standing Pat," 1.

76. "Alliance Vows Court Fight," *Albuquerque Tribune*, October 27, 1966, A-2.

77. For further evidence of this point, see Kelly, "Alliance Camps Out in Forest," D-1.

78. "200 Alianza Members Parade at Statehouse," *New Mexican*, April 18, 1967, Reies Tijerina Papers (MSS 654 BC, box 60, folder 12), CSWR; "Governor Offers His Office as Avenue for Alianza," *New Mexican*, April 23, 1967, Reies Tijerina Papers (MSS 654 BC, box 60, folder 12), CSWR; "Alianza Plans Tierra Amarilla Meeting," *New Mexican*, May 14, 1967, Reies Tijerina Papers (MSS 654 BC, box 60, folder 12), CSWR; "Land Grant Alliance Will 'Enforce Rights,'" *Portales News-Tribune*, May 15, 1967, Reies Tijerina Papers (MSS 654 BC, box 60, folder 12), CSWR; "Defunct Alliance Plans to Possess 700,000 Acres," *Carlsbad Current-Argus*, May 29, 1967, Reies Tijerina Papers (MSS 654 BC, box 60, folder 12), CSWR.

79. "Police Grab Guns in Land Issue, State, Federal United Mobilized in Rio Arriba," *Albuquerque Journal*, June 3, 1967, Reies Tijerina Papers (MSS 654 BC, box 60, folder 12), CSWR.

80. Reies López Tijerina, "News Release," June 4, 1967, Reies Tijerina Papers (MSS 654 BC, box 1, folder 1), CSWR.

81. "Naranjo Says Group Was After Sanchez," *New Mexican*, June 6, 1967, Reies Tijerina Papers (MSS 654 BC, box 60, folder 16), CSWR.

82. For more on the corridos about Tijerina, the Alianza, and the courthouse raid, see Bebout, "Hero Making in El Movimiento." The bulk of these corridos can be found in the Reies Tijerina Papers (MSS 654 BC, box 47, folder 54), CSWR.

83. Bebout, *Mythohistorical Interventions*, 84.

84. "The Word Is Revolution," *Albuquerque Tribune*, June 6, 1967, B-4, Reies Tijerina Papers (MSS 654 BC, box 60, folder 13), CSWR; Doyle Akers, "Daylight Raiders Leave Bloody Path," *Denver Post*, June 6, 1967, Reies Tijerina Papers (MSS 654 BC, box 60, folder 13), CSWR.

85. Clark S. Knowlton, "Spanish American Protest Movements in Northern New Mexico" (paper presented at the Center for Land Grant Studies at the University of Utah, Salt Lake City, n.d.), 43, 48, Reies Tijerina Papers (MSS 654 BC, box 50, folder 43), CSWR.

86. Condit and Lucaites, "Malcolm X and the Limits of the Rhetoric of Revolutionary Dissent," 309. For more on this point, see Busto, *King Tiger*, chapter 1.

87. Reies López Tijerina, "Tierra Amarilla—Junio 3–5, 1967," script for radio program *La Voz de la Justicia*, March 6, 1969, Reies Tijerina Papers (MSS 654 BC, box 35, folder 6), CSWR. The quotation above retains the typographical and grammatical errors of the original document. A version including the accent marks and corrections is as follows: "Todo esto fue lo que obligó al pueblo manso y humilde a tomar un paso histórico, y establecer un ejemplo nunca antes establecido en Nuevo México. Alfonso Sánchez obligó al pueblo a esforzar los derechos que la policía del Estado no esforzó. Esto fue un caso único en la historia de Nuevo México y

posible en todo el Sudoeste, en el cual, el pueblo fue obligado a corregir y enderezar la Justicia que los políticos han torcido. . . . Que Tierra Amarilla sea un buen ejemplo para todos los que juegan con los derechos del pueblo para todos los políticos ladeados."

88. Brouwer, "ACT-ing UP in Congressional Hearings," 89.

89. Terrill, "Colonizing the Borderlands," 76.

90. Pérez Firmat, *Literature and Liminality*, xiv.

91. Saldívar, *Border Matters*, 99.

92. Sandoval, *Methodology of the Oppressed*, 43, 30, 58.

93. I draw this idea of a rhetoric of difference and a rhetoric of sameness from Lisa A. Flores, "Creating Discursive Space," 142–56.

94. Mignolo, "Philosophy and the Colonial Difference," 82.

95. On this form of border discourse, see also Noe, "The Corrido."

96. Victor Witter Turner, *The Forest of Symbols*, 97.

97. Rudy Busto's *King Tiger* discusses the Alianza's later history.

98. Alarcón, "Traddutora, Traditora"; Moraga and Anzaldúa, *This Bridge Called My Back*.

99. For more on this point, see Bebout, *Mythohistorical Interventions*, 101–5; Rosales, *Chicano!* 327; Schmidt Camacho, *Migrant Imaginaries*, 152–55.

Chapter 3

This chapter is dedicated to "Nacho" Córdova, a wonderful scholar and kind friend who passed away well before his time and who is truly missed.

1. Loyd and Burridge, "La Gran Marcha." For analysis of these broader nationwide movements, see Chavez, *The Latino Threat*; Félix, González, and Ramírez, "Political Protest, Ethnic Media, and Latino Naturalization"; Pantoja, Menjívar, and Magaña, "The Spring Marches of 2006"; Voss and Bloemraad, *Rallying for Immigrant Rights*.

2. Globalization is a widely used term that arose in the context of economic changes such as the removal of tariffs and trade restrictions, the interconnection of national economies, and the greater transnational flow of capital but that now describes changes in a number of other sectors, from media and culture to politics and population. A classic summary can be found in Appadurai, *Modernity at Large*, chapter 1. See also von Werlhof, "The Consequences of Globalization and Neoliberal Policies."

3. Castles and Davidson, *Citizenship and Migration*, 153. Aleinikoff and Klusmeyer, *Citizenship Today*; Del Castillo, "Illegal Status and Social Citizenship"; Falk, "The Decline of Citizenship"; Friedman and Randeria, *Worlds on the Move*; Varsanyi, "'Getting out the Vote' in Los Angeles."

4. Though heretofore I have been discussing the border as a fairly contextual space and place in relation to Latina/os (in particular Mexicans and Chicana/os), there is also a broader literature, on which I will be drawing in this chapter, in which the border functions as a metaphor unconnected to a specific racial and ethnic group like Latina/os. Here the border helps us understand the impacts of neoliberal globalization, migration, and transculturation on citizenship and national sovereignty by theorizing a space at the interstices of territorial borders and nation-state sovereignty. Though this literature draws upon and deploys Chicana/o theories

of the border, such as those by Anzaldúa, it broadens its focus to what DeChaine calls "the social-spatial politics of movement, mobility, migration, and displacement." DeChaine, "Introduction," 5. In other words, this trajectory of border studies deploys it in perhaps the most expansive sense to refer to territorial, legal, and cultural borders of nation-states and the dimensions of life that take place at their intersections. On this point, see Bhabha, *The Location of Culture*, 206–8. More broadly, see Appadurai, *Modernity at Large*; García Canclini, *Hybrid Cultures*; Cunningham, "Mobilities and Enclosures after Seattle"; Gilbertson, "Regulating Transnational Citizens in the Post-1996 Welfare Reform Era"; Sparke, "Passports into Credit Cards."

5. William V. Flores and Benmayor, *Latino Cultural Citizenship*; Johnston, "The Emergence of Transnational Citizenship among Mexican Immigrants in California"; Joseph, *Nomadic Identities*; Aihwa Ong, *Flexible Citizenship*. It should go without saying that each of these theoretical developments of the citizenship literature is different. My intention here is not to conflate them but to point out that they all indicate the focus on transnational challenges facing borders and citizenship that was prevalent in scholarship at this time.

6. On battles against bilingual education, see Cisneros, "Latina/os and Party Politics"; Crawford, *Hold Your Tongue*; Lisa A. Flores, "Constructing National Bodies." For a discussion of these other anti-immigrant initiatives, see Daniels, *Coming to America*, chapters 16–17; Hasian and Delgado, "Trials and Tribulations of Racialized Critical Rhetorical Theory"; Holling, "Forming Oppositional Social Concord"; Ono and Sloop, *Shifting Borders*.

7. On the Minutemen, see Chavez, *The Latino Threat*; Cisneros, "Contaminated Communities"; DeChaine, "Bordering the Civic Imaginary"; Lyall, "Vigilante State."

8. One example is the seven-hundred-mile border fence that is still under construction at the cost of about $7 million per mile. See Garrett, "The Border Fence, Immigration Policy, and the Obama Administration." In fact, as the next chapter will show, despite the failure of federal immigration policy in general, and HR 4437 in particular, many of its most restrictive provisions came to be enacted through state and local immigration initiatives, creating a near-nationwide regime of anti-immigrant and nativist legislation.

9. Chavez, *The Latino Threat*, 8; Menchaca, *Naturalizing Mexican Immigrants*, 299. See *Border Protection, Antiterrorism, and Illegal Immigration Control Act of 2005*, HR 4437, December 16, 2005.

10. The presumption of alienization and otherization dominated even the more progressive Senate immigration bill introduced in May of 2006, which included paths to naturalization for undocumented immigrants but still featured a "border security and enforcement first" approach. See *Comprehensive Immigration Reform Act of 2006*, SB 2611, May 25, 2006. For more on the connection between rhetorics of terrorism and immigration, see DeChaine, "Bordering the Civic Imaginary"; Lugo-Lugo and Bloodsworth-Lugo, "475° from September 11"; Silva, "Brown."

11. Demo, "Sovereignty Discourse in Contemporary Immigration Politics," 306. See also Shafir, "Introduction"; Oboler, "Redefining Citizenship."

12. Ono and Sloop, *Shifting Borders*, 72.

13. DeChaine, "Bordering the Civic Imaginary," 50.

14. The history of "hybridity" has been traced in a level of detail I cannot hope to match

here, but suffice it to say that hybridity arose in the seventeenth century as a biological concept describing the cross-breeding of livestock and crops and then reached prominence during the mid-nineteenth century as a social and eugenic concept describing the intriguing but problematic (or so it was thought) fruits of miscegenation. Especially in the Western world, then, the concept of hybridity was used as a tool in the solidification of racial ideology and as a justification for racial hierarchy and racist sexualized violence. In Latin America and the Caribbean, a racialized concept of hybridity (as mestizaje or creolité) became a tool of national identity formation during the liberation movements of the nineteenth and early twentieth century. For example, in Mexico, as we have seen in the last two chapters, the idea of mestizaje or racial hybridity achieved preeminence as a nationalist myth. Hutnyk, "Hybridity"; Kraidy, *Hybridity*; Prabhu, *Hybridity*; Werbner and Modood, *Debating Cultural Hybridity*. For a review of hybridity as a critical cultural theory, see Kapchan and Strong, "Theorizing the Hybrid"; Stross, "The Hybrid Metaphor"; Werbner, "Introduction."

15. Valdivia, "Latinas as Radical Hybrid," 4. See also Bhabha, *The Location of Culture*; García Canclini, *Hybrid Cultures*; Kraidy, *Hybridity*; Papastergiadis, "Tracing Hybridity in Theory."

16. Kraidy, *Hybridity*, 156. For critiques of hybridity as a critical cultural theory, see Friedman, "Global Crises, the Struggle for Cultural Identity, and Intellectual Porkbarrelling"; Hutnyk, "Adorno at Womad"; van der Veer, "'The Enigma of Arrival.'"

17. Kraidy, "Hybridity in Cultural Globalization," 317. On hybridity as a strategic and performative rhetoric, see Enck-Wanzer, "A Radical Democratic Style?"; Maurice L. Hall, "The Postcolonial Caribbean as a Liminal Space"; Joseph, *Nomadic Identities*; Joseph, "Introduction"; Kraidy, *Hybridity*; Marotta, "The Hybrid Self and the Ambivalence of Boundaries."

18. DeChaine, "Bordering the Civic Imaginary," 50. See also Chavez, *The Latino Threat*; Molina-Guzmán, *Dangerous Curves*.

19. Ahmed, *Cultural Politics*, 44. See also De Genova, "The Legal Production of Mexican/Migrant Illegality"; Demo, "Sovereignty Discourse and Contemporary Immigration Politics."

20. For elaboration of these claims regarding Latina/os racialization as "hybrid," see Calafell, *Latina/o Communication Studies*; De Genova, "Introduction"; Gómez, *Manifest Destinies*; Molina-Guzmán, *Dangerous Curves*; Molina-Guzmán and Valdivia, "Brain, Brow, and Booty"; Moreman, "Hybrid Performativity South and North of the Border"; Moreman, "Qualitative Interviews of Racial Fluctuations"; Muñoz, *Disidentifications*; Shugart, "Crossing Over"; Valdivia, "Latinas as Radical Hybrid."

21. Appadurai, *Fear of Small Numbers*, 44.

22. Córdova, "*Nuestro Himno* as Heterotopic Mimicry," 121; Moreman, "Memoir as Performance," 347; Bhabha, *The Location of Culture*, 6–7. On this point, Ramón Grosfoguel argues that hybrid discourses need not be essentializing and hegemonic but can be "forms of resistance that resignify and transform dominant forms of knowledge from the point of view of the non-Eurocentric rationality of subaltern subjectivities thinking from border epistemologies . . . a redefinition/subsumption of citizenship, democracy, human rights, humanity, economic relations beyond the narrow definitions imposed by European modernity." As Grosfoguel argues here, critical to the transformative potential of vernacular hybridities is how they stand in relationship to racial, colonial, and national logics. Grosfoguel, "Transmodernity, Border

Thinking, and Global Coloniality." See also Cisneros, "(Re)Bordering the Civic Imaginary"; Joseph, *Nomadic Identities*; Werbner, "Introduction."

23. These texts include *Immigration March Draws Thousands of Protestors, CBS 2/KCAL 9 Los Angeles*, March 25, 2006, http://cbs2.com/video/?id=15998a/okcbs.dayport.com (accessed September 18, 2009); Cuerpo de Unidad, Inc., "La Gran Marcha 2006," 2006, http://www.granmarcha.org (accessed September 14, 2009); "La Gran Marcha, Los Angeles," *Internet Archive*, http://www.archive.org/details/LaGranMarchaLosAngeles (accessed September, 22, 2009). Though my analysis focuses on rhetorical fragments from La Gran Marcha, I also draw on discourse from throughout the protests of 2006 to construct a broad picture of these demonstrations. For more on this methodology, see McGee, "Text, Context, and the Fragmentation of Contemporary Culture."

24. Córdova, "*Nuestro Himno* as Heterotopic Mimicry," 117; Pineda and Sowards, "Flag Waving as Visual Argument," 171.

25. Teresa Watanabe and Hector Bercerra, "500,000 Pack Streets to Protest Immigration Bills: The Rally, Part of a Massive Mobilization of Immigrants and Their Supporters, May Be the Largest L.A. Has Seen," *Los Armeies Times*, March 26 2006, A1; Teresa Watanabe and Hector Bercerra, "How DJs Put 500,000 Marchers in Motion," *Los Angeles Times*, March 28 2006, A1.

26. Pineda and Sowards, "Flag Waving as Visual Argument."

27. Chavez, *The Latino Threat*.

28. Baker-Cristales, "Mediated Resistance."

29. Barreto et al., "Mobilization, Participation, and Solidaridad," 746. For further discussion of the organization and constituents of the protests, see Bloemraad, Voss, and Lee, "The Protests of 2006"; Alfonso Gonzales, "The 2006 Mega Marchas "; Wang and Winn, "Groundswell Meets Groundwork."

30. Alfonso Gonzales, "The 2006 Mega Marchas," 43. Wang and Winn, "Groundswell Meets Groundwork." For more on the lead-up to La Gran Marcha, see Bloemraad, Voss, and Lee, "The Protests of 2006." For a discussion of the role of churches and radio in organizing and mobilizing the demonstrations, see Félix, González, and Ramírez, "Political Protest, Ethnic Media, and Latino Naturalization"; Heredia, "From Prayer to Protest"; Ramírez, "Mobilization *en Español*."

31. Lisa A. Flores, "Creating Discursive Space."

32. This sign was distributed by the LA chapter of the left-wing protest organization the A.N.S.W.E.R. Coalition. Alfonso Gonzales, "The 2006 Mega Marchas," 43.

33. Levy and Chávez, *César Chávez*, 464; Sowards, "Rhetorical Agency as *Haciendo caras*," 224.

34. Navarro and Mejia, *Latino Americans and Political Participation*, 70–71; Enck-Wanzer, "Trashing the System."

35. McGee, "In Search of 'the People,'" 245. See also Lake, "Enacting Red Power."

36. Mattern, *Acting in Concert*, chapter 3.

37. Stephen, *Zapata Lives!*

38. Varsanyi, "The Paradox of Contemporary Immigrant Political Mobilization," 787.

39. Hariman and Lucaites, *No Caption Needed*, 100.

40. See Pineda and Sowards, "Flag Waving as Visual Argument," 168–70.

41. Quoted in Chavez, *The Latino Threat*, 158.

42. Bhabha, "DissemiNation," 300.

43. Lisa A. Flores, "Constructing Rhetorical Borders," 381.

44. Norton, *Republic of Signs*, 120.

45. DeLuca, "Unruly Arguments," 18.

46. See the video *Immigration March Draws Thousands of Protestors*.

47. DeChaine, "Bordering the Civic Imaginary," 49. See also Summers Sandoval, "Disobedient Bodies."

48. The videos of La Gran Marcha available at the Internet Archive are particularly telling on this point. *La Gran Marcha, Los Angeles*, http://www.archive.org/details/LaGranMarchaLosAngeles (accessed September 22, 2009).

49. Muñoz, "Feeling Brown," 69–70. In the same way that queer public kissing represents a "coming out" that flouts the heteronormativity and homophobia surrounding public expressions of intimacy by queer subjects, immigrants flouted the racialized affect of citizenship with a "coming out" of the shadows. See Morris and Sloop, "'What Lips These Lips Have Kissed.'"

50. For more on these demographic factors, see Barreto et al., "Mobilization, Participation, and Solidaridad."

51. Calafell, *Latina/o Communication Studies*, 33. See also Hasian and Delgado, "Trials and Tribulations of Racialized Critical Rhetorical Theory."

52. Bhabha, "DissemiNation," 293.

53. Watanabe and Bercerra, "How DJs Put 500,000 Marchers in Motion."

54. DeChaine, "Bordering the Civic Imaginary," 49.

55. Democracy Now, "Dallas High School Student Describes Organizing Mass Walkout," Democracynow.org, April 11, 2006, http://www.democracynow.org/2006/4/11/dallas_high_school_student_describes_organizing (accessed June 15, 2011).

56. Wang and Winn, "Groundswell Meets Groundwork." See also Bloemraad, Voss, and Lee, "The Protests of 2006"; Milkman, "L.A.'s Past, America's Future?"

57. DeChaine, "Bordering the Civic Imaginary," 60. On this notion of the "ideal citizen," see Greene, "John Dewey's Eloquent Citizen."

58. Enck-Wanzer, "Trashing the System," 191. See also Pezzullo, "Resisting 'National Breast Cancer Awareness Month.'"

59. Rosaldo, "Cultural Citizenship."

60. Bhabha, "Preface to the Routledge Classics Edition," xvii; Mignolo, "Delinking," 459, 461. See Enck-Wanzer, "Decolonizing Imaginaries."

61. Transcribed from the Spanish. Unfortunately, the crowd noise makes some of the organizer's speech unintelligible. The following is my Spanish transcription: "¡Marchamos todos juntos hasta la Victoria! ¡Hoy marchamos por la amnistía, mañana por la ciudadanía, y después para poder gobernar civilmente con el resto de los trabajadores de este país! ¡Para que haya justicia en este país y en todo el mundo!" See the video *Immigration March Draws Thousands of Protestors*. The phrase "Today we march, tomorrow we vote" (¡Hoy marchamos, mañana votamos!) became a rallying cry of the 2006 protests, according to Wang and Winn's "Groundswell Meets Groundwork." The phrase itself is pregnant with a hybrid performativity

since it enacts the conventional meaning of inclusion through incorporation into the national body (through legalization and the demand for the vote) but also presents the possibility of a participation in the polis without its explicit recognition (marching today despite one's illegal status).

62. Oboler, "Redefining Citizenship," 17.

63. Bloemraad, Voss, and Lee, "The Protests of 2006."

64. For a discussion of these events and the news coverage surrounding them, see Santa Ana, López, and Munguíya, "Framing Peace as Violence."

65. DeSipio, "Drawing New Lines in the Sand." For other assessments, see DeChaine, "Bordering the Civic Imaginary"; Milkman, "L.A.'s Past, America's Future?"; Pedraza, Segura, and Bowler, "The Efficacy and Alienation of Juan Q. Public."

66. Córdova, "*Nuestro Himno* as Heterotopic Mimicry," 120.

67. For further discussion of the political efficacy of the 2006 protests, see Pedraza, Segura, and Bowler, "The Efficacy and Alienation of Juan Q. Public"; Suro, "Out of the Shadows, into the Light."

Chapter 4

1. Conquergood, "Ethnography, Rhetoric, and Performance," 92.

2. On confrontational rhetoric, see Andrews, "Confrontation at Columbia"; Scott and Smith, "The Rhetoric of Confrontation."

3. The protest was described as such by Abby Goodnough in her story "Governors Voice Grave Concerns on Immigration," *New York Times*, July 12, 2010, A1.

4. §5, Arizona Revised Statues [ARS], §13–2929. See Arizona State Legislature, Senate, *The Support Our Law Enforcement and Safe Neighborhoods Act* (Senate Bill 1070).

5. Arizona State Legislature, House, *An Act Amending Sections 1–501 and 1–502*, Arizona Revised Statutes (House Bill 2162). I am citing here from §3[B] of the Arizona Revised Statues, §11–1051.

6. Kevin R. Johnson, "How Racial Profiling in America Became the Law of the Land," 1006.

7. Arizona Peace Officers Standards and Training Board, "Implementation of the 2010 Arizona Immigration Laws Statutory Provisions for Peace Officers," AZ POST Recommended Minimum Course of Training on Arizona Immigration Laws, June 2010, http://www.tucsonsentinel.com/documents/doc/070110_azpost_training_doc/ (accessed August 2, 2010).

8. Cisneros, "Looking 'Illegal,'" 146.

9. Jan Brewer, "Statement by Governor Jan Brewer on Senate Bill 1070," Office of the Governor, April 23, 2010, http://www.azgovernor.gov (accessed August 23, 2010). On state and local anti-immigrant measures, see Shahani and Greene, "Local Democracy on ICE"; Seth F. Wessler, "Hostile State Battles Now Define Immigration Debate," Colorlines.com, January 6, 2011, http://colorlines.com/archives/2011/01/sparing_no_time_in_the.html (accessed July 14, 2011).

10. Kevin Johnson, "The Debate over Immigration Reform Is Not Over until It's Over," *SCOTUS Blog*, June 25, 2012, http://www.scotusblog.com/?p=147582 (accessed October 2,

2012). For extensive discussion of the court's ruling, see the articles on the case page of the Supreme Court of the United States Blog at http://www.scotusblog.com/case-files/cases/arizona-v-united-states/.

11. Marisa Treviño, "Immigration Enforcement Has Gone from Public Policy to Public Domain," Latina Lista.com, July 13, 2010, http://www.latinalista.net/palabrafinal/2010/07/immigration_enforcement_has_gone_from_pu.html (accessed August 23, 2010).

12. Valeria Fernández, "Long before SB 1070 Arizona Put Squeeze on Immigrants," *New America Media*, July 29, 2010, http://newamericamedia.org/2010/07/long-before-sb-1070-arizona-put-squeeze-on-immigrants.php (accessed August 23, 2010); Seth F. Wessler, "A Year After SB 1070, the Deportation Pipeline Still Begins in Washington," Colorlines.com, April 25, 2011, http://colorlines.com/archives/2011/04/a_year_after_sb_1070_the_deportation_pipeline_still_begins_in_washington.html (accessed July 14, 2011).

13. Varsanyi, "Rescaling the 'Alien,'" 878–79. Neoliberalism is first and foremost a theory of political economy that has reached almost dogmatic status and that, in the words of David Harvey, is based on "individual entrepreneurial freedoms," the "free market," absolute free trade, and state deregulation. Here I focus on how this paradigm has come to influence immigration and border policy and understandings of U.S. identity. Harvey, *A Brief History of Neoliberalism*, 2. On neoliberalism and immigration, see Kretsedemas, "Immigration Enforcement and the Complication of National Sovereignty"; Aihwa Ong, *Neoliberalism as Exception.*

14. Goldberg, *Threat of Race*, 78. See also Bonilla-Silva, *Racism without Racists*; Enck-Wanzer, "Barack Obama, the Tea Party, and the Threat of Race"; Jones and Mukherjee, "From California to Michigan"; Melamed, "The Spirit of Neoliberalism."

15. Brewer, "Statement by Governor Jan Brewer on Senate Bill 1070"; Arizona Peace Officers Standards and Training Board, "Implementation of the 2010 Arizona Immigration Laws Statutory Provisions for Peace Officers," 3–4.

16. McKinnon, "Citizenship and the Performance of Credibility," 218. To clarify, affect describes a mode of perception that is prior to cognition, that is viscerally and materially felt, and that influences the process of meaning making we call emotion but is also distinct from it. As Brian Ott explains, affects are "incipient attitudes, as energies, intensities, and sensations that function as the first step towards an evolving attitude," i.e., emotion. Ott, "The Visceral Politics of *V* for *Vendetta*," 50. While affect is connected to visceral, embodied sensation, it is also connected to symbolization (rhetoric) because not only material experiences but also discourses stimulate, channel, and motivate those sensations. On this point, see Rice, "The New 'New'"; Lundberg, "Enjoying God's Death." In the case of SB 1070, discourses surrounding anti-immigrant laws stimulated affects of anger, fear, and so on, and these affects provided support for anti-immigration politics. At the same time, these affects surrounding immigration (fear, anger, etc.) also spurred anti-immigrant measures even in the relative absence of immigration/immigrants as "real" concerns for a community. A clear example of this is Alabama's HB 56, a law similar to SB 1070 passed at considerable expense. Affects surrounding the issue of immigration compelled the population of the state to support the law even in the absence of a measurable presence of unauthorized immigrants in the state. Such examples illustrate the complexity of affects of immigration and citizenship and their impact in evolv-

ing regimes of immigration policy. Immigration debates and policies channel, influence, and are motivated by affects of immigration such as those identified here.

17. On immigration and affective economies, see Ahmed, *Cultural Politics*; Cisneros, "Looking 'Illegal.'" On immigration and racial neoliberalism, see Hiemstra, "Immigrant 'Illegality' as Neoliberal Governmentality"; Kretsedemas, "Immigration Enforcement and the Complication of National Sovereignty"; Lugo-Lugo and Bloodsworth-Lugo, "475° from September 11"; McNevin, "Political Belonging in a Neoliberal Era"; Roberts and Mahtani, "Neoliberalizing Race, Racing Neoliberalism." My claims about SB 1070 sidestep even more problematic issues surrounding the legislation, particularly how Brewer's celebration of Arizona's diversity contradicted her regular public statements that Mexican and Latina/o immigrants brought crime and social and economic strife to the state. Brewer's public interviews during the debate over SB 1070 demonstrated that despite assurances to the contrary, there was a very specific racialized and gendered affective economy underlying the push for the legislation. For example, as Brewer stated on Fox News, undocumented immigrants brought "everything from the crime . . . to the drugs and the kidnappings and the extortion and the beheadings and the fact that people can't feel safe in their community." Also, during a televised gubernatorial debate she claimed that "the majority of [illegal immigrants] in my opinion and I think in the opinion of law enforcement . . . are not coming here to work. They are coming here and they're bringing drugs. And they're doing drop houses and they're extorting people and they're terrorizing the families." In these examples, Brewer drew on and stuck together racialized and gendered stereotypes of immigrants with affects of fear and threat. Paul Davenport and Amanda Lee Myers, "Jan Brewer Admits She Was Wrong about Beheadings," *Huffington Post*, September 4, 2010, http://www.huffingtonpost.com/2010/09/04/jan-brewer-admits-she-was_0_n_705722.html (accessed September 14, 2010); E. J. Montini, "What Part of Distortion Doesn't Brewer Understand?" AZCentral.com, June 23, 2010, http://www.azcentral.com/members/Blog/EJMontini/87586 (accessed October 5 2010).

18. DeChaine, "Bordering the Civic Imaginary," 54. See also Chavez, *The Latino Threat*. For an example of these efforts to end birthright citizenship, see Ezra Klein, "When Did Lindsey Graham Change His Mind on Immigration?" *Washington Post*, July 30, 2010, http://voices.washingtonpost.com/ezra-klein/2010/07/when_did_lindsey_graham_change.html (accessed August 30, 2010). See also Wessler, "Hostile State Battles."

19. I use the feminine pronoun here intentionally because concerns about economic and cultural impacts of immigration are increasingly positioned alongside of, if not behind, fears of the (racial and sociocultural) pollution and dilution of U.S. identity, the primary culprits of which are supposedly Mexicanas and Latinas. An example of this concern, which served as a public motivation for SB 1070 and other such legislation, was the discourse of "anchor babies" and "breeders." See Wright, "Challenging States of Illegality"; Hondagneau-Sotelo, "Women and Children First."

20. Craig Harris, Alia Beard Rau, and Glen Creno, "Arizona Governor Signs Immigration Law; Foes Promise Fight." *Arizona Republic*, April 24, 2010, http://www.azcentral.com/news/articles/2010/04/23/20100423arizona-immigration-law-passed.html (accessed September 2, 2011).

21. "Thousands Protest Ariz. Immigration Law," *CBSNews*, April 24, 2010, http://www.cbsnews.com/stories/2010/04/23/politics/main6426967.shtml?tag=mncol;lst;3 (accessed September 2, 2011).

22. Dianne Solís, "Protest of Immigration Law Planned," *Dallas Morning News*, April 27, 2010, B01; Dan Nowicki, "Arizona Immigration Law Ripples through History, U.S. Politics." *Arizona Republic*, July 25, 2010, http://www.azcentral.com/arizonarepublic/news/articles/2010/07/25/20100725immigration-law-history-politics.html (accessed September 2, 2011).

23. Teresa Watanabe and Richard Winton, "Mayor Backs Ariz. Boycott," *Los Angeles Times*, April 30, 2010.

24. National Network for Immigrant and Refugee Rights, "We Are ALL Arizona!" April 30, 2010, http://nnirr.blogspot.com/2010/04/nnirr-all-out-for-may-day-we-are-all.html (accessed March 25, 2013); National Network for Immigrant and Refugee Rights, "Join Us to Expand Immigrant Rights," July 19, 2012, http://www.nnirr.org/~nnirrorg/drupal/membership-letter (accessed March 25, 2013). See also the website of the group ¡Alto Arizona! (http://www.altoarizona.com/).

25. Valeria Fernández, "A Year After Arrest, Immigrant Family Marches against SB 1070," *Feet in 2 Worlds: Telling the Stories of Today's Immigrants*, May 31, 2010, http://news.feetintwoworlds.org/2010/05/31/a-year-after-arrest-immigrant-family-marches-against-sb-1070/ (accessed June 15, 2010).

26. Randal C. Archibols, with Anna Facio Contreras, "The Two Sides Intersect in Immigration Debate," *New York Times*, May 30, 2010, 14; Nicholas Riccardi, "Thousands Protest in Arizona," *Los Angeles Times*, May 30, 2010, A-16.

27. Julián Reséndiz, "Group to Join Arizona Protest," *Dallas Morning News*, May 14, 2010, B06; Ruben Vives, "Activists Protest as Napolitano Speaks," *Los Angeles Times*, May 17, 2010, AA3; Jen Wulf, "Camden Rally Defies Ariz. on Immigration," *Philadelphia Inquirer*, July 2, 2010, B01.

28. Treviño, "Immigration Enforcement."

29. For more on this recurrent trope of "dangerous" Latina fertility, see Chavez, *The Latino Threat*, chapter 3.

30. Goodnough, "Governors Voice Grave Concerns on Immigration"; "Protesters Blast Brewer at Boston Meeting," *East Valley Tribune*, July 10, 2010, http://www.eastvalleytribune.com/arizona/article_1d510de0–8c59–11df-a31d-001cc4c03286.html (accessed July 11, 2011). See also ANSWER Coalition, "Arizona Gov. Jan Brewer Met by Protestors during the National Governor's Association Meeting in Boston," *ANSWER Coalition*, July 20, 2010, http://www2.answercoalition.org/site/News2?abbr=ANS_&page=NewsArticle&id=9696&news_iv_ctrl=1621 (accessed July 14, 2011); Derek Ford, "Militant Protest Denounces SB1070 in Boston," *Party for Socialism and Liberation*, July 15, 2010, http://www.pslweb.org/site/News2?page=NewsArticle&id=14236&news_iv_ctrl=1030 (accessed July 11, 2011); "Pro-immigration Violence Escalates," *Washington Times*, May 4, 2010, 2. For TV news coverage, see ABC 5/WCVB Boston, "Arizona Immigration Protests Come to Boston," YouTube video, July 11, 2010, http://www.youtube.com/watch?v=QYvzxJF0R4I&list=PL1BA86A93465307D6 (accessed March 25, 2013).

31. Holling, "Forming Oppositional Social Concord." It is important to note, however, that the vilification of Governor Brewer in one instance took shape through problematic and misogynistic language when several protestors briefly chanted, "Abajo la vieja," or "Down with the old lady/'hag.'" In this case, Brewer was maligned not as a public figure representing a broader racist policy but rather as an ugly old woman or even a "witch." Though the trope of "la vieja" was not widespread in the protest, its use by a few male protestors in this one instance demonstrated that even within their demand for equality and against racism there remained for some protestors an unacknowledged dimension of sexism.

32. Jason Pramas and Annie Shreffler, "Arizona Gov. Jan Brewer Charged with Racism, Bigotry at Protest Outside National Governors Association Confab," Open Media Boston, July 14, 2010, http://www.openmediaboston.org/node/1367 (accessed October 24, 2012). More generally, see Alfonso Gonzales, "Beyond the Consensus"; Alfonso Gonzales, "The 2006 Mega Marchas."

33. Axel W. Caballero, "Do I Look 'Illegal'?—Latino Nationwide Movement Building," *Huffington Post*, April 30, 2010, http://www.huffingtonpost.com/axel-woolfolk/do-i-look-illegal-latino_b_558513.html (accessed September 12, 2011); Rachel Monahan, Erica Pearson, and Larry McShane, "From Sea to Angry Sea," *New York Daily News*, May 2, 2010, 9. To date, the slogan has been emblazoned on T-shirts, buttons, and even coffee mugs. It has appeared in activist documentaries and immigrants rights blogs and is the rallying cry for several Facebook fan pages and YouTube campaigns.

34. Muñoz, *Disidentifications*, 4, 12.

35. Chávez, "Counter-public Enclaves and Understanding the Function of Rhetoric in Social Movement Coalition-Building." For a list of sponsoring organizations, see ANSWER Coalition, "Arizona Gov. Jan Brewer Met by Protestors During the National Governor's Association Meeting in Boston."

36. Schmidt Camacho, *Migrant Imaginaries*.

37. Baker-Cristales, "Mediated Resistance."

38. Chávez, "Counter-public Enclaves and Understanding the Function of Rhetoric in Social Movement Coalition-Building"; Alfonso Gonzales, "Beyond the Consensus."

39. For examples, see Alfonso Gonzales, "Beyond the Consensus."

40. Wiesel, *And the Sea Is Never Full*, 94. On his coining of the phrase, see Chmiel, *Elie Wiesel and the Politics of Moral Leadership*, 72–75; Cohen, *No One Is Illegal*, 2.

41. Jakub Burkowicz, "No One Is Illegal," Affinity Project: Web of Struggles, http://affinityproject.org/groups/nooneisillegal.html (accessed September 29, 2011). See the group's manifesto at http://www.noii.org.uk/no-one-is-illegal-manifesto/.

42. Nyers, "No One Is Illegal between City and Nation," 137.

43. Alfonso Gonzales, "Beyond the Consensus," 15.

44. Saldívar, *Border Matters*, xii. On the logic of illegality, see De Genova, "Migrant 'Illegality' and Deportability in Everyday Life"; Hiemstra, "Immigrant 'Illegality' as Neoliberal Governmentality"; Inda, *Targeting Immigrants*; Aihwa Ong, "Cultural Citizenship as Subject-Making."

45. Nyers, "No One Is Illegal between City and Nation," 141.

46. Broadly speaking, cosmopolitanism is a name for an identity between local culture, national citizenship, and global relations. The ancient roots of cosmopolitanism lie in a Stoic belief in shared humanity and human spirit, and the modern rebirth of cosmopolitanism is often traced to Kant's cosmopolitan ethical/legal principle of universal hospitality for all humanity. As Mike Featherstone explains it, proponents of cosmopolitanism demand a rethinking of "the concept of society" and "our sphere of experience" as well as the development of "new ways of doing business and working, new forms of identity and politics, new forms of everyday life, time and space, new forms of sociability." Meanwhile, critics of cosmopolitanism argue that it represents an elitist and universalist orientation that violates local cultures, traditions, and identities. Featherstone, "Cosmopolis," 4. I believe that these criticisms are the result of overemphasis on cosmopolitanism as a universal theory and subsequent inattention to "actually existing" and multiple vernacular cosmopolitanism*s* in the discourses and practices of local communities. In other words, I am interested in cosmopolitanism as a situated, contingent, and rhetorical/performative strategy of identity and agency. For more on this point, see Nava, "Cosmopolitan Modernity"; Robbins, "Introduction, Part I"; Pollock et al., "Cosmopolitanisms." On the historical origins of cosmopolitan political theory, see Cheah and Robbins, *Cosmopolitics*; Nussbaum, "Kant and Stoic Cosmopolitanism"; Toulmin, *Cosmopolis*. For defenses of cosmopolitanism, see Beck, "The Cosmopolitan Society and Its Enemies"; Connolly, "Speed, Concentric Cultures, and Cosmopolitanism"; Bryan S. Turner, "Cosmopolitan Virtue, Globalization and Patriotism." For critiques of cosmopolitanism, see Mehta, "Cosmopolitanism and the Circle of Reason"; Glenister Roberts, "'Brand America'"; Schlesinger, "A Cosmopolitan Temptation."

47. Mignolo, *Darker Side of Western Modernity*, 293. While this idea of critical or vernacular cosmopolitanisms might seem to contradict the history of the term itself (as a universal model for community and identity), this is, in fact, one of the intentions of scholars who aim to rethink cosmopolitanism(s) as a form of vernacular discourse. As Mignolo puts it, the idea of multiple, localized, and performative cosmopolitanisms might seem like an oxymoron, but it is "an oxymoron that breaks away, delinks, from the imperial bend of Kantian cosmopolitan legacies." Ibid., 23. See Appadurai, "Spectral Housing and Urban Cleansing"; Diouf, "The Senegalese Murid Trade Diaspora and the Making of a Vernacular Cosmopolitanism"; Mignolo, "The Many Faces of Cosmo-Polis"; Pollock, "Cosmopolitan and Vernacular in History." This "pluriversal" cosmopolitanism is consistent with the ideas about rhetorics/performances of citizenship and borders I have been advancing throughout the book.

48. Pollock et al., "Cosmopolitanisms," 582. Peter Nyers argues that "all too often" cosmopolitan identification is a celebratory claim of the Western world: "[I]t is an 'us'—Westerners, Europeans, humanitarians, etc—who are the cosmopolitans, the champions of justice, human rights, and world order." Nyers, "Abject Cosmopolitanism," 1073.

49. Jonathan Corpus Ong, "The Cosmopolitan Continuum." On the connection between hybridity and cosmopolitanism, see Werbner and Modood, *Debating Cultural Hybridity*.

50. It is significant, to this end, that "No human is illegal" does not, in and of itself, imply a request for regularization or inclusion but merely rejects designations of illegality and demands that immigrants be allowed to live and work in peace. In this sense, the slogan seems

to privilege hospitality rather than inclusion and the right of presence rather than legalization. Another important distinction might be made between the border politics of Chicano movement(s), which were tied to the ethno-nationalist image of Aztlán, and the more fundamental challenge to borders and territorial nation-states implicit in "No human is illegal." These contrasts demonstrate the unique features of this vernacular rhetoric.

51. This is according to a flyer distributed by the Revolutionary Communist Party at the Boston protest. See http://revcom.us. According to Pheng Cheah and Walter Mignolo, Marxism itself represents a certain kind of (Western and universalist) cosmopolitan discourse. See Cheah, "Introduction, Part II"; Mignolo, *Darker Side of Western Modernity*.

52. Varsanyi, "Interrogating 'Urban Citizenship' vis-a-vis Undocumented Migration," 244.

53. Anguiano and Chávez, "Dreamers' Discourse." See the following activist websites for examples of these discourses: the Dream Activist website at http://www.dreamactivist.org and the Dream Act Portal at http://dreamact.info/.

54. Mignolo, "The Many Faces of Cosmo-Polis," 736.

55. Derrida, *On Cosmopolitanism and Forgiveness*.

56. Nyers, "Abject Cosmopolitanism," 1089.

57. See Agamben, "Beyond Human Rights."

58. I draw this concept of "reworlding" from Muthyala, *Reworlding America*.

59. Carla Hall, "Protesters Try to Put Arizona in Strike Zone," *Los Angeles Times*, June 1, 2010, AA2.

60. "Nine Inch Nails and More Join Zack de la Rocha's Arizona Boycott," *New Musical Express*, June 28, 2010; "Who Is Boycotting Arizona?" AZCentral.com, August 27, 2010, http://www.azcentral.com/business/articles/2010/05/13/20100513immigration-boycotts-list.html (accessed August 25, 2011); Jahna Berry, "$90 million at Risk in Boycott of Arizonam" AZ Central.com, May 11, 2010, http://www.azcentral.com/arizonarepublic/local/articles/2010/05/11/20100511phoenix-convention-center-boycott.html (accessed August 25, 2011). On the economic cost of the Arizona boycotts, see Chris Good, "Arizona's Immigration Law Comes with a Price," *Atlantic*, May 7, 2010, http://www.theatlantic.com/politics/archive/2010/05/arizonas-immigration-law-comes-with-a-price/56416/ (accessed September 12, 2011); Marshall Fitz and Angela Kelley, "Stop the Conference: The Economic and Fiscal Consequences of Conference Cancellations Due to Arizona's S.B. 1070," *Center for American Progress*, November 2010, http://www.americanprogress.org/issues/2010/11/az_tourism.html (accessed August 23, 2011). For a discussion of the rhetorical effectivity of boycotts, see Pezzullo, "Contextualizing Boycotts and Buycotts." On the Phoenix Suns controversy, see J. A. Adande, "Suns Using Jerseys to Send Message," ESPN.com, May 4, 2010, http://sports.espn.go.com/nba/playoffs/2010/columns/story?columnist=adande_ja&page=Sarver-100504 (accessed September 23, 2011); Craig Harris, "Political Gesture by Phoenix Suns, a Rarity in Sports, Angers Many Fans," *Arizona Republic*, May 6, 2010, http://www.azcentral.com/arizonarepublic/news/articles/2010/05/06/20100506arizona-immigration-law-phoenix-suns-los-suns-jerseys.html (accessed September 23, 2010).

61. As further evidence, supporters of these anti-immigrant measures also called for "buycotts" to combat the boycotts staged against Arizona, with the intent of promoting Arizo-

na's tourism industry and supporting locally housed corporations. On public opinion of the 2012 demonstrations, see Randal C. Archibold and Megan Thee-Brenan, "Poll of Americans Reveals Deepening Concerns about Illegal Immigration," *International Herald Tribune*, May 5, 2010, 5; Seema Mehta, "Los Angeles Times/USC Poll Voters Split on Arizona Law," *Los Angeles Times*, May 31, 2010, A1; Rudabeh Shahbazi, "SB 1070: To Boycott or 'Buycott' Arizona?" *ABC15.com, May* 16, 2010, http://www.abc15.com/dpp/news/state/sb-1070%3A-to-boycott-or-%27buycott%27-arizona%3F (accessed September 29, 2011). For an explanation of Governor Brewer's executive order, see Nataliya Binshteyn, "Arizona Responds to Deferred Action Program by Blocking Privileges for DREAMers," *National Law Review*, August 23, 2012, http://www.natlawreview.com/article/arizona-responds-to-deferred-action-program-blocking-privileges-dreamers (accessed October 2, 2012).

62. National Community Advisory Commission on Secure Communities, "Restoring Community: A National Community Advisory Report on ICE's Failed 'Secure Communities' Program," 2011, http://altopolimigra.com/documents/FINAL-Shadow-Report-regular-print.pdf (accessed June 19, 2012); Shahani and Greene, "Local Democracy on ICE"; Molly O'Toole, "Obama Deportations Raise Immigration Policy Questions," Reuters, September 20, 2011, http://www.reuters.com/article/2011/09/20/us-obama-immigration-idUSTRE78J05720110920 (accessed June 19, 2012).

63. An internal Department of Homeland Security report found that only about 2 percent of deportation cases had been halted because of prosecutorial discretion. Julia Preston, "While Seeking Support, Obama Faces a Frustrated Hispanic Electorate," *New York Times*, June 10, 2012, http://www.nytimes.com/2012/06/11/us/politics/obama-faces-a-frustrated-hispanic-electorate.html (accessed June 19, 2012). See Immigration Policy Center, "Prosecutorial Discretion: A Statistical Analysis," June 11, 2012, http://www.immigrationpolicy.org/just-facts/prosecutorial-discretion-statistical-analysis (accessed June 19, 2012). Because of these shortcomings similar criticisms were leveled at a later memo from 2012 promising discretion for some immigrants eligible under the DREAM Act (a policy called Deferred Action for Childhood Arrivals). See U.S. Citizenship and Immigration Services, "Consideration of Deferred Action for Childhood Arrivals Process," September 6, 2012, http://www.uscis.gov/childhoodarrivals (accessed October 2, 2012). As one Latina blogger summarized, "This is not administrative relief. This is not legalization. It is not even a cancellation of pending deportations. At best it is an abeyance, at worse [*sic*] it is another memo on top of the previous memos, like the Morton Memo, which have not been applied." Maegan Ortiz, "Hope or Hype? Behind the Washing(ton) Spin Cycle of an Alleged Immigration Policy Victory," VivirLatino.com, June 17, 2012, http://vivirlatino.com/2012/06/17/hope-or-hype-behind-the-washington-spin-cycle-of-an-alleged-immigration-policy-victory.php (accessed June 19, 2012).

64. Pezzullo, "Contextualizing Boycotts and Buycotts," 126.

Conclusion

1. Fry, *Latino Settlement in the New Century*. A compendium of this demographic information can be found in the August 6, 2012, edition of the U.S. Census Bureau's "Facts for Features" online newsletter, which compiles several different reports about Latina/o populations.

U.S. Census Bureau, "Facts for Features: Hispanic Heritage Month 2012: Sept. 15—Oct. 15," *Census.gov Newsroom*, August 6, 2012, http://www.census.gov/newsroom/releases/archives/facts_for_features_special_editions/cb12-ff19.html (accessed September 15, 2012).

2. Examples of these pronouncements abound. For example, Miranda and Quiroz, "The Decade of the Hispanic"; "The Latin Explosion," *New York Magazine*, September 6 1999; Geoffrey E. Fox, *Hispanic Nation*.

3. For further discussion of this "sleeping giant" trope, see Allatson, *Latino Dreams*, 50–51.

4. Thomas, "'How They Ignore Our Rights as American Citizens'"; Holling, "Retrospective on Latin@ Rhetorical and Performance Scholarship."

5. "Sotomayor's 'Wise Latina' Comment a Staple of Her Speeches," CNN.com, June 5, 2009, http://edition.cnn.com/2009/POLITICS/06/05/sotomayor.speeches/ (accessed April 30, 2011).

6. Sheryl Gay Stolberg, "Sotomayor Leaves Passion Behind," *New York Times*, July 14, 2009, http://www.nytimes.com/2009/07/15/us/politics/15judge.html (accessed April 30, 2011); Amy Goldstein, Robert Barnes, and Paul Kane, "Sotomayor Emphasizes Objectivity, Explains 'Wise Latina' Remark," *Washington Post*, July 15, 2009, http://www.washingtonpost.com/wp-dyn/content/article/2009/07/14/AR2009071400992.html (accessed April 30, 2011). While many journalists praised Sotomayor for performing a white, masculine citizen-subject, they also obsessed about Sotomayor's body language, dress, and demeanor, attempting to identify her true fiery Latina self underneath the façade she was presenting to the Senate Judiciary Committee. Thus, for example, the very same journalist who praised Sotomayor for her demeanor during the confirmation hearings also commented on the "flaming red jacket" and "manicured nails painted a pale pink," which supposedly "betray[ed]" Sotomayor's otherwise flawless performance. See Stolberg, "Sotomayor Leaves Passion Behind." This supports the point that the nomination debate over Sonia Sotomayor was in many ways a public debate about the boundaries of U.S. identity and the proper role for Latina/o and Latina/o "excess" within the U.S. civic imaginary. For more on this confirmation debate, see Kevin R. Johnson, "An Essay on the Nomination and Confirmation of the First Latina Justice on the U.S. Supreme Court"; Chambers-Letson, "Embodying Justice." On the representations of Latinas in popular culture, see Beltrán, "The Hollywood Latina Body"; Molina-Guzmán, *Dangerous Curves*.

7. I am drawing on this idea of the border as aberrant in part from the brilliant title of Ferguson's book, *Aberrations in Black*. Ferguson explores how African American culture has been constituted as nonnormative (that is, aberrant) through intersectional constructions of race, class, gender, sexuality, and nationality, and he traces situated African American texts, mainly novels, which responded to and critiqued those heteronormative constructions. In a similar vein, I am suggesting that the physical and figural borders of the civic imaginary work through discourses of aberration but themselves need to be denaturalized as aberrant and contestable constructions.

8. DeChaine, "Bordering the Civic Imaginary," 59; emphasis added.

9. Juan Flores helps us to contextualize this anger, writing that Puerto Ricans are subject to a "special, and especially unfavorable, position and representation" as the "exception" or

the "bottom rung" of the Latina/o community. For Flores, this racialized and gendered representation of Puerto Ricans in the national imaginary persists in part because of the colonial relationship between Puerto Rico and the United States. Juan Flores, *From Bomba to Hip-Hop*, 8–9.

10. Ramos-Zayas, *National Performances*. See also Enck-Wanzer, "Tropicalizing East Harlem." For more on the Boricuas for a Positive Image campaign, see Erica Lopez, "Puerto Ricans to ABC: We Are Not Drug Dealers!" *Fox News Latino*, January 5, 2012, http://latino.foxnews.com/latino/entertainment/2012/01/05/puerto-ricans-to-abc-are-not-drug-dealers/ (accessed April 25, 2012); "ABC Finally Issues Formal Apology to Boricuas for a Positive Image," Latino Rebels.com, May 1, 2012, http://www.latinorebels.com/2012/05/01/abc-finally-issues-formal-apology-to-boricuas-for-a-positive-image/ (accessed April 25, 2012). Also see the website of NYC Latino Politics, which has covered the group extensively: http://nyclatinopolitics.com/.

11. Ferguson, *Aberrations in Black*, 17–18; Ono and Sloop, "The Critique of Vernacular Discourse," 21.

12. Calafell and Holling, introduction, vii. See also Watts, "'Voice' and 'Voicelessness' in Rhetorical Studies."

13. Calafell, *Latina/o Communication Studies*; Juan Flores, *From Bomba to Hip-Hop*; De Genova and Ramos-Zayas, *Latino Crossings*; Oboler, *Ethnic Labels, Latino Lives*.

14. I discussed this "color-blind," neoliberal ideology in chapter 4. In brief, the idea is that purportedly race-neutral policies and "color-blind" identities are increasingly praised as progressive while racial and cultural difference and race-conscious politics are maligned as monocultural, regressive, or exclusionary. The problem is that this celebration of post-racial America obfuscates and entrenches the continued significance of race and institutional racism while neutralizing the possibility of antiracist struggle. See Goldberg, *The Threat of Race*; Melamed, "The Spirit of Neoliberalism."

15. Alcoff and Mohanty, "Reconsidering Identity Politics," 3; De Genova and Ramos-Zayas, *Latino Crossings*, 15.

16. Lisa A. Flores, "Creating Discursive Space," 142.

17. Acosta-Belén and Santiago, "Merging Borders," 36.

18. Ngai, *Impossible Subjects*.

19. Calafell, *Latina/o Communication Studies*, 6; Poblete, introduction, xx–xxi.

20. Butler, "Imitation and Gender Insubordination," 308.

21. See Calafell, *Latina/o Communication Studies*, chapter 6.

22. Molina-Guzmán and Valdivia, "Brain, Brow, and Booty," 219.

23. Singh, *Black Is a Country*, 52–53.

24. Joseph, *Nomadic Identities*, 5. See also Muñoz, *Disidentifications*; Shugart, "Counterhegemonic Acts."

25. According to Sloop and Ono, outlaw discourses are those that are outside of and represent challenges to the logics of the law, that "imagine new ways of constructing the world, and [new ways] to replace the logic of dichotomies with alternatives." Sloop and Ono, "Outlaw Discourse," 50.

26. Cristina Constantini, "Anti-Latino Hate Crimes Rise as Immigration Debate Intensifies,"

Huffington Post, October 18, 2011, http://www.huffingtonpost.com/2011/10/17/anti-latino-hate-crimes-rise-immigration_n_1015668.html (accessed October 3, 2012). For a broader discussion of this point, see the report by the National Institute of Justice, "Research Briefing: Understanding Trends in Hate Crimes against Immigrants and Hispanic-Americans," U.S. Department of Justice, May 25, 2011, http://www.nij.gov/topics/crime/hate-crime/immigrants-hispanics.htm (accessed October 3, 2012).

Bibliography

Acosta-Belén, Edna, and Carlos E. Santiago. "Merging Borders: The Remapping of America." In *The Latino Studies Reader: Culture, Economy, and Society*, edited by Antonia Darder and Rodolfo D. Torres, 29–42. Malden, MA: Blackwell, 1998.

Acuña, Rodolfo. *Occupied America: A History of Chicanos*. 5th ed. New York: Pearson Longman, 2004.

Agamben, Giorgio. "Beyond Human Rights." *Open: Cahier on Art in the Public Domain* 15 (2008): 90–95.

Ahmed, Sara. *The Cultural Politics of Emotion*. New York: Routledge, 2004.

Alaniz, Yolanda, and Megan Cornish. *Viva La Raza: A History of Chicano Identity and Resistance*. Seattle: Red Letter, 2008.

Alarcón, Norma. "Traddutora, Traditora: A Paradigmatic Figure of Chicana Feminism." *Cultural Critique* 13 (1989): 57–87.

Alcoff, Linda Martín. "Mignolo's Epistemology of Coloniality." *CR: The New Centennial Review* 7 (2007): 79–101.

Alcoff, Linda Martín, and Satya P. Mohanty. "Reconsidering Identity Politics: An Introduction." In *Identity Politics Reconsidered*, edited by Linda Martín Alcoff, Michael Hames-García, Satya P. Mohanty, and Paula M. L. Moya, 1–9. New York: Palgrave Macmillan, 2006.

Aldama, Arturo J. "Millennial Anxieties: Borders, Violence, and the Struggle for Chicana and Chicano Subjectivity." In *Decolonial Voices: Chicana and Chicano Cultural Studies in the 21st Century*, edited by Arturo J. Aldama and Naomi H. Quiñonez, 11–29. Bloomington: Indiana University Press, 2002.

Aldama, Arturo J., and Naomi H. Quiñonez, eds. *Decolonial Voices: Chicana and Chicano Cultural Studies in the 21st Century*. Bloomington: Indiana University Press, 2002.

Aleinikoff, Thomas Alexander, and Douglas B. Klusmeyer, eds. *Citizenship Today: Global Perspectives and Practices*. Washington, DC: Carnegie Endowment for International Peace, 2001.

Allatson, Paul. *Latino Dreams: Transcultural Traffic and the U.S. National Imaginary*. New York: Rodopi, 2002.

Almaguer, Tomás. *Racial Fault Lines: The Historical Origins of White Supremacy in California*. Berkeley: University of California Press, 1994.

Altschuler, Glenn C., and Stuart M. Blumin. "Limits of Political Engagement in Antebellum America: A New Look at the Golden Age of Participatory Democracy." *Journal of American History* 84 (1997): 855–85.

Amaya, Hector. "Dying American or, The Violence of Citizenship: Latinos in Iraq." *Latino Studies* 5 (2007): 3–24.

Amoore, Louise, and Alexandra Hall. "Border Theatre: On the Arts of Security and Resistance." *Cultural Geographies* 17 (2010): 299–319.

Anderson, Benedict R. *Imagined Communities: Reflections on the Origin and Spread of Nationalism*. Rev. ed. London: Verso, 2006.

Andrews, James R. "Confrontation at Columbia: A Case Study in Coercive Rhetoric." *Quarterly Journal of Speech* 55 (1969): 9–16.

Anguiano, Claudia A., and Karma R. Chávez. "DREAMers' Discourse: Young Latino/a Immigrants and the Naturalization of the American Dream." In *Latina/o Discourse in Vernacular Spaces: Somos de Una Voz?* edited by Michelle A. Holling and Bernadette Marie Calafell, 81–100. Lanham, MD: Lexington Books, 2011.

Annino, Antonio. "The Two-Faced Janus: The Pueblos and the Origins of Mexican Liberalism." In *Cycles of Conflict, Centuries of Change: Crisis, Reform, and Revolution in Mexico*, edited by Elisa Servín, Leticia Reina, and John Tutino, 60–90. Durham, NC: Duke University Press, 2007.

Anzaldúa, Gloria. *Borderlands/La Frontera: The New Mestiza*. San Francisco: Spinsters/Aunt Lute, 1987.

Anzaldúa, Gloria, and AnaLouise Keating. *This Bridge We Call Home: Radical Visions for Transformation*. New York: Routledge, 2002.

Aparicio, Frances R., and Susana Chávez-Silverman. Introduction to *Tropicalizations: Transcultural Representations of Latinidad*, edited by Frances R. Aparicio and Susana Chávez-Silverman, 1–17. Hanover, NH: Dartmouth College, 1997.

Appadurai, Arjun. *Fear of Small Numbers: An Essay on the Geography of Anger*. Durham, NC: Duke University Press, 2006.

———. *Modernity at Large: Cultural Dimensions of Globalization*. Minneapolis: University of Minnesota Press, 1996.

———. "Spectral Housing and Urban Cleansing: Notes on Millennial Mumbai." *Public Culture* 12 (2000): 627–51.

Arizona State Legislature. House. *An Act Amending Sections 1–501 and 1–502, Arizona Revised Statutes* (House Bill 2162). 49th leg., 2nd sess. (April 30, 2010). www.tucsonsentinel.com/files/pdf/hb2162.pdf (accessed August, 23, 2010).

Arizona State Legislature. Senate. *The Support Our Law Enforcement and Safe Neighborhoods Act* (Senate Bill 1070). 49th leg., 2nd sess. (April 23, 2010). www.azleg.gov/legtext/49leg/2r/bills/sb1070s.pdf (accessed August 23, 2010).

Asen, Robert. "A Discourse Theory of Citizenship." *Quarterly Journal of Speech* 90 (2004): 189–211.

Avant-Mier, Roberto. "Of Rocks and Nations: *Voces Rockeras* [Rock Music Voices] and the Discourse of 'Nationality.'" In *Latina/o Discourse in Vernacular Spaces: Somos de Una Voz?* edited by Michelle A. Holling and Bernadette Marie Calafell, 147–68. Lanham, MD: Lexington Books, 2011.

Baker, Houston A. *Blues, Ideology, and Afro-American Literature: A Vernacular Theory*. Chicago: University of Chicago Press, 1984.

Baker-Cristales, Beth. "Mediated Resistance: The Construction of Neoliberal Citizenship in the Immigrant Rights Movement." *Latino Studies* 7 (2009): 60–82.

Balibar, Etienne. "At the Borders of Citizenship: A Democracy in Translation?" *European Journal of Social Theory* 13 (2010): 315–22.

Bancroft, Hubert Howe. *California Pioneer Register and Index, 1542–1848*. Baltimore: Regional, 1964.

———. *History of California*. Vol. 6. Santa Barbara, CA: W. Hebberd, 1963.

Barreto, Matt A., Sylvia Manzano, Ricardo Ramirez, and Kathy Rim. "Mobilization, Participation, and *Solidaridad:* Latino Participation in the 2006 Immigration Protest Rallies." *Urban Affairs Review* 44 (2009): 736–64.

Beasley, Vanessa B., ed. *Who Belongs in America? Presidents, Rhetoric, and Immigration*. College Station: Texas A&M University Press, 2006.

———. *You, the People: American National Identity in Presidential Rhetoric*. College Station: Texas A&M University Press, 2004.

Bebout, Lee. "Hero Making in el Movimiento: Reies López Tijerina and the Chicano Nationalist Imaginary." *Aztlán: A Journal of Chicano Studies* 32 (2007): 93–121.

———. *Mythohistorical Interventions: The Chicano Movement and Its Legacies*. Minneapolis: University of Minnesota Press, 2011.

Beck, Ulrich. "The Cosmopolitan Society and Its Enemies." *Theory, Culture, and Society* 19, nos. 1–2 (2002): 17–44.

Beltrán, Mary C. "The Hollywood Latina Body as Site of Social Struggle: Media Constructions of Stardom and Jennifer Lopez's 'Cross-over Butt.'" *Quarterly Review of Film and Video* 19 (2002): 71–86.

Bennett, Jeffrey A. *Banning Queer Blood: Rhetorics of Citizenship, Contagion, and Resistance*. Tuscaloosa: University of Alabama Press, 2009.

Berlant, Lauren Gail. "Citizenship." In *Keywords for American Cultural Studies*, edited by Bruce Burgett and Glenn Hendler, 37–42. New York: New York University Press, 2007.

———. *The Queen of America Goes to Washington City: Essays on Sex and Citizenship*. Durham, NC: Duke University Press, 1997.

Bhabha, Homi K. "DissemiNation: Time, Narrative and the Margins of the Modern Nation." In *Nation and Narration*, ed. Homi K. Bhabha. London: Routledge, 1990.

———. *The Location of Culture*. London: Routledge, 1994.

———. "Preface to the Routledge Classics Edition." In *The Location of Culture*, 2nd ed., ix–xxv. London: Routledge, 2004.

Biesecker, Barbara A., and John Louis Lucaites, eds. *Rhetoric, Materiality, and Politics*. New York: Peter Lang, 2009.

Bizzell, Patricia, and Bruce Herzberg. *The Rhetorical Tradition: Readings from Classical Times to the Present*. 2nd ed. Boston: St. Martin's, 2001.

Blawis, Patricia Bell. *Tijerina and the Land Grants: Mexican Americans in Struggle for Their Heritage*. New York: International, 1971.

Bloemraad, Irene, Anna Korteweg, and Gökçe Yurdakul. "Citizenship and Immigration: Multiculturalism, Assimilation, and Challenges to the Nation-State." *Annual Review of Sociology* 34 (2008): 153–79.

Bloemraad, Irene, Kim Voss, and Taeku Lee. "The Protests of 2006: What Were They, How Do We Understand Them, and Where Do We Go?" In *Rallying for Immigrant Rights: The Fight for Inclusion in 21st Century America*, edited by Kim Voss and Irene Bloemraad. Berkeley: University of California Press, 2011.

Bonilla-Silva, Eduardo. *Racism without Racists: Color-blind Racism and the Persistence of Racial Inequality in the United States*. 3rd ed. Lanham, MD: Rowan & Littlefield, 2010.

Border Protection, Antiterrorism, and Illegal Immigration Control Act of 2005. HR 4437, December 16, 2005. THOMAS (Library of Congress), http://thomas.loc.gov.

Bosniak, Linda. *The Citizen and the Alien: Dilemmas of Contemporary Membership*. Princeton, NJ: Princeton University Press, 2006.

Brady, Mary Pat. "Border." In *Keywords for American Cultural Studies*, edited by Bruce Burgett and Glenn Hendler, 29–32. New York: New York University Press, 2007.

Brouwer, Daniel C. "ACT-ing UP in Congressional Hearings." In *Counterpublics and the State*, edited by Robert Asen and Daniel C. Brouwer, 87–109. Albany: State University of New York Press, 2001.

Brown, Fahamisha Patricia. *Performing the Word: African American Poetry as Vernacular Culture*. New Brunswick, NJ: Rutgers University Press, 1999.

Brown, Wendy. "Neo-liberalism and the End of Liberal Democracy." *Theory and Event* 7, no. 1 (2003). http://muse.jhu.edu/journals/theory_and_event/v007/7.1brown.html (accessed March 23, 2013).

Browne, J. Ross. *Report of the Debates in the Convention of California on the Formation of the State Constitution, in September and October, 1849*. Washington, DC: John T. Towers, 1850.

Burke, Kenneth. *A Rhetoric of Motives*. Berkeley: University of California Press, 1969.

Burns, John F. "Taming the Elephant: An Introduction to California's Statehood and Constitutional Era." In *Taming the Elephant: Politics, Government, and Law in Pioneer California*, edited by John F. Burns and Richard J. Orsi, 1–26. Berkeley: University of California Press, 2003.

Busto, Rudy V. *King Tiger: The Religious Vision of Reies López Tijerina*. Albuquerque: University of New Mexico Press, 2005.

Butler, Judith. *Gender Trouble: Feminism and the Subversion of Identity*. 2nd ed. New York: Routledge, 1999.

———. "Imitation and Gender Insubordination." In *The Lesbian and Gay Studies Reader*, edited by Henry Abelove, Michèle Aina Barale, and David M. Halperin, 300–15. New York: Routledge, 1993.

———. *Undoing Gender*. New York: Routledge, 2004.

Calafell, Bernadette Marie. "In Our Own Image? A Rhetorical Criticism of *Latina* Magazine." *Voces: A Journal of Chicana and Latina Studies* 3 (2001): 12–46.

———. *Latina/o Communication Studies: Theorizing Performance*. New York: Peter Lang, 2007.

———. "Love, Loss, and Immigration: Performative Reverberations between a Great-grandmother and Great-granddaughter." In *Border Rhetorics: Citizenship and Identity on the US-Mexico Frontier*, edited by D. Robert DeChaine, 151–62. Tuscaloosa: University of Alabama Press, 2012.

Calafell, Bernadette Marie, and Fernando Delgado. "Reading Latina/o Images: Interrogating Americanos." *Critical Studies in Media Communication* 21 (2004): 1–21.

Calafell, Bernadette Marie, and Michelle A. Holling. Introduction to *Latina/o Discourse in Vernacular Spaces: Somos de Una Voz?* edited by Michelle A. Holling and Bernadette Marie Calafell, xv–xxvi. Lanham, MD: Lexington Books, 2011.

Camarillo, Albert. *Chicanos in California: A History of Mexican Americans in California*. San Francisco: Boys & Fraser, 1984.

Castles, Stephen, and Alastair Davidson. *Citizenship and Migration: Globalization and the Politics of Belonging*. New York: Routledge, 2000.

Chambers-Letson, Josh Takano. "Embodying Justice: The Making of Justice Sonia Sotomayor." *Women and Performance: A Journal of Feminist Theory* 20 (2010): 149–72.

Chávez, Karma R. "Border (In)Securities: Normative and Differential Belonging in LGBTQ and Immigrant Rights Discourse." *Communication and Critical/Cultural Studies* 7 (2010): 136–55.

———. "Border Interventions: The Need to Shift from a Rhetoric of Security to a Rhetoric of Militarization." In *Border Rhetorics: Citizenship and Identity on the US-Mexico Frontier*, edited by D. Robert DeChaine, 48–64. Tuscaloosa: University of Alabama Press, 2012.

———. "Counter-public Enclaves and Understanding the Function of Rhetoric in Social Movement Coalition-Building." *Communication Quarterly* 59 (2011): 1–18.

Chavez, Leo R. *Covering Immigration: Popular Images and the Politics of the Nation*. Berkeley: University of California Press, 2001.

———. *The Latino Threat: Constructing Immigrants, Citizens, and the Nation*. Stanford, CA: Stanford University Press, 2008.

Cheah, Pheng. "Introduction, Part II: The Cosmopolitical–Today." In *Cosmopolitics: Thinking and Feeling beyond the Nation*, edited by Pheng Cheah and Bruce Robbins, 20–39. Minneapolis: University of Minnesota Press, 1998.

Cheah, Pheng, and Bruce Robbins, eds. *Cosmopolitics: Thinking and Feeling beyond the Nation*. Minneapolis: University of Minnesota Press, 1998.

Chmiel, Mark. *Elie Wiesel and the Politics of Moral Leadership*. Philadelphia: Temple University Press, 2001.

Cho, Eunice Hyunhye. "Beyond the Day without an Immigrant: Immigrant Communities Building a Sustainable Movement." In *Immigrant Rights in the Shadows of Citizenship*, edited by Rachel Buff, 94–121. New York: New York University Press, 2008.

Cisneros, J. David. "Contaminated Communities: The Metaphor of 'Immigrant as Pollutant' in Media Representations of Immigration." *Rhetoric and Public Affairs* 11 (2008): 569–601.

———. "Latina/os and Party Politics in the California Campaign against Bilingual Education: A Case Study in Argument from Transcendence." *Argumentation and Advocacy* 45 (2009): 115–34.

———. "Looking 'Illegal': Affect, Rhetoric, and Performativity in Arizona's Senate Bill 1070." In *Border Rhetorics: Citizenship and Identity on the US-Mexico Frontier*, edited by D. Robert DeChaine, 133–50. Tuscaloosa: University of Alabama Press, 2012.

———. "(Re)Bordering the Civic Imaginary: Rhetoric, Hybridity, and Citizenship in *La Gran Marcha*." *Quarterly Journal of Speech* 97 (2011): 26–49.

———. "Reclaiming the Rhetoric of Reies López Tijerina: Border Identity and Agency in 'The Land Grant Question.'" *Communication Quarterly* 60 (2012): 561–87.

Cloud, Dana L. "Hegemony or Concordance? The Rhetoric of Tokenism in 'Oprah' Winfrey's Rags-to-Riches Biography." *Critical Studies in Mass Communication* 13 (1996): 115–37.

Cohen, Steve. *No One Is Illegal: Asylum and Immigration Control Past and Present*. Stoke-on-Trent, UK: Trentham Books, 2003.

Comprehensive Immigration Reform Act of 2006. SB 2611, May 25, 2006. THOMAS (Library of Congress), http://thomas.loc.gov.

Condit, Celeste Michelle, and John Louis Lucaites. *Crafting Equality: America's Anglo-African Word*. Chicago: University of Chicago Press, 1993.

———. "Malcolm X and the Limits of the Rhetoric of Revolutionary Dissent." *Journal of Black Studies* 23 (1993): 291–313.

Conmy, Peter Thomas. *The Constitutional Beginnings of California*. San Francisco: Grand Parlort, 1959.

Connolly, W. E. "Speed, Concentric Cultures, and Cosmopolitanism." *Political Theory* 28 (2000): 596–618.

Conquergood, Dwight. "Ethnography, Rhetoric, and Performance." *Quarterly Journal of Speech* 78 (1992): 80–97.

———. "Rethinking Elocution: The Trope of the Talking Book and Other Figures of Speech." *Text and Performance Quarterly* 20 (2000): 325–41.

Córdova, Nathaniel I. "The Incomplete Subject of Colonial Memory: Puerto Rico and the Post/Colonial Biopolitics of Congressional Recollection." *Communication Review* 11 (2008): 42–75.

———. "*Nuestro Himno* as Heterotopic Mimicry: On the Ambivalences of a Latin@ Voicing." In *Latina/o Discourse in Vernacular Spaces: Somos de Una Voz?* edited by Michelle A. Holling and Bernadette Marie Calafell, 101–22. Lanham, MD: Lexington Books, 2011.

Crawford, James. *Hold Your Tongue: Bilingualism and the Politics of "English Only."* Reading, MA: Addison-Wesley, 1992.

Cunningham, Hilary. "Mobilities and Enclosures After Seattle: Politicizing Borders in a 'Borderless' World." *Dialectical Anthropology* 33 (2009): 143–56.

Daniels, Roger. *Coming to America: A History of Immigration and Ethnicity in American Life*. 2nd ed. New York: Perennial, 2002.

Dávila, Arlene M. *Latino Spin: Public Image and the Whitewashing of Race*. New York: New York University Press, 2008.

de Certeau, Michel. *The Practice of Everyday Life*. Berkeley: University of California Press, 1988.

DeChaine, D. Robert. "Bordering the Civic Imaginary: Alienization, Fence Logic, and the Minuteman Civil Defense Corps." *Quarterly Journal of Speech* 95 (2009): 43–65.

———, ed. *Border Rhetorics: Citizenship and Identity on the US-Mexico Frontier*. Tuscaloosa: University of Alabama Press, 2012.

———. "Introduction: For a Rhetorical Border Studies." In *Border Rhetorics: Citizenship and Identity on the US-Mexico Frontier*, edited by D. Robert DeChaine, 1–15. Tuscaloosa: University of Alabama Press, 2012.

De Genova, Nicholas. "Introduction: Latino and Asian Racial Formation at the Frontiers of U.S. Nationalism." In *Racial Transformations: Latinos and Asians Remaking the United States*, edited by Nicholas De Genova, 1–20. Durham, NC: Duke University Press, 2006.

———. "The Legal Production of Mexican/Migrant 'Illegality.'" In *Latinos and Citizenship: The Dilemma of Belonging*, edited by Suzanne Oboler, 61–90. New York: Palgrave Macmillan, 2006.

———. "Migrant 'Illegality' and Deportability in Everyday Life." *Annual Review of Anthropology* 31 (2002): 419–47.

———, ed. *Racial Transformations: Latinos and Asians Remaking the United States*. Durham, NC: Duke University Press, 2006.

De Genova, Nicholas, and Ana Y. Ramos-Zayas. *Latino Crossings: Mexicans, Puerto Ricans, and the Politics of Race and Citizenship*. New York: Routledge, 2003.

Del Castillo, Adelaida R. "Illegal Status and Social Citizenship: Thoughts on Mexican Immigrants in a Postnational World." *Aztlán: A Journal of Chicano Studies* 27 (2002): 11–32.

Delgado, Fernando P. "Chicano Ideology Revisited: Rap Music and the (Re)Articulation of Chicanismo." *Western Journal of Communication* 62 (1998): 95–113.

———. "Chicano Movement Rhetoric: An Ideographic Interpretation." *Communication Quarterly* 43 (1995): 446–55.

———. "When the Silenced Speak: The Textualization and Complications of Latina/o Identity." *Western Journal of Communication* 62 (1998): 420–38.

DeLuca, Kevin Michael. "Unruly Arguments: The Body Rhetoric of Earth First!, ACT UP, and Queer Nation." *Argumentation and Advocacy* 36 (1999): 9–21.

Demo, Anne T. "Sovereignty Discourse and Contemporary Immigration Politics." *Quarterly Journal of Speech* 91 (2005): 291–311.

Derrida, Jacques. *On Cosmopolitanism and Forgiveness*. Translated by Mark Dooley and Michael Hughes. London: Routledge, 2001.

DeSipio, Louis. "Drawing New Lines in the Sand: Evaluating the Failure of Immigration Reforms from 2006 to the Beginning of the Obama Administration." In *Rallying for Immigrant Rights: The Fight for Inclusion in 21st Century America*, ed. Kim Voss and Irene Bloemraad. Berkeley: University of California Press, 2011.

Dickinson, Greg. "Selling Democracy: Consumer Culture and Citizenship in the Wake of September 11." *Southern Communication Journal* 70 (2005): 271–84.

Diouf, Mamadou. "The Senegalese Murid Trade Diaspora and the Making of a Vernacular Cosmopolitanism." Translated by Steven Rendall. *Public Culture* 12 (2000): 679–702.

Dow, Bonnie J. "Criticism and Authority in the Artistic Mode." *Western Journal of Communication* 65 (2001): 336–48.

Edbauer Rice, Jenny. "The New 'New': Making a Case for Critical Affect Studies." *Quarterly Journal of Speech* 94 (2008): 200–12.

Enck-Wanzer, Darrel. "Barack Obama, the Tea Party, and the Threat of Race: On Racial Neoliberalism and Born Again Racism." *Communication, Culture, and Critique* 4 (2011): 23–30.

———. "Decolonizing Imaginaries: Rethinking 'the People' in the Young Lord's Church Offensive." *Quarterly Journal of Speech* 98 (2012): 1–23.

———. "Gender Politics, Democratic Demand and Anti-essentialism in the New York Young Lords." In *Latina/o Discourse in Vernacular Spaces: Somos de Una Voz?* edited by Michelle A. Holling and Bernadette Marie Calafell, 59–80. Lanham, MD: Lexington Books, 2011.

———. "A Radical Democratic Style? Tradition, Hybridity, and Intersectionality." *Rhetoric and Public Affairs* 11 (2008): 459–65.

———. "Trashing the System: Social Movement, Intersectional Rhetoric, and Collective Agency in the Young Lords Organization's Garbage Offensive." *Quarterly Journal of Speech* 92 (2006): 174–201.

———. "Tropicalizing East Harlem: Rhetorical Agency, Cultural Citizenship, and Nuyorican Cultural Production." *Communication Theory* 21 (2011): 344–67.

Fahnestock, Jeanne. *Rhetorical Style: The Uses of Language in Persuasion*. New York: Oxford University Press, 2011.

Falk, R. "The Decline of Citizenship in an Era of Globalization." *Citizenship Studies* 4 (2000): 5–17.

Featherstone, Mike. "Cosmopolis: An Introduction." *Theory, Culture, and Society* 19, nos. 1–2 (2002): 1–16.

Félix, Adrián, Carmen González, and Ricardo Ramírez. "Political Protest, Ethnic Media, and Latino Naturalization." *American Behavioral Scientist* 52 (2008): 618–34.

Ferguson, Roderick A. *Aberrations in Black: Toward a Queer of Color Critique.* Minneapolis: University of Minnesota Press, 2004.

Fernandez, Ruby Ann, and Richard J. Jensen. "Reies Lopez Tijerina's 'The Land Grant Question': Creating History through Metaphors." *Howard Journal of Communications* 6 (1995): 129–45.

Fisher, Andrew B., and Matthew D. O'Hara. "Introduction: Racial Identities and Their Interpreters in Colonial Latin America." In *Imperial Subjects: Race and Identity in Colonial Latin America*, edited by Andrew B. Fisher and Matthew D. O'Hara, 1–37. Durham, NC: Duke University Press, 2009.

Flores, Juan. *From Bomba to Hip-Hop: Puerto Rican Culture and Latino Identity.* New York: Columbia University Press, 2000.

Flores, Lisa A. "Constructing National Bodies: Public Argument in the English-Only Movement." In *Argument at Century's End: Reflecting on the Past and Envisioning the Future*, edited by Thomas A. Hollihan, 436–45. Annandale, VA: National Communication Association, 2000.

———. "Constructing Rhetorical Borders: Peons, Illegal Aliens, and Competing Narratives of Immigration." *Critical Studies in Media Communication* 20 (2003): 362–87.

———. "Creating Discursive Space through a Rhetoric of Difference: Chicana Feminists Craft a Homeland." *Quarterly Journal of Speech* 82 (1996): 142–56.

Flores, Lisa A., Dreama G. Moon, and Thomas K. Nakayama. "Dynamic Rhetorics of Race: California's Racial Privacy Initiative and the Shifting Grounds of Racial Politics." *Communication and Critical/Cultural Studies* 3 (2006): 181–201.

Flores, William V. "Citizens vs. Citizenry: Undocumented Immigrants and Latino Cultural Citizenship." In *Latino Cultural Citizenship: Claiming Identity, Space, and Rights*, edited by William V. Flores and Rina Benmayor, 255–78. Boston: Beacon, 1997.

Flores, William V., and Rina Benmayor, eds. *Latino Cultural Citizenship: Claiming Identity, Space, and Rights*. Boston: Beacon, 1997.

Foucault, Michel. "Governmentality." In *The Foucault Effect: Studies in Governmentality*, edited by Graham Burchell, Colin Gordon, and Peter Miller, 87–104. Chicago: University of Chicago Press, 1991.

———. *The History of Sexuality: An Introduction*, Vol 1. Translated by Robert Hurley. New York: Vintage Books, 1990.

———. *"Society Must Be Defended": Lectures at the Collège de France, 1975–76*. Edited by Mauro Bertani, Alessandro Fontana, François Ewald, and David Macey. Translated by David Macey. New York: Picador, 2003.

———. "The Subject and Power." Translated by Leslie Sawyer. *Critical Inquiry* 8 (1982): 777–95.

Fox, Geoffrey E. *Hispanic Nation: Culture, Politics, and the Constructing of Identity*. New York: Carol, 1996.

Fox, Jonathan. "Unpacking 'Transnational Citizenship.'" *Annual Review of Political Science* 8 (2005): 171–201.

Friedman, Jonathan. "Global Crises, the Struggle for Cultural Identity, and Intellectual Pork-barrelling: Cosmopolitans versus Locals, Ethnics and Nationals in an Era of De-hegemonisation." In *Debating Cultural Hybridity: Multi-cultural Identities and the Politics of Anti-racism*, edited by Pnina Werbner and Tariq Modood, 70–89. New York: Zed Books, 1997.

Friedman, Jonathan, and Shalini Randeria, eds. *Worlds on the Move: Globalization, Migration, and Cultural Security*. New York: Palgrave Macmillan, 2004.

Fry, Richard. *Latino Settlement in the New Century*. Washington, DC: Pew Hispanic Center, 2008.

Gaonkar, Dilip Parameshwar. "Toward New Imaginaries: An Introduction." *Public Culture* 14 (2002): 1–19.

García, Ignacio M. *Chicanismo: The Forging of a Militant Ethos among Mexican Americans*. Tucson: University of Arizona Press, 1997.

García Canclini, Néstor. *Hybrid Cultures: Strategies for Entering and Leaving Modernity*. Minneapolis: University of Minnesota Press, 1995.

Gardner, Richard. *Grito! Reies Tijerina and the New Mexico Land Grant War of 1967*. Tierra Amarilla, NM: Bobbs-Merrill, 1970.

Garrett, T. M. "The Border Fence, Immigration Policy, and the Obama Administration: A Cautionary Note." *Administrative Theory and Praxis* 32 (2010): 129–33.

Garza, Teresita. "The Rhetorical Legacy of Coyolxauhqui: (Re)Collecting and (Re)Membering Voice." In *Latina/o Discourse in Vernacular Spaces: Somos de Una Voz?* edited by Michelle A. Holling and Bernadette Marie Calafell, 31–56. Lanham, MD: Lexington Books, 2011.

Gencarella, Stephen Olbrys, and Phaedra C. Pezzullo, eds. *Readings on Rhetoric and Performance*. State College, PA: Strata, 2010.

Gilbertson, Greta A. "Regulating Transnational Citizens in the Post-1996 Welfare Reform Era: Dominican Immigrants in New York City." In *Latinos and Citizenship: The Dilemma of Belonging*, edited by Suzanne Oboler, 91–112. New York: Palgrave Macmillan, 2006.

Glenister Roberts, Kathleen. "'Brand America': Media and the Framing of 'Cosmopolitan' Identities." *Critical Studies in Media Communication* 28 (2011): 68–84.

Goldberg, David Theo. *The Threat of Race: Reflections on Racial Neoliberalism*. Malden, MA: Wiley-Blackwell, 2009.

Goltz, Dustin Bradley, and Kimberlee Pérez. "Borders without Bodies: Affect, Proximity, and Utopian Imaginaries through 'Lines in the Sand.'" In *Border Rhetorics: Citizenship and Identity on the US-Mexico Frontier*, edited by D. Robert DeChaine, 151–62. Tuscaloosa: University of Alabama Press, 2012.

Gómez, Laura E. *Manifest Destinies: The Making of the Mexican American Race*. New York: New York University Press, 2007.

Gonzales, Alfonso. "Beyond the Consensus: Oppositional Migrante Politics in the Obama Era." *NACLA Report on the Americas* 43, no. 6 (2010): 15–19.

———. "The 2006 Mega Marchas in Greater Los Angeles: Counter-Hegemonic Moment and the Future of El Migrante Struggle." *Latino Studies* 7 (2009): 30–59.

Gonzales, Manuel G. *Mexicanos: A History of Mexicans in the United States*. Bloomington: Indiana University Press, 1999.

González, Alberto. "Listening to Our Voices: Latina/os and the Communities They Speak." In *Latina/o Discourse in Vernacular Spaces: Somos de Una Voz?* edited by Michelle A. Holling and Bernadette Marie Calafell, 3–16. Lanham, MD: Lexington Books, 2011.

González, Juan. *Harvest of Empire: A History of Latinos in America*. New York: Viking, 2000.

Goodale, Greg. *Sonic Persuasion: Reading Sound in the Recorded Age*. Urbana: University of Illinois Press, 2011.

Goodwin, Leonidas Cardinal. *The Establishment of State Government in California, 1846–1850*. New York: Macmillan, 1914.

Gottheimer, Josh. *Ripples of Hope: Great American Civil Rights Speeches*. New York: Basic Civitas Books, 2003.

Gracia, Jorge J. E., ed. *Latin American Philosophy in the Twentieth Century: Man, Values, and the Search for Philosophical Identity*. Buffalo, NY: Prometheus Books, 1986.

Greenberg, Amy S. *Manifest Manhood and the Antebellum American Empire*. Cambridge: Cambridge University Press, 2005.

Greene, Ronald Walter. "John Dewey's Eloquent Citizen: Communication, Judgment, and Postmodern Capitalism." *Argumentation and Advocacy* 39 (2003): 189–200.

Griswold del Castillo, Richard. *The Treaty of Guadalupe Hidalgo: A Legacy of Conflict*. Norman: University of Oklahoma Press, 1990.

Grodin, Joseph R., Calvin R. Massey, and Richard B. Cunningham. *The California State Constitution: A Reference Guide*. Westport, CT: Greenwood, 1993.

Grosfoguel, Ramón. "The Epistemic Decolonial Turn: Beyond Political-Economy Paradigms." *Cultural Studies* 21 (2007): 211–23.

———. "Transmodernity, Border Thinking, and Global Coloniality: Decolonizing Political Economy and Postcolonial Studies." *Eurozine*, July 4, 2008. http://www.eurozine.com/articles/2008-07-04-grosfoguel-en.html (accessed March 23, 2013).

Guerra, François-Xavier. "Mexico from Independence to Revolution: The Mutations of Liberalism." In *Cycles of Conflict, Centuries of Change: Crisis, Reform, and Revolution in Mexico*, edited by Elisa Servín, Leticia Reina, and John Tutino, 129–52. Durham, NC: Duke University Press, 2007.

Gunn, Joshua. "On Speech and Public Release." *Rhetoric and Public Affairs* 13 (2010): 175–215.

Gutiérrez, Gabriel. "Affirmative Action of the First Kind: Social and Legal Constructions of Whiteness and White Male Privilege in Nineteenth-Century California." *Latino Studies Journal* 11 (2000): 14–48.

Gutiérrez, José Angel. Introduction to *They Called Me "King Tiger": My Struggle for the Land and Our Rights*, by Reies L. Tijerina, xi–vxii. Houston: Arte Público, 2000.

Hall, Maurice L. "The Postcolonial Caribbean as a Liminal Space: Authoring Other Modes of Contestation and Affirmation." *Howard Journal of Communications* 18 (2007): 1–13.

Hall, Stuart. "When Was the 'Post-colonial'? Thinking at the Limit." In *The Post-colonial Question: Common Skies, Divided Horizons*, edited by Iain Chambers and Lidia Curti, 242–60. London: Routledge, 1996.

Hall Kells, Michelle. *Héctor P. García: Everyday Rhetoric and Mexican American Civil Rights*. Carbondale: Southern Illinois University Press, 2006.

Hammerback, John C., and Richard J. Jensen. "Ethnic Heritage as Rhetorical Legacy: The Plan of Delano." *Quarterly Journal of Speech* 80 (1994): 53–70.

———. "Reies López Tijerina: Founder of the Alianza, Minority Leader." In *Leaders from the 1960s: A Biographical Sourcebook of American Activism*, edited by David DeLeon, 166–76. Westport, CT: Greenwood, 1994.

———. *The Rhetorical Career of César Chávez*. College Station: Texas A&M University Press, 1998.

———. "The Rhetorical Worlds of César Chávez and Reijes Tijerina." *Western Journal of Speech Communication* 44 (1980): 166–76.

Hammerback, John C., Richard J. Jensen, and Jose Angel Gutierrez. *A War of Words: Chicano Protest in the 1960s and 1970s*. Westport, CT: Greenwood, 1985.

Haney-López, Ian. *White by Law: The Legal Construction of Race*. 10th anniversary ed. New York: New York University Press, 2006.

Hariman, Robert, and John Louis Lucaites. *No Caption Needed: Iconic Photographs, Public Culture, and Liberal Democracy*. Chicago: University of Chicago Press, 2007.

Harvey, David. *A Brief History of Neoliberalism*. New York: Oxford University Press, 2005.

Hasian, Marouf, Jr., and Fernando Delgado. "Trials and Tribulations of Racialized Critical Rhetorical Theory: Understanding the Rhetorical Ambiguities of Proposition 187." *Communication Theory* 8 (1998): 245–70.

Hasian, Marouf, Jr., and George F. McHendry Jr. "The Attempted Legitimation of the Vigilante Civil Border Patrols, the Militarization of the Mexico-US Border, and the Law of Unintended Consequences." In *Border Rhetorics: Citizenship and Identity on the US-Mexico Frontier*, edited by D. Robert DeChaine, 103–16. Tuscaloosa: University of Alabama Press, 2012.

Hauser, Gerard A. *Vernacular Voices: The Rhetoric of Publics and Public Spheres*. Columbia: University of South Carolina Press, 1999.

Heidenreich, Linda. *"This Land Was Mexican Once": Histories of Resistance from Northern California*. Austin: University of Texas Press, 2007.

Heizer, Robert F., and Alan F. Almquist. *The Other Californians: Prejudice and Discrimination under Spain, Mexico, and the United States to 1920*. Berkeley: University of California Press, 1971.

Heredia, Luisa. "From Prayer to Protest: The Immigrant Rights Movement and the Catholic Church." In *Rallying for Immigrant Rights: The Fight for Inclusion in 21st Century America*, edited by Kim Voss and Irene Bloemraad. Berkeley: University of California Press, 2011.

Herzog, Tamar. *Defining Nations: Immigrants and Citizens in Early Modern Spain and Spanish America*. New Haven, CT: Yale University Press, 2003.

Hiemstra, Nancy. "Immigrant 'Illegality' as Neoliberal Governmentality in Leadville, Colorado." *Antipode* 42 (2010): 74–102.

Holling, Michelle A. "Forming Oppositional Social Concord to California's Proposition 187 and Squelching Social Discord in the Vernacular Space of CHICLE." *Communication and Critical/Cultural Studies* 3 (2006): 202–22.

———. "Retrospective on Latin@ Rhetorical and Performance Scholarship: From 'Chicano Communication' to 'Latina/o Communication?'" *Communication Review* 11 (2008): 293–322.

Holling, Michelle A., and Bernadette Marie Calafell. "Identities on Stage and Staging Identities: Chicanobrujo Performances as Emancipatory Practices." *Text and Performance Quarterly* 27 (2007): 58–83.

———, eds. *Latina/o Discourse in Vernacular Spaces: Somos de Una Voz?* Lanham, MD: Lexington Books, 2011.

———. "Tracing the Emergence of Latin@ Vernaculars in the Studies of Latin@ Communication." In *Latina/o Discourse in Vernacular Spaces: Somos de Una Voz?* edited by Michelle A. Holling and Bernadette Marie Calafell, 17–29. Lanham, MD: Lexington Books, 2011.

Hondagneau-Sotelo, Pierette. "Women and Children First: New Directions in Anti-immigrant Politics." In *American Families: A Multicultural Reader*, edited by Stephanie Coontz, 288–304. New York: Routledge, 1999.

Hutchings, K., and R. Dannreuther, eds. *Cosmopolitan Citizenship*. London: Macmillan, 1999.

Hutnyk, John. "Adorno at Womad: South Asian Crossovers and the Limits of Hybridity-Talk." In *Debating Cultural Hybridity: Multi-cultural Identities and the Politics of Anti-racism*, edited by Pnina Werbner and Tariq Modood, 106–36. New York: Zed Books, 1997.

———. "Hybridity." *Ethnic and Racial Studies* 28 (2005): 79–102.

Inda, Jonathan Xavier. *Targeting Immigrants: Government, Technology, and Ethics*. Malden, MA: Blackwell, 2006.

Isin, Engin F. "Theorizing Acts of Citizenship." In *Acts of Citizenship*, edited by Engin F. Isin and Greg Marc Nielsen, 15–43. New York: Zed Books, 2008.

Isin, Engin F., and Greg Marc Nielsen, eds. *Acts of Citizenship*. New York: Zed Books, 2008.

Johnson, Julia R. "Bordering as Social Practice: Intersectional Identifications and Coalitional Possibilities." In *Border Rhetorics: Citizenship and Identity on the US-Mexico Frontier*, edited by D. Robert DeChaine, 33–47. Tuscaloosa: University of Alabama Press, 2012.

Johnson, Kevin R. "An Essay on the Nomination and Confirmation of the First Latina Justice on the U.S. Supreme Court: The 'High-Tech Lynching' of a 'Wise Latina'?" *UC Davis Legal Studies Research Paper No. 188*, August 24, 2009. http://dx.doi.org/10.2139/ssrn.1460932 (accessed September 24, 2012).

———. "How Racial Profiling in America Became the Law of the Land: *United States v. Brignoni-Ponce* and *Whren v. United States* and the Need for Truly Rebellious Lawyering." *Georgetown Immigration Law Journal* 98 (2010): 1005–77.

Johnston, Paul. "The Emergence of Transnational Citizenship among Mexican Immigrants in California." In *Citizenship Today: Global Perspectives and Practices*, edited by T. Alexander Aleinikoff and Douglas B. Klusmeyer, 253–77. Washington, DC: Carnegie Endowment for International Peace, 2001.

Jones, Bradley, and Roopali Mukherjee. "From California to Michigan: Race, Rationality, and Neoliberal Governmentality." *Communication and Critical/Cultural Studies* 7 (2010): 401–22.

Joseph, May. "Introduction: New Hybrid Identities and Performance." In *Performing Hybridity*, edited by May Joseph and Jennifer Fink, 1–24. Minneapolis: University of Minnesota Press, 1999.

———. *Nomadic Identities: The Performance of Citizenship*. Minneapolis: University of Minnesota Press, 1999.

Joseph, May, and Jennifer Fink, eds. *Performing Hybridity*. Minneapolis: University of Minnesota Press, 1999.

Kapchan, Deborah A., and Pauline Turner Strong. "Theorizing the Hybrid." *Journal of American Folklore* 112 (1999): 239–53.

Klusmeyer, Douglas B. Introduction to *Citizenship Today: Global Perspectives and Practices*, edited by T. Alexander Aleinikoff and Douglas B. Klusmeyer, 1–15. Washington, DC: Carnegie Endowment for International Peace, 2001.

Kraidy, Marwan M. "Hybridity in Cultural Globalization." *Communication Theory* 12 (2002): 316–39.

———. *Hybridity; or, The Cultural Logic of Globalization*. Philadelphia: Temple University Press, 2005.

Kretsedemas, Philip. "Immigration Enforcement and the Complication of National Sovereignty: Understanding Local Enforcement as an Exercise in Neoliberal Governance." *American Quarterly* 60 (2008): 553–73.

Kymlicka, Will. "Multicultural Citizenship." In *The Citizenship Debates*, edited by Gershon Shafir, 167–88. Minneapolis: University of Minnesota Press, 1998.

Lacy, Michael G., and Kent A. Ono, eds. *Critical Rhetorics of Race*. New York: New York University Press, 2011.

———. Introduction to *Critical Rhetorics of Race*, edited by Michael G. Lacy and Kent A. Ono, 1–20. New York: New York University Press, 2011.

Lake, Randall A. "Enacting Red Power: The Consummatory Function in Native American Protest Rhetoric." *Quarterly Journal of Speech* 69 (1983): 127–42.

Leff, Michael, and Ebony A. Utley. "Instrumental and Constitutive Rhetoric in Martin Luther King Jr.'s 'Letter from Birmingham Jail.'" *Rhetoric and Public Affairs* 7 (2004): 37–52.

Levy, Jacques E., and César Chávez. *César Chávez: Autobiography of La Causa*. New York: Norton, 1975.

Longeaux y Vásquez, Enriqueta, John Treadwell Nichols, Dionne Espinoza, and Lorena Oropeza. *Enriqueta Vasquez and the Chicano Movement: Writings from El Grito del Norte*, Houston: Arte Público, 2006.

Loyd, Jenna M., and Andrew Burridge. "La Gran Marcha: Anti-racism and Immigrants Rights in Southern California." *ACME: An International E-Journal for Critical Geographies* 6 (2007): 1–35.

Lucaites, John Louis, and Celeste Michelle Condit. "Reconstructing <Equality>: Culturetypal and Counter-cultural Rhetorics in the Martyred Black Vision." *Communication Monographs* 57 (1990): 5–24.

Lugo-Lugo, Carmen R., and Mary K. Bloodsworth-Lugo. "475° from September 11." *Cultural Studies* 24 (2010): 234–55.

Lundberg, Christian. "Enjoying God's Death: *The Passion of the Christ* and the Practices of an Evangelical Public." *Quarterly Journal of Speech* 95 (2009): 387–411.

Lyall, James D. "Vigilante State: Reframing the Minuteman Project in American Politics and Culture." *Georgetown Immigration Law Journal* 23 (2009): 257–91.

Maciel, David, and Erlinda Gonzales-Berry, eds. *The Contested Homeland: A Chicano History of New Mexico*. Albuquerque: University of New Mexico Press, 2000.

Maciel, David R., and Juan José Peña. "La Reconquista: The Chicano Movement in New Mexico." In *The Contested Homeland: A Chicano History of New Mexico*, edited by David Maciel and Erlinda Gonzales-Berry, 269–301. Albuquerque: University of New Mexico Press, 2000.

Madison, D. Soyini, and Judith Hamera. "Performance Studies at the Intersections." In *The Sage Handbook of Performance Studies*, edited by D. Soyini Madison and Judith Hamera, xi–xxv. Thousand Oaks, CA: Sage, 2006.

Maldonado-Torres, Nelson. *Against War: Views from the Underside of Modernity*. Durham, NC: Duke University Press, 2008.

———. "On the Coloniality of Being: Contributions to the Development of a Concept." *Cultural Studies* 21 (2007): 240–70.

Marotta, Vince P. "The Hybrid Self and the Ambivalence of Boundaries." *Social Identities* 14 (2008): 295–312.

Martínez, Katynka Zazueta. "*Latina* Magazine and the Invocation of a Panethnic Family: Latino Identity as It Is Informed by Celebrities and Papis Chulos." *Communication Review* 7 (2004): 155–74.

Martinez, Ruben. "Fighting 187: The Different Opposition Strategies." *NACLA Report on the Americas* 29, no. 3 (1995): 29–34.

Mattern, Mark. *Acting in Concert: Music, Community, and Political Action*. New Brunswick, NJ: Rutgers University Press, 1998.

McGee, Michael C. "In Search of 'the People': A Rhetorical Alternative." *Quarterly Journal of Speech* 61 (1975): 235–49.

———. "Text, Context, and the Fragmentation of Contemporary Culture." *Western Journal of Communication* 54 (1990): 274–89.

McKerrow, Raymie E. "Critical Rhetoric: Theory and Praxis." *Communication Monographs* 56 (1989): 91–111.

McKinnon, Sara L. "Citizenship and the Performance of Credibility: Audiencing Gender-Based Asylum Seekers in U.S. Immigration Courts." *Text and Performance Quarterly* 29 (2009): 205–21.

McNevin, Anne. "Political Belonging in a Neoliberal Era: The Struggle of the Sans-Papiers." *Citizenship Studies* 10 (2006): 135–51.

Mehan, Hugh. "The Discourse of the Illegal Immigration Debate: A Case Study in the Politics of Representation." *Discourse and Society* 8 (1997): 249–70.

Mehta, Pratab Bhanu. "Cosmopolitanism and the Circle of Reason." *Political Theory* 28 (2000): 619–39.

Meier, Matt S., and Feliciano Ribera. *The Chicanos: A History of Mexican Americans*. New York: Hill & Wang, 1972.

Melamed, Jodi. "The Spirit of Neoliberalism: From Racial Liberalism to Neoliberal Multiculturalism." *Social Text* 24, no. 4 (2006): 1–24.

Menchaca, Martha. *Naturalizing Mexican Immigrants: A Texas History*. Austin: University of Texas Press, 2011.

———. *Recovering History, Constructing Race: The Indian, Black, and White Roots of Mexican Americans*. Austin: University of Texas Press, 2001.

Mignolo, Walter. *The Darker Side of Western Modernity: Global Futures, Decolonial Options*. Durham, NC: Duke University Press, 2011.

———. "Delinking: The Rhetoric of Modernity, the Logic of Coloniality, and the Grammar of De-coloniality." *Cultural Studies* 21 (2007): 449–514.

———. *Local Histories/Global Designs: Coloniality, Subaltern Knowledges, and Border Thinking*. Princeton, NJ: Princeton University Press, 2000.

———. "The Many Faces of Cosmo-Polis: Border Thinking and Critical Cosmopolitanism." *Public Culture* 12 (2000): 721–48.

———. "Philosophy and the Colonial Difference." In *Latin American Philosophy: Currents, Issues, Debates*, edited by Eduardo Mendieta, 80–86. Bloomington: Indiana University Press, 2003.

Milkman, Ruth. "L.A.'s Past, America's Future? The 2006 Immigrant Rights Protests and Their Antecedents." In *Rallying for Immigrant Rights: The Fight for Inclusion in 21st Century America*, ed. Kim Voss and Irene Bloemraad. Berkeley: University of California Press, 2011.

Miller, Toby. *Cultural Citizenship: Cosmopolitanism, Consumerism, and Television in a Neoliberal Age*. Philadelphia: Temple University Press, 2007.

———. "Culture, Dislocation, and Citizenship." In *Global Migration, Social Change, and Cultural Transformation*, edited by Emory Elliot, Jasmine Payne, and Patricia Ploesch, 165–86. New York: Palgrave Macmillan, 2007.

Miranda, Leticia, and Julia Teresa Quiroz. "The Decade of the Hispanic: An Economic Retrospective." Washington, DC: Office of Research Advocacy and Legislation, National Council of La Raza, 1990.

Molina-Guzmán, Isabel. *Dangerous Curves: Latina Bodies in the Media*. New York: New York University Press, 2010.

Molina-Guzmán, Isabel, and Angharad Valdivia. "Brain, Brow, and Booty: Latina Iconicity in U.S. Popular Culture." *Communication Review* 7 (2004): 205–21.

Monroy, Douglas. "Guilty Pleasures: The Satisfactions of Racial Thinking in Early-Nineteenth-Century California." In *Race and Nation: Ethnic Systems in the Modern World*, edited by Paul R. Spickard, 33–52. New York: Routledge, 2004.

Moraga, Cherríe, and Gloria Anzaldúa. *This Bridge Called My Back: Writings by Radical Women of Color*. 2nd ed. New York: Kitchen Table, Women of Color, 1983.

Morelli, Federica. "Entre el antiguo y el nuevo régimen: La historia política hispanoamericana del siglo XIX." *Historia crítica* 33 (2007): 122–55.

Moreman, Shane T. "Hybrid Performativity South and North of the Border: *Entre la teoría y la materialidad de hibridación*." In *Latina/o Communication Studies Today*, edited by Angharad N. Valdivia, 91–111. New York: Peter Lang, 2008.

———. "Memoir as Performance: Strategies of Hybrid Ethnic Identity." *Text and Performance Quarterly* 29 (2009): 346–66.

———. "Qualitative Interviews of Racial Fluctuations: The 'How' of Latina/o-White Hybrid Identity." *Communication Theory* 21 (2011): 197–216.

Moreman, Shane T., and Bernadette Marie Calafell. "Buscando para Nuestra Latinidad: Utilizing La Llorona for Cultural Critique." *Journal of International and Intercultural Communication* 1 (2008): 309–26.

Morris, Charles E., III, and John M. Sloop. "'What Lips These Lips Have Kissed': Refiguring the Politics of Queer Public Kissing." *Communication and Critical/Cultural Studies* 3 (2006): 1–26.

Muñoz, José Esteban. *Disidentifications: Queers of Color and the Performance of Politics*. Minneapolis: University of Minnesota Press, 1999.

———. "Feeling Brown, Feeling Down: Latina Affect, the Performativity of Race, and the Depressive Position." *Signs: A Journal of Women in Culture and Society* 31 (2006): 675–88.

Murphy, John M. "The Language of the Liberal Consensus: John F. Kennedy, Technical Reason, and the 'New Economics' at Yale University." *Quarterly Journal of Speech* 90 (2004): 133–62.

———. "Theory and Public Address: The Allusive Mr. Bush." In *The Handbook of Rhetoric and Public Address*, edited by Shawn J. Parry-Giles and J. Michael Hogan, 271–90. Malden, MA: Wiley-Blackwell, 2010.

Muthyala, John. *Reworlding America: Myth, History, and Narrative*. Athens: Ohio University Press, 2006.

Nabokov, Peter. *Tijerina and the Courthouse Raid*. 2nd ed. Berkeley, CA: Ramparts, 1970.

Nakayama, Thomas K., and R. L. Krizek. "Whiteness: A Strategic Rhetoric." *Quarterly Journal of Speech* 81 (1995): 291–309.

Nava, Mica. "Cosmopolitan Modernity: Everyday Imaginaries and the Register of Difference." *Theory, Culture, and Society* 19, nos. 1–2 (2002): 81–99.

Navarro, Sharon Ann, and Armando Xavier Mejia. *Latino Americans and Political Participation: A Reference Handbook*. Santa Barbara, CA: ABC-CLIO, 2004.

Ngai, Mae M. *Impossible Subjects: Illegal Aliens and the Making of Modern America*. Princeton, NJ: Princeton University Press, 2004.

Noe, Mark. "The Corrido: A Border Rhetoric." *College English* 71 (2009): 596–605.

Noriega, Chon A. "El Hilo Latino: Representation, Identity and National Culture." *Jump Cut: A Review of Contemporary Media* 38 (1993): 45–50.

Norton, Anne. *Republic of Signs: Liberal Theory and American Popular Culture*. Chicago: University of Chicago Press, 1993.

Nussbaum, Martha C. "Kant and Stoic Cosmopolitanism." *Journal of Political Philosophy* 5 (1997): 1–25.

Nyers, Peter. "Abject Cosmopolitanism: The Politics of Protection in the Anti-deportation Movement." *Third World Quarterly* 24 (2003): 1069–93.

———. "No One Is Illegal between City and Nation." *Studies in Social Justice* 4 (2010): 127–43.

Oboler, Suzanne. *Ethnic Labels, Latino Lives: Identity and the Politics of (Re)Presentation in the United States*. Minneapolis: University of Minnesota Press, 1995.

———. "Redefining Citizenship as a Lived Experience." In *Latinos and Citizenship: The Dilemma of Belonging*, edited by Suzanne Oboler, 3–30. New York: Palgrave Macmillan, 2006.

Olson, Lester C., Cara A. Finnegan, and Diane S. Hope, eds. *Visual Rhetoric: A Reader in Communication and American Culture*. Los Angeles: Sage, 2008.

Omi, Michael, and Howard Winant. *Racial Formation in the United States: From the 1960s to the 1990s*. New York: Routledge, 1994.

Ong, Aihwa. "Cultural Citizenship as Subject-Making: Immigrants Negotiate Racial and Cultural Boundaries in the United States." *Current Anthropology* 37 (1996): 737–62.

———. *Flexible Citizenship: The Cultural Logics of Transnationality*. Durham, NC: Duke University Press, 1999.

———. *Neoliberalism as Exception: Mutations in Citizenship and Sovereignty*. Durham, NC: Duke University Press, 2006.

Ong, Jonathan Corpus. "The Cosmopolitan Continuum: Locating Cosmopolitanism in Media and Cultural Studies." *Media, Culture and Society* 31 (2009): 449–66.

Ono, Kent A. "Borders That Travel: Matters of the Figural Border." In *Border Rhetorics: Citizenship and Identity on the US-Mexico Frontier*, edited by D. Robert DeChaine, 19–32. Tuscaloosa: University of Alabama Press, 2012.

Ono, Kent A., and John M. Sloop. "Commitment to Telos—A Sustained Critical Rhetoric." *Communication Monographs* 59 (1992): 48–60.

———. "The Critique of Vernacular Discourse." *Communication Monographs* 62 (1995): 19–46.

———. *Shifting Borders: Rhetoric, Immigration, and California's Proposition 187*. Philadelphia: Temple University Press, 2002.

Oropeza, Lorena. "The Heart of Chicano History: Reies Lopez Tijerina as a Memory Entrepreneur." *The Sixties: A Journal of History, Politics, and Culture* 1 (2008): 49–67.

Orozco, Cynthia. *No Mexicans, Women, or Dogs Allowed: The Rise of the Mexican American Civil Rights Movement*. Austin: University of Texas Press, 2009.

Ott, Brian L. "The Visceral Politics of *V for Vendetta*: On Political Affect in Cinema." *Critical Studies in Media Communication* 27 (2010): 29–54.

Pantoja, Adrian D., Cecilia Menjívar, and Lisa Magaña. "The Spring Marches of 2006: Latinos, Immigration, and Political Mobilization in the 21st Century." *American Behavioral Scientist* 52 (2008): 499–506.

Papastergiadis, Nikos. "Tracing Hybridity in Theory." In *Debating Cultural Hybridity: Multicultural Identities and the Politics of Anti-racism*, edited by Pnina Werbner and Tariq Modood, 257–81. New York: Zed Books, 1997.

Pedraza, Francisco I., Gary M. Segura, and Shaun Bowler. "The Efficacy and Alienation of Juan Q. Public: The Immigration Marches and Latino Orientations toward American Political Institutions." In *Rallying for Immigrant Rights: The Fight for Inclusion in 21st Century America*, edited by Kim Voss and Irene Bloemraad. Berkeley: University of California Press, 2011.

Perelman, Chaim, and Lucie Olbrechts-Tyteca. *The New Rhetoric: A Treatise on Argumentation*. Notre Dame, IN: University of Notre Dame Press, 1969.

Pérez, Emma. *The Decolonial Imaginary: Writing Chicanas into History*. Bloomington: Indiana University Press, 1999.

Pérez Firmat, Gustavo. *Literature and Liminality: Festive Readings in the Hispanic Tradition*. Durham, NC: Duke University Press, 1986.

Pezzullo, Phaedra C. "Contextualizing Boycotts and Buycotts: The Impure Politics of Consumer-Based Advocacy in an Age of Global Ecological Crises." *Communication and Critical/Cultural Studies* 8 (2011): 124–45.

———. "Resisting 'National Breast Cancer Awareness Month': The Rhetoric of Counterpublics and Their Cultural Performances." *Quarterly Journal of Speech* 89 (2003): 345–65.

Pineda, Richard D., and Stacey K. Sowards. "Flag Waving as Visual Argument: 2006 Immigration Demonstrations and Cultural Citizenship." *Argumentation and Advocacy* 43 (2007): 164–74.

Pitt, Leonard. *The Decline of the Californios: A Social History of the Spanish-Speaking Californians, 1846–1890*. Berkeley: University of California Press, 1966.

Poblete, Juan. Introduction to *Critical Latin American and Latino Studies*, ix–xli. Minneapolis: University of Minnesota Press, 2003.

Pollock, Sheldon. "Cosmopolitan and Vernacular in History." *Public Culture* 12 (2000): 591–625.

Pollock, Sheldon, Homi K. Bhabha, Carol A. Breckenridge, and Dipesh Chakrabarty. "Cosmopolitanisms." *Public Culture* 12 (2000): 577–89.

Prabhu, Anjali. *Hybridity: Limits, Transformations, Prospects*. Albany: State University of New York Press, 2007.

Quijano, Aníbal. "Coloniality and Modernity/Rationality." *Cultural Studies* 21, nos. 2–3 (2007): 168–78.

Quiñonez, Naomi H. "Re(Riting) the Chicana Postcolonial: From Traitor to 21st Century Interpreter." In *Decolonial Voices: Chicana and Chicano Cultural Studies in the 21st Century*, edited by Arturo J. Aldama and Naomi H. Quiñonez, 129–51. Bloomington: Indiana University Press, 2002.

Ramirez, Pablo A. "Toward a Borderlands Ethics: The Undocumented Migrant and Haunted

Communities in Contemporary Chicana/o Fiction." *Aztlán: A Journal of Chicano Studies* 35 (2010): 49–67.

Ramírez, Ricardo. "Mobilization *en Español*: Spanish-Language Radio and the Activation of Political Identities." In *Rallying for Immigrant Rights: The Fight for Inclusion in 21st Century America*, edited by Kim Voss and Irene Bloemraad. Berkeley: University of California Press, 2011.

Ramos-Zayas, Ana Yolanda. *National Performances: The Politics of Class, Race, and Space in Puerto Rican Chicago*. Chicago: University of Chicago Press, 2003.

Ray, Angela G. "The Permeable Public: Rituals of Citizenship in Antebellum Men's Debating Clubs." *Argumentation & Advocacy* 41 (2004): 1–16.

———. "The Rhetorical Ritual of Citizenship: Women's Voting as Public Performance, 1868–1875." *Quarterly Journal of Speech* 93 (2007): 1–26.

Ray, Angela G., and Cindy Koenig Richards. "Inventing Citizens, Imagining Gender Justice: The Suffrage Rhetoric of Virginia and Francis Minor." *Quarterly Journal of Speech* 93 (2007): 375–402.

Reies Tijerina Papers, MSS 654 BC. Center for Southwest Research, University Libraries, University of New Mexico.

Reina, Leticia, Elisa Servín, and John Tutino. "Introduction: Crises, Reforms, and Revolutions in Mexico, Past and Present." In *Cycles of Conflict, Centuries of Change: Crisis, Reform, and Revolution in Mexico*, edited by Elisa Servín, Leticia Reina, and John Tutino, 1–20. Durham, NC: Duke University Press, 2007.

Rivera-Servera, Ramon H. "Exhibiting Voice/Narrating Migration: Performance-Based Curatorial Practice in *¡Azúcar! The Life and Music of Celia Cruz*." *Text and Performance Quarterly* 29 (2009): 131–48.

Robbins, Bruce. "Introduction, Part I: Actually Existing Cosmopolitanism." In *Cosmopolitics: Thinking and Feeling beyond the Nation*, edited by Pheng Cheah and Bruce Robbins, 1–19. Minneapolis: University of Minnesota Press, 1998.

Roberts, David J., and Minelle Mahtani. "Neoliberalizing Race, Racing Neoliberalism: Placing 'Race' in Neoliberal Discourses." *Antipode* 42 (2010): 248–57.

Robinson, W. W. *Land in California: The Story of Mission Lands, Ranchos, Squatters, Mining Claims, Railroad Grants, Land Scrip [and] Homesteads*. Berkeley: University of California Press, 1948.

Rocco, Raymond. "Transforming Citizenship: Membership, Strategies of Containment, and the Public Sphere in Latino Communities." In *Latinos and Citizenship: The Dilemma of Belonging*, edited by Suzanne Oboler, 301–28. New York: Palgrave Macmillan, 2006.

Rodriguez, Gregory. *Mongrels, Bastards, Orphans, and Vagabonds: Mexican Immigration and the Future of Race in America*. New York: Pantheon Books, 2007.

Roediger, David R. *Working toward Whiteness: How America's Immigrants Became White*. New York: Basic Books, 2005.

Rosaldo, Renato. "Cultural Citizenship, Inequality, and Multiculturalism." In *Latino Cultural Citizenship: Claiming Identity, Space, and Rights*, edited by William V. Flores and Rina Benmayor, 27–38. Boston: Beacon, 1997.

Rosales, Francisco A. *Chicano! The History of the Mexican American Civil Rights Movement*. Houston: Arte Público, 1996.

Royce, Josiah. *California: From the Conquest in 1846 to the Second Vigilance Committee in San Francisco; A Study of American Character*. New York: Knopf, 1948.

Russel y Rodríguez, Mónica. "Mexicanas and Mongrels: Policies of Hybridity, Gender and Nation in the US-Mexican War." *Latino Studies Journal* 11 (2000): 49–73.

Saldívar, José David. *Border Matters: Remapping American Cultural Studies*. Berkeley: University of California Press, 1997.

———. "On the Bad Edge of *La Frontera*." In *Decolonial Voices: Chicana and Chicano Cultural Studies in the 21st Century*, edited by Arturo J. Aldama and Naomi H. Quiñonez, 262–96. Bloomington: Indiana University Press, 2002.

———. *Trans-Americanity: Subaltern Modernities, Global Coloniality, and the Cultures of Greater Mexico*. Durham, NC: Duke University Press, 2012.

———. "Unsettling Race, Coloniality, and Caste: Anzaldúa's *Borderlands/La Frontera*, Martinez's *Parrot in the Oven*, and Roy's *The God of Small Things*." *Cultural Studies* 21 (2007): 339–67.

Sandoval, Chela. *Methodology of the Oppressed*. Minneapolis: University of Minnesota Press, 2000.

Santa Ana, Otto. *Brown Tide Rising: Metaphors of Latinos in Contemporary American Public Discourse*. Austin: University of Texas Press, 2002.

Santa Ana, Otto, with Laya López and Edgar Munguíya. "Framing Peace as Violence: Television News Depictions of the 2007 Police Attack on Immigrant Rights Marchers in Los Angeles." *Aztlán: A Journal of Chicano Studies* 35 (2010): 69–101.

Schiwy, Freya. "Decolonization and the Question of Subjectivity: Gender, Race, and Binary Thinking." *Cultural Studies* 21 (2007): 271–94.

Schlesinger, Philip. "A Cosmopolitan Temptation." *European Journal of Communication* 22 (2007): 413–26.

Schmidt Camacho, Alicia R. *Migrant Imaginaries: Latino Cultural Politics in the U.S.-Mexico Borderlands*. New York: New York University Press, 2008.

Scholz, T. M. Linda. "Hablando por (Nos)Otros, Speaking for Ourselves: Exploring the Possibilities of 'Speaking por' Family and Pueblo in the Bolivian Testimonio *Si me permiten hablar*." In *Latina/o Discourse in Vernacular Spaces: Somos de Una Voz?* edited by Michelle A. Holling and Bernadette Marie Calafell, 203–22. Lanham, MD: Lexington Books, 2011.

Schudson, Michael. *The Good Citizen: A History of American Civic Life*. New York: Martin Kessler Books, 1998.

Schutte, Ofelia. *Cultural Identity and Social Liberation in Latin American Thought*. Albany: State University of New York Press, 1993.

Scott, Robert L., and Donald K. Smith. "The Rhetoric of Confrontation." *Quarterly Journal of Speech* 55 (1969): 1–8.

Selzer, Jack, and Sharon Crowley. *Rhetorical Bodies*. Madison: University of Wisconsin Press, 1999.

Shafir, Gershon. "Introduction: The Evolving Tradition of Citizenship." In *The Citizenship Debates*, edited by Gershon Shafir, 1–28. Minneapolis: University of Minnesota Press, 1998.

Shahani, Aarti, and Judith Greene. *Local Democracy on ICE: Why State and Local Governments Have No Business in Federal Immigration Law Enforcement*. Brooklyn, NY: Justice Strategies, 2009.

Shugart, Helene A. "Counterhegemonic Acts: Appropriation as a Feminist Rhetorical Strategy." *Quarterly Journal of Speech* 83 (1997): 210–29.

———. "Crossing Over: Hybridity and Hegemony in the Popular Media." *Communication and Critical/Cultural Studies* 4 (2007): 115–41.

Silva, Kumarini. "Brown: From Identity to Identification." *Cultural Studies* 24 (2010): 167–82.

Singh, Nikhil Pal. *Black Is a Country: Race and the Unfinished Struggle for Democracy*. Cambridge, MA: Harvard University Press, 2004.

Sloop, John M. *Disciplining Gender: Rhetorics of Sex Identity in Contemporary U.S. Culture*. Amherst: University of Massachusetts Press, 2004.

Sloop, John M., and Kent A. Ono. "Out-law Discourse: The Critical Politics of Material Judgment." *Philosophy and Rhetoric* 30 (1997): 50–69.

Smith, Rogers M. *Civic Ideals: Conflicting Visions of Citizenship in U.S. History*. New Haven, CT: Yale University Press, 1997.

Solnit, Rebecca. *Storming the Gates of Paradise: Landscapes for Politics*. Berkeley: University of California Press, 2007.

Sowards, Stacey. "Rhetorical Agency as *Haciendo caras* and Differential Consciousness through Lens of Gender, Race, Ethnicity, and Class: An Examination of Dolores Huerta's Rhetoric." *Communication Theory* 20 (2010): 223–47.

———. "Rhetorical Functions of Letter Writing: Dialogic Collaboration, Affirmation, and Catharsis in Dolores Huerta's Letters." *Communication Quarterly* 60 (2012): 295–315.

Sowards, Stacey, and Richard D. Pineda. "*Latinidad* in *Ugly Betty*: Authenticity and the Paradox of Representation." In *Latina/o Discourse in Vernacular Spaces: Somos de Una Voz?* edited by Michelle A. Holling and Bernadette Marie Calafell, 123–44. Lanham, MD: Lexington Books, 2011.

Sparke, Matthew. "Passports into Credit Cards: On the Borders and Spaces of Neoliberal Citizenship Identities and Local Practices." In *Boundaries and Belonging: States and Societies in the Struggle to Shape Identities and Local Practices*, edited by Joel S. Migdal, 251–83. Cambridge: Cambridge University Press, 2004.

Spickard, Paul R., ed. *Race and Nation: Ethnic Systems in the Modern World*. New York: Routledge, 2004.

Steiner, Stan. *La Raza: The Mexican Americans*. London: Minority Rights Group, 1979.

Stephen, Lynn. *Zapata Lives! Histories and Cultural Politics in Southern Mexico*. Berkeley: University of California Press, 2002.

Stewart, Charles J. "The Evolution of a Revolution: Stokely Carmichael and the Rhetoric of Black Power." *Quarterly Journal of Speech* 83 (1997): 429–46.

Stross, Brian. "The Hybrid Metaphor: From Biology to Culture." *Journal of American Folklore* 112 (1999): 254–67.

Summers Sandoval, Tomás F., Jr. "Disobedient Bodies: Racialization, Resistance, and the Mass

(Re)Articulation of the Mexican Immigrant Body." *American Behavioral Scientist* 52 (2008): 580–97.

Suro, Roberto. "Out of the Shadows, into the Light: Questions Raised by the Spring of 2006." In *Rallying for Immigrant Rights: The Fight for Inclusion in 21st Century America*, edited by Kim Voss and Irene Bloemraad. Berkeley: University of California Press, 2011.

Swisher, Carl B. *Motivation and Political Technique in the California Constitutional Convention, 1878–1879*. New York: Da Capo, 1969.

Tavárez, David. "Legally Indian: Inquisitorial Readings of Indigenous Indentity in New Spain." In *Imperial Subjects: Race and Identity in Colonial Latin America*, edited by Andrew B. Fisher and Matthew D. O'Hara, 80–99. Durham, NC: Duke University Press, 2009.

Taylor, Charles. *Modern Social Imaginaries*. Durham, NC: Duke University Press, 2004.

Terrill, Robert E. "Colonizing the Borderlands: Shifting Circumference in the Rhetoric of Malcolm X." *Quarterly Journal of Speech* 86 (2000): 67–85.

———. *Malcolm X: Inventing Radical Judgment*. East Lansing: Michigan State University Press, 2004.

Thomas, Lorrin. "'How They Ignore Our Rights as American Citizens': Puerto Rican Migrants and the Politics of Citizenship in the New Deal Era." In *Latinos and Citizenship: The Dilemma of Belonging*, edited by Suzanne Oboler, 33–58. New York: Palgrave Macmillan, 2006.

Tice, Robert. "The Rhetoric of La Raza." Unpublished book manuscript. Hayden Library, Arizona State University, Tempe, 1971.

Tijerina, Reies L. "From Prison: Reies López Tijerina." In *The Chicanos: Mexican American Voices*, edited by Ed Ludwig and James Santibañez, 215–22. Baltimore: Penguin Books, 1971.

———. "The Land Grant Question." In "The Rhetoric of La Raza," by Robert Tice, 1–25. Hayden Library, Arizona State University, Tempe, 1971.

———. "A Letter from Jail." In *We Are Chicanos: An Anthology of Mexican American Literature*, edited by Philip D. Ortega, 88–98. New York: Simon & Schuster, 1973.

———. *They Called Me "King Tiger": My Struggle for the Land and Our Rights*. Houston: Arte Público, 2000.

Toulmin, Stephen. *Cosmopolis: The Hidden Agenda of Modernity*. Chicago: University of Chicago Press, 1992.

Turner, Bryan S. "Cosmopolitan Virtue, Globalization and Patriotism." *Theory, Culture, and Society* 19, nos. 1–2 (2002): 45–63.

Turner, Victor Witter. *The Forest of Symbols: Aspects of Ndembu Ritual*. Ithaca, NY: Cornell University Press, 1967.

Valdivia, Angharad. *Latina/o Communication Studies Today*. New York: Peter Lang, 2008.

———. "Latinas as Radical Hybrid: 'Transnationally Gendered Traces in Mainstream Media.'" *Global Media Journal* 3 (2004): 1–21.

van der Veer, Peter. "'The Enigma of Arrival': Hybridity and Authenticity in the Global Space." In *Debating Cultural Hybridity: Multi-cultural Identities and the Politics of Anti-racism*, edited by Pnina Werbner and Tariq Modood, 90–105. New York: Zed Books, 1997.

Varsanyi, Monica W. "'Getting out the Vote' in Los Angeles: The Mobilization of Undocumented Migrants in Electoral Politics." In *Latinos and Citizenship: The Dilemma of Belonging*, edited by Suzanne Oboler, 219–46. New York: Palgrave Macmillan, 2006.

———. "Interrogating 'Urban Citizenship' vis-a-vis Undocumented Migration." *Citizenship Studies* 10 (2006): 229–49.

———. "The Paradox of Contemporary Immigrant Political Mobilization: Organized Labor, Undocumented Migrants, and Electoral Participation in Los Angeles." *Antipode* 37 (2005): 775–95.

———. "Rescaling the 'Alien,' Rescaling Personhood: Neoliberalism, Immigration, and the State." *Annals of the Association of American Geographers* 98 (2009): 877–96.

Vasconcelos, José. *La Raza Cósmica*. Translated by Didier Tisdel Jaén. Baltimore: Johns Hopkins University Press, 1979.

von Werlhof, Claudia. "The Consequences of Globalization and Neoliberal Policies: What Are the Alternatives?" *Centre for Research on Globalization*, February 11, 2008. http://www.globalresearch.ca/the-consequences-of-globalization-and-neoliberal-policies-what-are-the-alternatives (accessed June 12, 2010).

Voss, Kim, and Irene Bloemraad, eds. *Rallying for Immigrant Rights: The Fight for Inclusion in 21st Century America*. Berkeley: University of California Press, 2011.

Wander, Philip C., Judith N. Martin, and Thomas K. Nakayama. "Whiteness and Beyond: Sociohistorical Foundations of Whiteness and Contemporary Challenges." In *Whiteness: The Communication of Social Identity*, edited by Thomas K. Nakayama and Judith N. Martin, 13–26. Thousand Oaks, CA: Sage, 1999.

Wang, Ted, and Robert C. Winn. "Groundswell Meets Groundwork: Building on the Mobilizations to Empower Immigrant Communities." In *Rallying for Immigrant Rights: The Fight for Inclusion in 21st Century America*, edited by Kim Voss and Irene Bloemraad. Berkeley: University of California Press, 2011.

Watts, Eric King. "'Voice' and 'Voicelessness' in Rhetorical Studies." *Quarterly Journal of Speech* 87 (2001): 179–96.

Werbner, Pnina. "Introduction: The Dialectics of Cultural Hybridity." In *Debating Cultural Hybridity: Multi-cultural Identities and the Politics of Anti-racism*, edited by Pnina Werbner and Tariq Modood, 1–26. New York: Zed Books, 1997.

Werbner, Pnina, and Tariq Modood, eds. *Debating Cultural Hybridity: Multi-cultural Identities and the Politics of Anti-racism*. New York: Zed Books, 1997.

Westgate, Christopher Joseph. "When Sexual Becomes Spiritual: Lila Downs and the Body of Voice." In *Latina/o Discourse in Vernacular Spaces: Somos De Una Voz?* edited by Michelle A. Holling and Bernadette Marie Calafell, 169–84. Lanham, MD: Lexington Books, 2011.

Wiesel, Elie. *And the Sea Is Never Full: Memoirs, 1969*. New York: Knopf, 1999.

Willis, E. B., and P. K. Stockton. *Debates and Proceedings of the Constitutional Convention of the State of California, Convened at the City of Sacramento, Saturday, September 28, 1879*. Sacramento, CA: State Printing, 1881.

Wilson, Kirt H. "The Racial Politics of Imitation in the Nineteenth Century." *Quarterly Journal of Speech* 89 (2003): 90–108.

Wright, Cynthia. "Challenging States of Illegality: From 'Managed Migration' to a Politics of No Borders." *Labour/Le travail* 62 (2008): 185–98.

Zarefsky, David. "Four Senses of Rhetorical History." In *Doing Rhetorical History: Concepts and Cases*, edited by Kathleen J. Turner, 19–32. Tuscaloosa: University of Alabama Press, 1998.

Index